the church
and the
second sex

Emily Oddwoman

The Church and the Second Sex

MARY DALY

WITH THE FEMINIST
POSTCHRISTIAN INTRODUCTION
AND
NEW ARCHAIC AFTERWORDS
BY THE AUTHOR

Beacon Press   Boston

Beacon Press
25 Beacon Street
Boston, Massachusetts 02108

Beacon Press books are published under the auspices
of the Unitarian Universalist Association
of Congregations in North America.

92   8 7 6 5 4

Library of Congress Cataloging-in-Publication Data

Daly, Mary
        The church and the second sex.

        Includes bibliographical references and index.
        1. Feminism.   2. Women in Christianity.   I. Title.
BV639.W7D28.   1985   261.8'344   85-47519
ISBN 0-8070-1101-0

This book is dedicated to the memory of my mother and my father with love and gratitude.

Acknowledgement

Quotations in Chapter One from Simone de Beauvoir, *The Second Sex*, are from the English translation by H. M. Parshley, published by Alfred A. Knopf Inc., New York, and Jonathan Cape Ltd., London, and are used by permission.

Contents

New Archaic Afterwords

Wicked Afterthoughts concerning The Church and the
Second Sex *and its 1975* A.F. (Anno Feminarum)
"Feminist Postchristian Introduction," *understood from
perspectives of 1985* A.F. . . . *and Afterwards.*

These *Afterwords* are coming into be-ing seventeen years after the
original publication of *The Church and the Second Sex* and just ten years
after the appearance of the 1975 edition, which contains the "Autobiographical Preface" and "Feminist Postchristian Introduction."
Recalling the process of writing that Preface and Introduction is re-
membering an ecstatic experience. That writing was a celebra-
tion/cerebration of my departure from the catholic church in particular
and christianity in general.

My actual parting had taken place a few years before that, gradually
and — in more senses than one — by degrees. As I look back at that
process, my attention is drawn to its inherent relentless logic — a
logic that was/is both complex and simple at the same time.

Musing upon that parting, I was moved to reread Nietzsche's
famous passages concerning the "death of God." The following sentences
were thought-provoking:

> This tremendous event is still on its way, still wandering — it has
> not yet reached the ears of man. Lightning and thunder require
> time, the light of the stars requires time, deeds require time even
> after they are done, before they can be seen and heard. This deed
> is more distant from them than the most distant stars — *and yet
> they have done it themselves.*[1]

Despite the intellectual passion of the passage, it is clear that Nietzsche
had no conscious understanding of the Truly Tremendous Event that
is the death of the patriarchal god. Certainly he could rant, rave, and
even at times write coherently about shifts *within* the patriarchal
symbol system, but his patriarchal mentality could not break out of
that system. Consequently, the "death of God" that was accessible to
his imagination is a dreary soap opera. To a radical feminist it is a
most unimpressive affair. It can hardly seem "tremendous" to a woman
who realizes that something inherently dead — such as a system of
dead phallic symbols — cannot logically be said to die.

XI

Yet from the radical feminist perspective of 1985 *Anno Feminarum* it can be seen that Nietzsche was saying more than he consciously knew he was saying (a condition frequently observable in the ravings of phallocracy's Great Prophets). For there IS a Truly Tremendous Event that is "still on its way, still wandering — it has not yet reached the ears of man." And women have done it ourSelves. This Event is the Self-Realizing of women who have broken free from the stranglehold of patriarchal religion, with its deadly symbols, its ill logic, its gynocidal laws and other poisonous paraphernalia.

The bringing about of this Event, exorcism of the poisonous patriarchal god and his attendant pathologies, has required and continues to require Courage — the Courage to Leave and, more than this, the Courage to Live beyond the godfathers' gruesome grasp. In 1985 *Anno Feminarum* it is crucial that we consider the meaning of such Courage.

The Courage to Leave

The Courage to Leave such an institution as the catholic church and, beyond that, christianity in general and all patriarchal religion in all of its forms — both sacral and secular — is often born of desperation. If the motivating force that propels one to Leave is Realization of one's own Elemental/Spiritual Powers, this Leaving involves Leap after Leap of Living Faith.[2] It is my observation and conviction that Living Faith propels women out of patriarchal religion, whereas blind faith in dead symbols keeps women lost/trapped inside its gynocidal, spirit-deadening maze.[3]

From the perspective of 1985 A.F. it can be seen clearly, and more clearly than ever, that a tragic error/terror manages to lock women within the prisons of blind/blinded faith. The basic terror-engendering error is belief that the church* has something special to offer, that something irreplaceable is bestowed upon women by and through the churchly godfathers, and that leaving the church means spiritual death.[4]

---

* I use the word *church* here and elsewhere not only specifically to refer to the catholic church but also generally to include all churches and other institutionalized manifestations of patriarchal religion. As I wrote in *Gyn/Ecology*: "*Patriarchy is itself the prevailing religion of the entire planet,* and its essential message is necrophilia. All of the so-called religions legitimating patriarchy are mere sects subsumed under its vast umbrella/canopy. They are essentially similar, despite the variations. All — from buddhism and hinduism to islam, judaism, christianity, to secular derivatives such as freudianism, jungianism, marxism, and maoism — are infra-

Acceptance of this error gives rise to terror of Leaving. This terror is itself a major cause of spiritual death. It causes crippling emotional and intellectual paralysis, blinding women to the most self-evident contradictions inherent in patriarchal faith. The terror and the belief system to which it is attached are exorcised only when women break through to the Elemental Realization that we owe the church Nothing, since the church has given us precisely Nothing. We then see that we have Nothing to lose by Leaving. Indeed, the loss of Nothing posing as Something brings almost inexpressible relief.

The Courage to Leave springs from deep knowledge of the nucleus of nothingness which is at the core of the fallacious faith that freezes/fixes its victims. It is essential, then, to turn to a consideration of this faith that is used to frame women, together with its partners, false hope and dead love (charity). I will examine some of the ways in which this deadly trio of patriarchal virtues blocks women's potential for Living Faith, Hopping Hope, and Biophilic Bonding.

fallacious faith, false hope, and dead love

The triumvirate of vacuous virtues which sustain the illusion that Nothing is Something requires special attention. I will examine them in the traditional order, which has its own ill logic.

Fallacious faith, carefully planted and cultivated by the churchly hierarchy/liararchy, takes root in women's psyches in the absence of a context of woman-identified spirituality. The religious framers/fixers of women, having rendered that Life-affirming context nearly invisible, set up a situation of confusion. Women who have experienced our spiritual powers within the patriarchal context — in which males are purported to be the divinely ordained donors of all spiritual gifts — have been pressured into confusing this contrived context with the true source of these powers, our own Elemental Selves as we participate in Be-ing.[5]

---

structures of the edifice of patriarchy. All are erected as parts of the male's shelter against anomie. And the symbolic message of all the sects of the religion which is patriarchy is this: Women are the dreaded anomie. Consequently, women are the objects of male terror, the projected personifications of 'The Enemy,' the real objects of attack in all the wars of patriarchy." See Mary Daly, *Gyn/Ecology: The Metaethics of Radical Feminism* (Boston: Beacon Press, 1978), p. 39.

Deceived in this way, women under patriarchal religious control become grateful to the paternal predators for their priestly ministrations, believing their dogmas, little suspecting that what these fathers, sons, and holy ghosts bestow upon their faithful followers, who are victims of mass hypnosis, is a bag of illusions. The tricksters can never actually give what they envy and have attempted to steal from women — Natural, Elemental, Spiritual Power. What they *can* do very successfully, however, is create an artificial environment of spiritual deprivation and illusion, in which women experiencing our own spiritual energy are duped into attributing the source of this energy to the very males who have betrayed us.

Women under the treacherous tutelage of these tricksters are prevented from seeing the abject, degraded condition in which they are framed/fixed. They are tracked and tamed into believing that all Self-affirming transcendent experiences come from outside. They are prevented from Realizing their relation to the Ultimate/Intimate Reality in which we all naturally participate. Blinded to the Source(s) of their own transcendence, believing in the supernatural benevolence of the malegod and his earthly surrogates, they are frozen in their tracks by fallacious faith.

This fallacious faith is the foundation of false hope spooned out by the sadospiritual churchmen. When women's Inner Eyes have been sealed by the ghoulish gift of fallacious faith, it is inevitable that they hope for the wrong things. The ultimate plastic hope, of course, is for happiness in a malegod-controlled "otherworld," reachable only after death. In the meantime, women are permitted to hope for modest gains in this life, but these gains, too, are attainable only after what amounts to spiritual death — a death of the Wild, Independent Self.

These earthly rewards for the Selfless include full-fillment in feminine roles for the majority and — for the "privileged" minority — an opportunity to be drained in the no-win struggle for equality in an inherently woman-hating, gynocidal institution. This struggle is literally endless, since its basic direction is intrinsically self-contradictory. Having been actively engaged in that struggle (in the 1960s, when this book was originally written and published), I have experienced its inner dynamics or, rather, statics. These are the dynamics/statics of imposed ignorance. In 1985 A.F. it is clearer than ever that this ignorance can become willfully chosen if the pathology of fallacious faith and false hope has become deeply embedded in a woman's psyche.

Ignorance of woman-identified powers of be-ing is ingrained by means of all "literature," from nursery rhymes and fairy tales to the most sophisticated of theological texts, and it is perpetuated through the usual patriarchal strategies of mind-rape, such as erasure, reversal, and doublethink.[6] In the Sadostate of Ignorance, women's complicity is cultivated, so that no Way Out is visible. Trapped in the mazes of phallocracy, women can become lost in a frenzy of running from one patriarchal institution to another, seeking a Great Change. In the State of Ignorance, a fundamental secret of patriarchy is hidden from us. Once the secret is out, we see its simplicity: Phallocracy does not and in fact cannot essentially change. It cannot reverse its destructive mechanisms that massacre women and nature, for these are essential to its necrophilic existence. They are its vital, i.e., lethal, functions.

There are, however, variations among patriarchy's manifestations, and these serve to manufacture illusions of change, thus sustaining false hope. One example can illustrate this mechanism: Two basic divisions of christianity — roman catholicism and (liberal) protestantism — function to keep women running back and forth in their masters' mazes, driven by false hope. To use another metaphor, these "branches" of christianity form a two-pronged pitchfork designed to impale women struggling for Self-actualization within the confines of the church(es). Thus liberal protestant women can see the blatant oppression of catholic women as a source of encouragement, making their own situation appear better than it really is ("At least, I'm not one of *them*!"). This comparison with greater hopelessness feeds the false hope of protestant women seeking equality within patriarchal churches. The other side of the pitchfork jabs/pricks catholic women, for seeing the apparently better protestant situation stirs hope that they too may one day reach such heights.[7]

Fallacious faith and false hope require a third vacuous virtue, dead love, in order to function optimally for the massacre of women's spirits. Cut off from Elemental connections with their own Powers, women experience a false need to belong to the fathers, to be befriended by them, and to appear appealing/desirable/"bewitching" to them.[8] When deprived of healthy, healing Self-love, women can be full-filled with plastic longing for paternal "divine love" — mediated by woman-loathing popes, priests, and bible-thumping preachers who screech endlessly on the subject of "love." Women hooked by churchly love-hysteria are victims of necrophilic love that loves to see women possessed, marching zombie-like in the ranks of the living dead.

The strategies of churchly love-mongers are essentially the same as those of other pimps, pornographers, woman-batterers, child-molesters. To describe the complex of strategies for female possession, pimps (the honest kind) use the expression "seasoning." As Kathleen Barry has explained, seasoning is intended to break its victim's will, shrink her ego, and separate her from her previous life. Affection and "love-making" are used to make a woman dependent emotionally and psychologically.[9]

Women are seasoned by religious patriarchs as well. This seasoning — through preaching, confession, misogynist "moral" teachings, et cetera — is equally intended to break its victim's will, reduce her ego, separate her from her Original Life. "Love" is intended to hook a woman, making her dependent emotionally and psychologically. She is taught to believe that this "love" is mutual.

A common theme in the master-minded strategy of pimps, pornographers, woman-batterers, child-molesters, and other priests of patriarchy is the creation of an addiction in the victim. All count on the tactic of reducing the woman's—or child's—Self-esteem, separating her from her own Deep Memory. All hook and fix their victims systematically, by physical and psychic degradation. A common experience recounted by women who as children were molested by their fathers is emotional confusion. Physical molestation was accompanied by mind molestation. Having been robbed of their ability to believe in their Selves, they were driven back to Daddy for love. So also, women robbed of the capacity to know their Selves as Sources of spiritual power are driven to "spiritual fathers," the sources of pseudolove. Only the Courage to Live can break the grip of this chilling charity, which is dead/deadening love.

The Courage to Live: An Archaic Analysis

The Way Out of the mazes of fallacious faith, false hope, and dead love begins with a Leap of Living Faith. Unlike the christian "leap of faith" into blind acceptance of gynocidal, biocidal religion, this is Self-confident Leaping. It is thinking, moving, be-ing in accord with Faith in one's Self. This requires Courage — not merely to Leave, but primarily to Live.

What does it mean to Live in 1985 . . . and Afterwards? This question itself brings the questioner into the Presence of the mystery of time. The "Feminist Postchristian Introduction" to this book was dated 1975 *Anno Feminarum* in order to convey that Feminist Time/Space

IS *on the boundary* of patriarchal time and space. That piece, then, was written *on the boundary* of 1975 a.d. (*anno domini*, the year of the lord). To continue to Live ten woman-light years later, on the boundary of 1985 a.d., is yet an Other experience.

The "year of the lord" — any year of the lord — is a time and space of patriarchal possession, that is, the foreground.[10] As I have suggested, this state is always essentially the same, but there are variations in style, method, and degree of overtness of its attacks. To those who have experienced the boundary-living of the seventies and who have spiritually survived, the overtness of the oppression and deception of 1985 is unavoidably obvious. Therefore our Journeying into and in 1985 A.F. involves acknowledgment of and confrontation with this shift in murderous methodology.

Many women, attempting to describe the experience of transition from foreground conditions of a decade or so ago to the "today" of the mid-eighties, grope for expressions. One frequently hears: "Time seems to be rushing backwards." Although it is understandable that this way of describing the phenomenon would come to mind, it is not completely adequate. The question arises: Backwards to *what*? To boundary-living observers of the year of the lord 1985, it is clear that at least one answer to this question is "Backwards into the timelessness of the patriarchal archetypes." The direction of the regression is into the deadly grip of the models and roles of phallocracy — to such an extent that individuals seem to blend into roles, to fuse with fixed forms. Under the archetypal leadership of an actor president and a media made-up pope, the possessed victims of 1985 a.d. (which is, yes, worse than 1984) goose-step into archetypal alignment, Selflessly acting out their assigned roles.

Leaping beyond these processions of possession, Lusty women experience Archaic Time. By Archaic I do not merely mean ancient. The word is derived from the Greek *arche,* meaning "first principle or origin." Archaic time is Original Time — beyond the stifling grasp of archetypal molds. I define *time* here in the classic philosophical sense of "measure of motion."[11] Archaic Time is the measure of Original Motion, Original Movement.

Women living on the boundary of 1985 a.d., by explicitly countering archetypes, are claiming/re-claiming our own Original Motion/ E-Motion/Movement. Refusing to join the archetypal act, we move into Time that is measured by Original Acts. Original Movements/Acts are by definition creative. Original Women,[12] Spinning off limits imposed by the archetypal actors of the year of the lord 1985, create an Original Future, an Archaic Future. We create 1985 A.F. — Archaic Future . . . and Afterwards. This creation moves us into Other years of Archaic Time. Each Event on the way is truly New, to the extent that it is a Movement of further Realizing Archaic Originality.

The timelessness of recession/procession into archetypes which characterizes the mid-eighties a.d. is a pathological mirror image of the Elemental shedding of patriarchal time that is essential to Movement into and creation of an Archaic Future. As women move more and more into Living Archaic Time, our Original, Creative Time, we Realize ourSelves and realize that the year of the lord — any year a.d. — is *archetypal deadtime*.

The extreme explicitness of the oppression/regression of the mid-eighties, *archetypal deadtime*, can serve as a forceful warning to Wild women. Refusing to be lulled into the sleeping death of archetypal deadtime/bedtime, we reject the role of comatose, done-in, Sleeping Beauty. Wise women know that this role/model is being force-fed through media images of women — from Nancy Reagan to Sunny von Bulow. We take on the prevailing pathology as a challenge.

Even the dulled-out mid-eighties can be turned to advantage. The very explicitness of the archetypal molds of this deadtime can be used to awaken women to Live in Archaic Time. Refusing to be lulled/dulled by the deadly daydreams of daddyland, defiant women can exploit the explicitness of the explorers. A few examples will illustrate this point: We see that the pornographic plague which has been extended into an eight-billion-dollar industry infects/infests the lives of millions of women in the playpens and penthouses of the world. This can be a challenge to proclaim and live Female Pride, the Lusty virtue of Self-affirming women.[13] We see that violence against women is becoming more explicit — including violence of the maniacal "right-to-lifers," "pro-lifers." This fact can call forth from our depths the Courage to Live, to be truly Pro-Life, without compromise. We observe the omnipresent sterile play-acting — the manufacture and spread of a deceptive dummy world — as manifested and legitimated in the insane recitations of the great dummy — reagan — and his cohorts schultz, falwell, et cetera. This horror can be a challenge to Lusty women to Act out of our deepest potential/potency.

Many characteristics of this deadtime can serve as demands/commands to Daring women to transcend the domination of dronedom/clonedom. Thus righteous contempt for the prevailing overt as well as subliminal lying of "leaders" can serve as an incentive to Soothsaying women to be totally truthful to our Selves. Fury over the fragmentation imposed by the infernal fraternities that rule the world can fuel our determination to reclaim Original Integrity. Rage over the imposed uniformity/ deformity/conformity of clonedom can fire/inspire us to re-member our Radiant Diversity.

To accept the challenge of archetypal deadtime in this way is not mere reaction. It is A-Mazing Action. Indeed, it is in part inspired by Disgust. I suggest that in 1985 A.F. Disgust be proclaimed a Necessary Virtue for Viragos. It is High Time for the celebration of Disgust — a Queenly, Dragon-identified Virtue. The verb *disgust* means "to provoke to loathing, repugnance, or aversion." The phallocrats of the eighties provoke Proud, Prudent women to all of these responses and more. Clearly, Disgust is an asset to Amazons and Spinsters, inspiring us to Spin on our heels into Other dimensions. Therefore it deserves special attention at this Time.

A Brief Discussion of Disgust

In countless conversations with women concerning prevailing fore-ground conditions I have heard expressions of almost inexpressible Disgust. Women are Disgusted at the increase of rape, of child-molestation, of woman-battering, of poverty, of gynecological abuse. Women are Disgusted over the nuclear arms build-up, chemical con-tamination, the escalating exploitation of the Third World, the torture of animals in laboratories and agribusiness, medical experimentation, the torture of women (flaunted on the "news" as scientific progress).[14] Women are Disgusted at the apparent absence of Disgust in those around them. It seems that to many persons, dulled out in archetypal deadtime, no exploitation, no atrocity, no degradation is disgusting enough to elicit honest Disgust. Deadened in the state of sleeping death, comatose, possessed occupants of deadtime cannot distinguish fancy from fact, the lies of paternal propagandists from the loathsome realities these are intended to disguise.

Many feminists, vehemently anti-pornography, have told me that they have found media coverage of the pope and his cardinals more Disgusting than pornography. While the latter is woman-hating to its (hard) core, it is, by comparison, almost straightforward in its intent. In contrast to this, the papal and hierarchical processions, parades, performances, and preachments are absolutely hypocritical about their intent.[15] For this reason, many feminists, having inadvertently glanced at television or picked up a *Deadtime Magazine* featuring these fatherly imposters, have experienced the necessity to disgorge and to laugh simultaneously. Indeed, Lusty Laughter is the only preventive medicine for incurable Nausea.

Women have described this Nausea to me in some detail. It is spiritual; it is physical. It is a Natural reaction to the fact of being force-fed insufferable lies, and *especially to being force-fed the tragic spectacle of women manipulated and humiliated by this hypocrisy, accepting the humiliation as benevolence, as a blessing.*

The *New York Times,* in the context of an article concerning the pope's 1985 visit to the Netherlands and Belgium, featured an Associated Press photo of a middle-aged woman in Brussels kneeling at the feet of the pope, her gaze turned upward, her hand clutching the sleeve of his immaculate white robe.[16] Countless pornographic magazines feature stories and photographs of women kneeling before men to perform fellatio under explicit or implicit threat of violence.[17] No present overt violence forces women to writhe and grovel and kneel before the holy father.[18] The act appears voluntary. Hence the spectacle elicits Nausea. Moreover, the Nausea is intensified if a feminist tries not to acknowledge her Disgust, for the simple reason that she wants to identify with this woman as her sister. She does not want to feel the Disgust she may be feeling.

I suggest that it is Time to let Disgust out of its closet, to celebrate its public Emergence — not disgust for bamboozled women but Disgust for the sacred set-up, the subliminal pornographic seduction, the hidden hard-ons of the holy fathers who induce such grotesque Self-abasement. It is Time to proclaim that the Disgust of a Wholly Disgusted Woman is Holy. This is Her Holiness, refusing to kneel before his nothingness, calling to other women to rise from their knees, laugh at his lies, acknowledge their own Powers — the Powers of Holy Crones who throw off the chains of hypocrisy, who refuse to allow our strength to be turned against us.

In 1985 a.d. the *Boston Globe* printed an Associated Press article reporting on pope john paul two's "firm message to rebels in the Dutch Roman Catholic hierarchy that he would not ease the Vatican's ban against women entering the priesthood."* According to the article,

---

*I am *not* advocating the ordination of women to the catholic priesthood. One of the most devastating things the catholic church could do, I think, would be to ordain women, thereby masking its deep-rooted misogyny and further promoting fallacious faith, false hope, and dead love.

that same afternoon, before a formal session of the World Court, "the pontiff attacked 'discrimination — in law or in fact — on the basis of race, origin, color, culture, sex, or religion.' "[19]

In the endless 1984 a.d. world such examples of doublethink are omnipresent and require no comment. They do, however, illustrate the climate of mind-rape that pervades contemporary deadtime/deadspace and that continues to bring women "willingly" to their knees. Without such tactics and without such kneeling women the church would literally lose its power and cease to exist, for there would be no female energy for it to feed upon. It is essential to realize that *without the loyalty of women the church and its churchmen would shrivel and die.* Hence, it is important to move to a brief analysis of this loyalty, the lies that maintain it, and the unnatural dependence and need for love that make it appear necessary to vulnerable women.

On Loyalty, Lies, and Luv

Feminist theorist Andrea Dworkin has written of the promises of the ultra-Right which entrap women. The Right offers *form* (which banishes the confusion women feel in a senseless society), *shelter* (which allays women's deep fear of homelessness in a world owned by men), *safety* (in a gynocidal world), *rules* (so that women can know how to survive in servitude), and *love* (especially the love of jesus).[20] In Dworkin's analysis, which applies accurately to the plight of conservative catholic women, mormon women, fundamentalist women, et cetera, these lethal gifts are payments for loyalty to the divine males.

The word *loyal* is derived from the Latin *legalis,* meaning "legal." One meaning of *loyal* is "faithful in allegiance to one's lawful sovereign or government." Believing that churchmen are their lawful sovereigns, women give them allegiance. It is enlightening to note that a basic definition of *allegiance* is "the obligation of a feudal vassal to his liege lord." Under patriarchal religion all women are vassals. A vassal is "a person under the *protection* of another who is his [*sic*] feudal lord and to whom he has vowed homage and fealty" (emphasis mine).

Feminists are familiar with the syndrome of the "protection racket" as it operates in rapist society. Briefly, in exchange for loyalty to one sovereign male, a woman receives his protection against other males who would rape her. Applying this paradigm to the realm of spiritual rape, we see that churchly sovereigns protect their female vassals from other mind-rapers, reserving to themselves the right to such rape and the rites of mind-rape. On the deepest level, this protection is about shielding women from knowledge of our own Elemental Powers. The lords know that these Powers, unleashed, would overturn their rapist reign.

The most effective strategy for shielding/"protecting" women from knowledge of our own Powers is degradation and female complicity in women's degradation. This is a clue to the hidden connections among the strategies of pornographers, pimps, and priests. Women as vassals, whether as porn models, prostitutes, or pious adherents to patriarchal religion, are vessels of Self-hatred, protected from their own strength, independence, intelligence, health, passion, and spiritual development. Rewarded for Self-destructive and woman-hating behavior, women are recruited into loyal service to the sovereigns of sadosociety.

In her brilliant work *Three Guineas*, Virginia Woolf — foresister of exceptional genius — writes of various forms of "brain prostitution,"[21] and she advises women to accept several "teachers," including "freedom from unreal loyalties." This is "freedom from loyalty to old schools, old colleges, old churches, old ceremonies, old countries."[22] Attached to phallic institutions by unreal loyalties, women are lured into "living" lies, converted to the habit of loving lies.

Women are hooked into unreal loyalty through an embedded need for false love. This "love," or luv, is junk food for the soul. As spiritual junk food junkies, robbed of Self-love, women go to the sovereign church. Their hunger is not really assuaged, since the cannibalistic "love" offered by a woman-hating priesthood does not nourish and strengthen; rather it assimilates/drains gynergy, increasing hunger, increasing addiction.

Seething masses chanting "John Paul Two, We love you," have been greeted by the papal response: "I love you *more*."[23] Any thoughtful observer would feel impelled to ask what this interchange could possibly mean. It might seem the height of *hubris* for a head hierarch to state that he can "love" a crowd of hundreds of thousands of people more than they, collectively, can "love" him. Yet, in a sense, the papal proclamation is correct. For, in his archetypal role, this replicant of the great mother assumes gigantic unreal proportions, eliciting unreal loyalties from millions who are oppressed by the dogmas he pontifically proclaims.

I suggest that the massive response to this archetypal illusion is due in large measure to the fact that it/he wields symbolic power precisely by making people believe that no matter how much they "love" him, he "loves" them MORE. Draining symbolic power from the image of the "Great Mother," whose robes and gestures he unashamedly assumes, the papal mother drains his flock. In this sense he exercises his symbolic power to luv them more than they can ever luv in return. Countless newspaper articles allude to the fact that john paul two is energized by the cheers and adulation of the crowds. Bearing in mind that these crowds adoring the misogynist pope are comprised largely of women, one can have some insight into the nature of the energy transaction that prevails in this wholly unwholesome, unholy luv affair.

Addiction to archetypal manipulation is hardly restricted to roman catholics in relation to their hierarchy.* I have suggested that women incestuously abused by their fathers are similarly addicted. The mechanisms of the loyalty, lies, and luv syndrome function in analogous ways in a variety of situations. Thus women who are victims of experimentation by the patriarchs of the medical profession are hooked by luv into Self-destructive unreal loyalty.[24] Battered women are addicted to murderous situations of patriarchal marriage. Women who are possessed by pimps are hooked on luv. All of these scenarios seemingly are lived/died out in isolation. Yet there are threads of commonality. The scenarios take place under the hypnotic influence of the same archetypal symbol system, with male motherhood as a central theme and addiction as a primary consequence.[25]

---

*Nor is the loyalty, lies, and luv syndrome confined to religious priesthoods and their believers/followers. The nuclear priesthood, for example, together with its acolytes, is brimful of luv. In June 1985 the *Boston Globe* printed an article illustrating this syndrome in the lower echelons of the nuclear establishment. Charles Sweeney, "who as a 25-year-old Air Force major piloted the B-29 'Bock's Car' that dropped the atomic bomb on Nagasaki," is described as "hoping to return to that Japanese city on Aug. 9 — the 40th anniversary of the mission that led to the end of World War II." In case some readers would be naive enough to imagine that this bearer of hideous death and disease to tens of thousands of people forty years ago would be returning on his knees (symbolically, at least) to beg forgiveness, it is important to emphasize that this is precisely *not* how the syndrome of loyalty, lies, and luv works. Sweeney would expect to return as a hero.

Maintaining (parroting the official line) that "an estimated 1 million US casualties anticipated in an invasion of the Japanese mainland" were "saved" by his mission and that the ensuing quick end to the conflict was "welcomed by the Japanese people," Sweeney proudly proclaims that he would "do the same thing again if called upon." Moreover (in case some persistently naive reader might think that the Japanese would officially lynch this "hero"), readers are assured that, as the Japanese industrialist Sumio Shimodoi told Sweeney, "even in the days that followed the killing of some 180,000 people at both cities, there was no hatred of the Americans by the Japanese civilians."

The case of the papal projection of male motherhood, luv, and consequent addiction to unreal loyalty is of particular interest largely because the display of deception is so explicit, so obvious, so brazen, and apparently so successful. The extraordinary explicitness is useful, for it gives the wholly holey show away. The papal re-production of primary partiarchal archetypal reversals is writ large enough for all to see. This raises the obvious question: Why, then, do so many still not see? The problem, I think, centers on the nature of addiction itself, for this is what prevents seeing. Hooked, the victim *lacks the emotional distance* that is necessary to see and to judge.

It is significant that the victims of lies/luv are prevented from laughing at the palpably absurd pomposity, the unbelievable costumes and performances, the ineffable charade of ghoulish female impersonators who parade shamelessly under the umbrella of luv. This is because humor implies the *seeing through* which requires distance/detachment

---

Sweeney himself says that he never questioned the morality of what he was doing. In his view, the moral question of the use of nuclear weapons "is up to the philosophers to decide." He does luv the Japanese people. In his own words: "I love the people, the beauty and the culture of Japan . . . I hope to return" (*Boston Globe*, 10 June 1985, pp. 21, 24).

I offer this example not as unusual but as ineffably commonplace, banal. Sweeney, who, like Adolf Eichmann, experiences no moral responsibility since he was acting under orders, exemplifies the qualities of intellect and emotion characteristic of the agents and tools of patriarchal priesthoods. The complicity of the hierarchs of the Japanese — or any other — industrial priesthoods should not be surprising. Moreover, members of religious priesthoods have been enthusiastically complicit. As Richard Falk has noted: "The great [*sic*] French Jesuit philosopher-anthropologist Teilhard de Chardin greeted the test explosion in the New Mexico desert with wild enthusiasm" (Robert J. Lifton and Richard Falk, *Indefensible Weapons* [New York: Basic Books, Inc., 1982], p. 193). The words of the renowned jesuit thinker concerning the test explosion deserve attention here. He wrote that it "disclosed to human existence a supreme purpose: the purpose of pursuing ever further, to the very end, the forces of Life. In exploding the atom we took our first bite at the fruit of the great discovery, and this was enough for a taste to enter our mouths that can never be washed away: the taste for super-creativeness" (Pierre Teilhard de Chardin, *The Future of Man* [New York: Harper Colophon Books, 1964], p. 151).

The response of the victims/survivors of such luv commonly involves a great deal of denial, as Robert J. Lifton has shown. (See his book *Death in Life: Survivors of Hiroshima* [New York: Touchstone Books, 1967].) While the victims include men as well as women, the men are also reduced to the archetypal feminine role of victim. The syndrome of loyalty, lies, luv can be detected in the mechanisms of racism, classism, ageism and is illustrated in such institutions as modern patriarchal medicine, in which clients are degraded to the role of "patient." (See Denise D. Connors, "Sickness unto Death: Medicine as Mythic, Necrophilic, and Iatrogenic," *Advances in Nursing Science*, vol. 2, no. 3 [April 1980], pp. 39–51.)

from the absurd spectacle. Lusty Laughter, the uninhibited expression of recognizing the absurd, also presupposes a woman's Realizing of her Rage. It implies not only the Virtue of Disgust but also the Virtue of Courage and the Virtue of Wild Prudence, which is the practical wisdom of Prudes. [26] For deviant/defiant Shrewd Prudes see that it is Wise to Laugh Out Loud and publicly at the patently absurd processions of the infernal pseudomaternal predators. (Imagine hundreds of thousands of women lining the streets, howling and roaring at pompous processions of the pope and cardinals whenever/wherever they try to process!) It is important, then, to turn to a discussion of Laughing Out Loud, the Lusty Virtue of women who have the Courage to Leave/Live.

The Virtue of Laughing Out Loud

When women are victimized as vassals, chained by unreal loyalty to the liege lords of archetypal deadland, they are, as Jane Caputi has remarked, vessels containing their own laughter. [27] Undone by unreal loyalties, women are prisoners of the serious. Certainly, there is much to be serious about: the enslavement and indirect murder of women by means of legislation and moral (i.e., immoral) dictates against abortion, birth control, lesbianism, and, in general, against Self-government and expansion of woman-identified be-ing/spiritual Life. Yet it would be a mistake (quite literally, a *serious* mistake) to be so transfixed by the horror of what is being done to women and all oppressed people that attention is drawn away from the *agents* of the atrocities. When this happens, we can fail to assess the agents accurately, overlooking their absurdity and radical ontological impotence.

This mistake of fixing only on victimization can itself be addictive, inhibiting the instinct to take distance, to see the oppressors' absurdity and Laugh Out Loud. This mistake is not only a psychological error; it is a political failure and ultimately an ontological one. It is failure to evoke the Powers of Be-Fooling. As I have written elsewhere, Be-Fooling is ontological Fooling; it is pronouncing the predators' snoolish stupidity to be blameworthy and evil. It punctures the pomposity of wantwits and windbags, whose malignant mindlessness would destroy the world. Be-Fooling is Elemental humor, an explosive expression of Elemental Power. [28]

The archetypal headmen/deadmen are grave men. These grave diggers are deadly serious. Simone de Beauvoir, in *The Ethics of Ambiguity*, gives radical insight into the mentality of "the serious man," who "puts nothing into question." She writes:

Therefore, the serious man is dangerous. It is natural that he makes himself a tyrant. Dishonestly ignoring the subjectivity of his choice, he pretends that the unconditioned value of the object is being asserted through him; and by the same token he also ignores the value of the subjectivity and freedom of others, to such an extent that, sacrificing them to the thing, he persuades himself that what he sacrifices is nothing.[29]

The predators do not question what they are doing. They are tyrants who dishonestly ignore the subjectivity of their choices — pretending total "objectivity" and correctness, asserting "unconditioned value of the object," for example, by designing and enforcing anti-abortion laws. The priests of the professions of patriarchy ignore the subjectivity and freedom of others, sacrificing them to the thing (their god, their science, their sadism), persuading themselves that what they sacrifice is nothing.[30]

There is no "appropriate response" to sadoseriousness. The point is not to respond/react, but spontaneously to Act — inappropriately. Seeing the absurdity, a responsible/response-able woman Laughs Out Loud. Her Laughter sends out clear vibrations, cracking the hypocritical hierarchs' house of mirrors: the world of illusions/delusions in which they are encased. Priorities are important here. The point is not merely to rid the deluders of their delusions/illusions (this could be an impossible project) but to crack their power of deluding others. The more women Laugh Out Loud, the more women Hear ourSelves Laughing, the bigger the cracks in the masters' mirrors.

Laughing Out Loud cracks the man-made universe.[31] It creates a crack though which women can escape into the Wild. When Crones crack our own Jokes, the world splits open.[32] There is a cosmic thunder, pealing as Prudes' Laughter peals. The peals of thunder-laughter peal away the plastic films that limit Life-Lust. They peel away the plastic passions from our souls, unleashing Passion.[33] As Crackpots, Crones unpot the potted passions, freeing them to grow.[34]

Laughing Out Loud is Archaically Timely. Mimicking the gimmicks of archetypal deadtime, Archimagical Musing women unmask the male mothers. For example, we fashion New Archaic Fairy Tales about The Cardinals' New Clothes.[35] When tired of this entertainment, we leave the exposed prelates to tinker with their boys' toys, propped up by the stage props of a passing age/stage. Laughing women then move on to consider the Cardinal Virtue of Lust.

The Cardinal Virtue of Lust

There are many bright virtues in Archaic Time/Space, but the greatest of these is Lust, Ontological Lust. The Courage to Leave implies the Courage to Live, which implies the Courage to Lust for Elemental Happiness. This Lust reaches beyond Wildest imagination. It is, in fact, about Creation. Wonderlusting women Dream ourSelves into Archaic Futures — unimaginable now, but dawning in our souls.

Crackpot Crones peer through the cracks and glimpse the crack of dawn. Our cackling, awakening new vibrations, elicits invitations from within our own Original be-ing. These Calls of the Wild, beckonings of the Wonderlust in every Witch-Woman's heart, inspire us to shed the last husks of fallacious faith, false hope, and dead luv. Ontological Lust is an Outbreak of Courage — the Courage to Break Out.

Ontological Lust is a Cardinal Virtue. The word *cardinal*, of course, means "of basic importance, MAIN, CHIEF, PRIMARY." It is derived from the Latin *cardo*, meaning "hinge." All other virtues of Wild women hinge on Ontological Lust, which is the hinge of the door to freedom, to the possibility of Breaking Out. Without the Cardinal Virtue of Ontological Lust, women become unhinged, attempting to hinge ourSelves to whatever appears stable. The stable owners of Stag-Nation — hierarchical opportunists — hustle their services, attempting to hook/hinge women to their fraudulent frameworks, framing their prey. The framers thus work to fix women, to bolt the doors of our souls, ourSelves.

The Powers to break the framers' frameworks are within women. Dis covering our Lust of Be-ing, we can easily swing open the doors to our freedom. We work to attain the Prudence of Prudes, the Courage of Crones, the Distemper of Dragon-identified Fire-breathing Furies. Furiously focused, we find our Final Cause.[36]

Wicked Conclusions

No longer hinging on frameworks of framers, Lusty women are positively Unhinged. Unhinged, Unhooked, we Spin our spiritual powers. Freed from preying/praying priestly predators, Wicked Women practice Natural Magic.

Ontological/Logical Lust leads to logical conclusions. We conclude our complicity in Crone-killing professions, freeing ourSelves from fascist physicians of body and soul. We sever relations with rakes and rippers, the prickers revered in rapist religion. We refuse the "wisdom" of wantwits and frauds, the academented[37] hucksters of "higher" learning. Declining a-Musement by drones, we dream our own dreams. Refusing confinement in boys' boxes for women — from porn peddlars' playpens to misogynists' churches — we end the endless tedium of the State of Boredom.

Unhinged women end delusions by drawing Crone-logical conclusions. These conclusions are the Wicked Work of Wild Wiccen women.[38] They are, in fact, radical beginnings of Spinsters' Spinnings into 1985 A.F. . . . and Afterwards. Wanderlusting into Archaic Time, Wiccen women Weave Archaic Futures. Deep Memories — Metamemories — erupt into our Real Present/Presence, making possible Real Futures. No longer trapped in the years of the lord — archetypal deadtime — Original Women, in touch with our Origins, bring forth Original thoughts, words, deeds. Forgetting to remember old creeds, we conjure new and ancient Faith. Ignoring false promises/premises, we hop with Living Hope. Riding the Tides of Present Promise, we bond in the chorus of Be-ing.

1985 and afterwards a.d. is the time of the archetypal act. It is rehearsal time for the armageddon staged and planned in the disneyworld of huckster presidents, premiers, prelates, and their fundamentalist flunkies and other professional puppets. On the Other hand, 1985 A.F. and Afterwards is the Time of Ultimate Opportunity. It is now that the dis-covering of women's submerged Elemental/Spiritual Powers can make all the difference. In Archaic Time, of course, this is always so. In the Present moment, however, the urgency is especially obvious. The Call of the Wild from the depths of our souls, to the depths of our souls, is particularly poignant and clear. Those who have ears to Hear, Let them Hear.

[1] Friedrich Nietzsche, *The Gay Science*, in *The Portable Nietzsche*, selected and translated by Walter Kaufmann (New York: The Viking Press, 1954, 1968), p. 96.

[2] This Leaving has nothing in common with mere apathetic "dropping out" that is not inspired by an ardent Lust for transcendence.

[3] Analysis of these dead symbols and how they work can be found in my books: *Beyond God the Father: Toward a Philosophy of Women's Liberation* (Boston: Beacon Press, 1973; reissued with an Original Reintroduction, 1985); *Gyn/Ecology: The Metaethics of Radical Feminism* (Boston: Beacon Press, 1978); *Pure Lust: Elemental Feminist Philosophy* (Boston: Beacon Press, 1984). All of these books give copious references to other works offering historical and analytic materials on the subject of patriarchal symbols and myths.

[4] This terrifying false belief is summarized in the doctrine/cliché "Outside the church there is no salvation."

[5] Conversation with Emily Culpepper, Boston, March 1985.

[6] *Mind-rape* is the violation of women's minds. *Erasure* is the obliteration of women's history and women's lives. I have analyzed this at length in *Gyn/Ecology*, especially in Chapters 3 through 7. *Reversal* is exemplified in the idea that Eve was born from Adam; in the naming of the MX missile "Peacekeeper"; in descriptions of strong, witty women as "humorless." *Doublethink* is the perverted psychological mechanism which makes reversals acceptable and even invisible.

[7] Conversation with Emily Culpepper, Boston, April 1985. It is a positive advantage of the situation of catholic women, I think, that ordination is denied them. This makes the situation of oppression clearer and thus enhances the chances of escape. The pitfalls of tokenism and of the use of women by the hierarchy as priestly token torturers of other women are inadvertently avoided. Yet even the most lucid discussions of "advantages" on either side of such a wholly unadvantageous situation as closure in patriarchal religion can reinforce the patterns of the maze. As Culpepper has remarked, women's energies are endlessly misfocused in defending aspects of their respective woman-hating traditions to each other. (Conversation, Boston, June 1985.)

[8] I have discussed these traps in *Pure Lust*, with an emphasis on Ways Out of them, namely, *Be-Longing* (the Lust for Happiness), *Be-Friending* (the Lust to share Happiness), and *Be-Witching* (the Lust for Metamorphosis). See Chapters 9 through 12.

[9] See Kathleen Barry, *Female Sexual Slavery* (Englewood Cliffs, N.J.: Prentice-Hall, Inc., 1979), especially pp. 73–102.

[10] The term *foreground* was invented by Denise Connors to Name the male-centered, monodimensional level on which objectification and alienation take place. Connors has contrasted this with the *Background* which is "the realm of the wild reality of women's Selves." (Conversation, Boston, October 1976.) This terminology, now commonly used among feminist theorists, is an essential cornerstone of the theory developed in *Gyn/Ecology* and *Pure Lust*.

[11] See Aristotle, *Physics*, Book IV, Ch. 12.

[12] This expression is used by Jan Raymond in her article "A Genealogy of Female Friendship," *Trivia: A Journal of Ideas*, vol. 1 (Fall 1982), p. 7. Raymond develops this concept in her book *A Passion for Friends: Toward a Philosophy of Female Affection* (Boston: Beacon Press, 1986).

[13] Such Pride is manifested in the work of Andrea Dworkin and Catharine MacKinnon, in their unflagging efforts to initiate antipornography legislation.

[14] Medical experimentation on and torture of women is exposed at length by Gena Corea in her books *The Hidden Malpractice* (New York: Harper Colophon Books, 1977, 1985) and *The Mother Machine* (New York: Harper and Row, 1985).

[15] See *Pure Lust*, pp. xi, 82–83. Pornographers such as the editors of *Penthouse* are, of course, also hypocritical, but this is a different genre of hypocrisy.

[16] *New York Times*. 21 May 1985, p. 2.

[17] As psychologist Joyce Contrucci has stated, many women, bombarded by these images, have taken the pornographic image into their core. (Conversation, Norwell, Mass., May 1985.)

[18] As Emily Culpepper has suggested, however, it is important to look behind the scenes at the history of gynocide, for example, at the Witchcraze in Western Europe, in the course of which hundreds of thousands, possibly millions, of women were massacred. Women have been affected — in many cases, broken — by this legacy, which has been trivialized and ignored in patriarchal accounts of history. (Conversation, Boston, June 1985.) See *Gyn/Ecology*, Chapter 6.

[19] *Boston Globe*, 14 May 1985, pp. 1, 13.

[20] Andrea Dworkin, *Right-Wing Women* (New York: G. P. Putnam's Sons, Harbinger Books, 1983), pp. 13–35.

[21] Virginia Woolf, *Three Guineas* (New York: Harcourt, Brace & World, Harbinger Books, 1938), p. 94.

[22] Woolf, *Three Guineas*, p. 78.

[23] *Boston Globe*, 9 October 1979, p. 1.

[24] Gena Corea recounts the case of a woman who had been horribly and unnecessarily genitally mutilated by her physician. The victimized woman described herself as having been "ridiculously loyal" to her doctor. See *The Hidden Malpractice* (1985 edition), pp. 313–14.

[25] I have discussed the phenomenon of male motherhood in *Beyond God the Father*, *Gyn/Ecology*, and *Pure Lust*.

[26] *Prude* is derived from the French *prudefemme*, meaning "wise or good woman," and is rooted in the Old French *prode*, meaning "good, capable, brave." *Prude* has the same origins as *proud*. Of course, within phallocracy, this is used disparagingly of women, and it should be reclaimed.

[27] Conversation, Boston, June 1985.

[28] This concept is developed in the forthcoming book *Websters' First New Intergalactic Wickedary of the English Language*, Conjured by Mary Daly, in Cahoots with Jane Caputi.

[29] Simone de Beauvoir, *The Ethics of Ambiguity*, trans. Bernard Frechtman (Secaucus, N.J.: The Citadel Press, 1948), p. 49.

[30] It is thought provoking that the man who died in Brazil in 1979, believed to be the Nazi war criminal Josef Mengele, was described by an admirer as "a serious man." *Boston Globe*, 8 June 1985, p. 1.

[31] This idea was suggested by Jane Caputi (conversation, Boston, June 1985).

[32] This was inspired by the poet Muriel Rukeyser's famous lines:
What would happen if one woman told the truth about her life?
The world would split open.
From "Käthe Kollwitz," III, st. 4, *The Speed of Darkness* (New York: Random House, 1968), p. 103.

[33] See Daly, *Pure Lust*, Chapter 5.

[34] See Daly, *Pure Lust*, Chapter 5.

[35] Virginia Woolf has set a splendid example for this in *Three Guineas*.

[36] See Daly, *Beyond God the Father*, Chapter 7.

[37] This word was suggested by Diana Davies (personal communication, February 1985).

[38] The adjective *wiccen* is here constructed from the noun *wicce*, the Old English word for "witch."

THE CHURCH
AND THE
SECOND SEX

Autobiographical Preface
to the 1975 Edition

The Church and the Second Sex was published in 1968, before the cresting of the second wave of feminism. The writing began in 1965 in a small medieval city, Fribourg, Switzerland, where I lived for seven years. It was completed in 1967 in Boston. Not counting doctoral dissertations, it was my first book. It was written with a great sense of pride, anger, and hope.

In 1971, after a brief, turbulent history, *The Church and the Second Sex* went out of print.[1] It formally died. I tried to "reason" with the publisher that there was a demand for it, pointing out that I had received many letters and telephone calls, especially from women taking or teaching Feminist Studies, asking why the book wasn't available. But reason, as I had always understood the term, had no effect upon the publishing house patriarchs, who refused to move. So I moved on to other things, including a dramatic/traumatic change of consciousness from "radical Catholic" to postchristian feminist. My graduation from the Catholic church was formalized by a self-conferred diploma, my second feminist book, *Beyond God the Father: Toward a Philosophy of Women's Liberation,* which appeared in 1973.[2] The journey in time/space that took place between the publication dates of the two books could not be described adequately by terrestrial calendars and maps. Experientially, it was hardly even a mere trip to the moon, but more like leap-frogging galaxies in a mind voyage to further and further stars. Several woman-light years had separated me from *The Church and the Second Sex,* whose author I sometimes have trouble recalling.

Then, in 1974, with the imponderable logic that characterizes the Divinities of the Publishing World, its publishers informed me of their celestial desire that the book appear on earth once again. O Goddess: a Second Coming? Startled, I contemplated this new revelation. The Divine Word had been spoken. Now, what response should I give about this strange book and its strange author who had

[1] Published by Harper & Row, 1968, reprinted with Autobiographical Preface and Feminist Postchristian Introduction, 1975.

[2] Published in Boston by Beacon Press.

inhabited a distant world? There was of course the biblical answer: "Let it be done according to Thy Word." However, to a postchristian feminist that hardly seemed an appropriate response. Therefore, I would have to devise some unique solution to the subtle and intriguing problem posed by these Godfathers. What were the possibilities? An updated, revised edition, perhaps? I went to my bookcase and took the book off the shelf. Opening it with a sense of reluctance, I felt as if this were the journal of a half-forgotten foremother, whose quaintness should be understood in historical context and treated with appropriate respect.

Opening the book at random, I found myself in Chapter Seven, "Toward Partnership: Some Modest Proposals." I read a few pages and discovered that the author was proposing that there be equality between men and women in the Church (sic, with capital "C"). Why, I wondered, would anyone want "equality" in the church? In a statement that I had given to the press only three or four womanlight years distant from now, I had explained that a woman's asking for equality in the church would be comparable to a black person's demanding equality in the Ku Klux Klan. How could the author of this book have been so obtuse . . . ? But then, the publication date was 1968 A.D. Flipping through a few pages, I noted that the author had used the rather pompous editorial "we" instead of "I" and had written "they" to refer to women, instead of "we." Why did she say "we" when she meant "I" and "they" when she meant "we"? I noted with a sense of embarrassment for her that she used the term "man" as if it were a generic term. I perceived that she had hoped to reform Christianity. Clearly, it would be impossible to "revise" this book in the year 1975 of feminist postchristian time/space (hereafter referred to as A.F., which is to say *Anno Feminarum*).[3]

---

[3] The question naturally arose: why not begin renumbering the years, instead of merely using a numbering system which coincides with the A.D. system? But the fact is that women have not entered feminist postchristian time/space "all at once" *en bloc* with military precision. This is an important difference between our time and the linear patriarchal time of "A.D." I cannot assume that there was one single or supreme moment of revelation in the past upon which we must forever fix a backward gaze. Rather, since the women's movement *moves,* its revelation moves. Women enter it freely, as unique selves. Indeed, some who are lodged in 1975 A.D. can be expected to move into 1975 A.F. Feminist time/space is *on the boundary* of patriarchal time and space. As we are living *now,* the matter of numbering our time does not seem of central significance, and so for the sake of convenience, and in order to communicate our boundary-living situation, I have retained the

What to do? Since the Christian model of resignation to the will of the Proprietor of the Word is dysfunctional in the year 1975 A.F., I considered simply refusing to allow this Second Coming of *The Church and the Second Sex*. However, I hesitated at the prospect of such a drastic refusal, partly because women continued to ask for the book. Then another possibility occurred to me: let it become incarnate again, with a new postchristian introduction by myself. The advantages of this last option became apparent the longer I reflected upon the dilemma posed by time warp. First, since the book is a carefully researched historical record and since the material it contains is difficult to obtain anywhere else, this Second Coming would make the data available again for those engaged in Feminist Studies. Second, the book itself is now part of women's history, and as such it is revealing. It represents a stage of thought, feelings, hope, politics that can now be reflected upon from the perspective of new feminist time/space. Since I was, in an earlier incarnation, the author of that book, I am in a unique position to bring it forth again in a new light, to tell its story and then, in the new introduction, to become its critic and reviewer. And so it was the Morning of the Second Daly. I saw that it was a good idea.

THE STORY OF *The Church and the Second Sex*

In the early sixties Europe, and specifically Fribourg, was home. Stranger in a strange land, I felt free in the strangeness, doing just what I had chosen to do in a seemingly unlikely place. I was accumulating doctoral degrees, the first in theology and the second in philosophy, at the University of Fribourg, Switzerland, while at the same time earning enough money for survival by teaching philosophy courses to American students at three different "junior year abroad" programs. Life was made easier by a Velosolex motorbicycle on which I zoomed back and forth between the university, where I was lectured at by pompous professors, and the American villas, where I learned more relevant things from my own students.

---

old numbers. It may be that at some point in our future, women will think that this transitional dating is no longer appropriate and adopt a new expression, such as "Amazon Infinity" (A.I.), which was suggested by Emily Culpepper during a conversation in June, 1974 A.F.

There seems to be no way of explaining adequately how I got to Fribourg, storybook medieval town whose streets transported me to the thirteenth century. My passion had been to study philosophy and theology. To a person who had grown up in the Catholic ghetto, theology then meant "Catholic" theology. There was no place in the United States where a female was allowed to study for the "highest degree" in this field, the "canonical" Doctorate in Sacred Theology. Since I would settle for nothing less than "highest degrees," I applied to study in Fribourg, where the theological faculty was state-controlled and therefore could not legally exclude women.

Why anyone would want such a degree is an unfathomable mystery if the question is asked from the perspective of 1975 A.F. It may seem equally mad that I persisted and obtained yet another doctorate, this time in philosophy, from the same university. But in the otherworld of the 1960's A.D. these appeared to be two doorways to the life of a philosopher-theologian, the life of a woman who could think, write and teach about the most fascinating of all questions and earn her living by doing just this. It now appears that the naiveté that gave rise to and sustained such an ambition was astonishing. I can only say that it was a tough innocence that was willing to cross oceans and face unknown dragons to obtain its objectives.

I have said that Fribourg was an unlikely place. It was an improbable place to have existed at all, let alone for a feminist book to have been conceived in. Fribourg was, in fact, an experience—a mad series of improbable situations with multidimensional meanings. For example, it meant sitting in classes taught in Latin by white-robed Dominican priests whose lectures often made more sense when you didn't comprehend the language than when you did. The oddness of this situation was compounded by the fact that my classmates were nearly all priests and male seminarians, many of whom were from Latin countries. It was further compounded by the fact that in the crowded classrooms there frequently were empty places on each side of me, because my "fellow" students feared the temptations that might arise from sitting next to a female. But this "outfreaking" experience was only part of the scene.

Fribourg also meant freedom—a fact which I frequently celebrated in its unique tea rooms and cafés with other American students, mainly my own students. We rejoiced about many things: travel, adventure, mindblowing discoveries of a different culture.

We also rejoiced over the fact that the Statue of Liberty was still far away. Tired and poor, we had escaped that stifling embrace for yet a little while. Fribourg meant learning the intense intellectual discipline of a culture that even then had long ago disappeared from most places on the planet earth, but which retained its fascination for me, at least. A seven years' ecstatic experience interspersed with brief periods of gloom, it was a sort of lengthy spiritual-intellectual chess game, interrupted by side trips to less ethereal realms such as London, Dublin, Paris, Vienna, Madrid, Athens, Damascus, Cairo. Most significantly, it was interrupted by one very special side trip to Rome.

The Church and the Second Sex might never have happened if there had not been one great carnival of an event, the Second Vatican Council of the Roman Catholic Church, and if I had not managed to go to that carnival in the fall of 1965. In some ways it was the opposite of the experience of Fribourg. While the latter was an internationally populated island of isolation, the Rome of Vatican II was a sea of international communication—the place/ time where the Catholic church came bursting into open confrontation with the twentieth century. It seemed to everyone, except to the strangely foreseeing "conservatives," prophets of doom who in some perverse way knew what was really going on, that the greatest breakthrough of nearly two thousand years was happening. We met —theologians, students, journalists, lobbyists for every imaginable cause—and found that our most secret thoughts about "the church" were not solitary aberrations. They were shared, spoken out loud, allowed credibility. There was an ebullient sense of hope. Most of us thought then that this meant there was hope for the church. Years later, some would manage to understand that the hope was real even though its focus was misplaced. Some would learn to transfer the primary force of that hope away from the church and to ourselves and each other. We would even learn to stop misnaming ourselves as "the church." But then all eyes were turned to the church.

For the species "Catholic Feminist," this misplaced hope was comparable to the euphoria experienced in a slightly later period by the species "New Left Feminist." To both groups, which were distinct but partly overlapping, it appeared that a door had opened *within* patriarchy which could admit an endless variety of human possibilities. The gradual extinction of both groups was inevitable and desirable, although not yet desired, at least, not by their members. It would take time to learn that *all* male-controlled "revolutions" are essentially movements in circles within the same senescent patriarchal system.

Every day during that month-long visit in Rome was fascinating, but one day in particular was important. I borrowed a journalist's identification card and went into St. Peter's for one of the major sessions. Sitting in the section reserved for the press, I saw in the distance a multitude of cardinals and bishops—old men in crimson dresses. In another section of the basilica were the "auditors": a group which included a few Catholic women, mostly nuns in long black dresses with heads veiled. The contrast between the arrogant bearing and colorful attire of the "princes of the church" and the humble, self-deprecating manner and somber clothing of the very few women was appalling. Watching the veiled nuns shuffle to the altar rail to receive Holy Communion from the hands of a priest was like observing a string of lowly ants at some bizarre picnic. (In retrospect it seems to have been an ant-poisonous picnic.) Speeches were read at the session, but the voices were all male, the senile, cracking whines of the men in red. The few women, the nuns, sat docilely and listened to the reading of documents in Latin, which neither they nor the readers apparently understood. When questioned by the press afterward, the female "auditors" repeatedly expressed their gratitude for the privilege of being present. Although there were one or two exceptions, for the most part they were cautious about expressing any opinion at all. Although I did not grasp the full meaning of the scene all at once, its multileveled message burned its way deep into my consciousness. No Fellini movie could have outdone this unintended self-satire of Catholicism.

When I returned home to Fribourg, I really began to work on *The Church and the Second Sex*. But it was not only the experience of the Vatican Council in Rome that made this written expression of anger and hope possible. Another important catalyst had been an article by Rosemary Lauer, a Catholic philosopher, which had appeared two years earlier in *Commonweal* (December, 1963). That piece had been only moderately critical of the church's treatment of women, but the fact that a woman who retained her identity as "Catholic" had said these things was an astounding breakthrough. It somehow bestowed upon me the psychological freedom to "write out loud" my own thoughts. That article functioned in a special way that the more radical works of Simone de Beauvoir and Betty Friedan, which I greatly admired, could not function at that point in time: it legitimated the possibility of my own creative feminist writing.

I wrote a letter supporting the Lauer article, and my own first article on sexism and religion, "A Built-In Bias," appeared in *Commonweal* in January, 1965. Some weeks later a letter from a British publisher in London found its way to me in Fribourg, after visiting several wrong addresses. It contained an invitation to write a book on women and the church, developing the ideas in the *Commonweal* article, which had been spotted by someone who worked for the publishing house. The letter was like a summons, and I knew clearly that the time was right for the First Coming of *The Church and the Second Sex*. The contract was signed in May, 1965. But it was in the fall of that year, after the crimson and black of the Roman circus in Saint Peter's basilica broke through the surface of my mind, that my visionary anger began to incarnate itself in the form of this book.

The first five chapters were written in Fribourg. When I returned to the United States I finished the book. Soon afterward the book almost finished me. I was fired from my teaching job at Jesuit-run Boston College, that is, given a terminal contract. Although the administrators never bothered to give any reason for the termination of our happy relationship, the press and just about everyone else put two and two together. An uppity Second Sex was just too much for the church. And for Boston College students that was precisely the issue: Was their university a place where ideas could be expressed freely, or was it "the church"?

My "case" became a *cause célèbre*. It was 1969, a year of demonstrations, and the students wanted a symbol in their crusade for "academic freedom." I was it. There were several months of struggle. An estimated fifteen hundred students demonstrated. Twenty-five hundred signed a petition. All of this was ignored by the administration, whose nonresponse brought forth a seven hour teach-in. Several professors fired from other universities spoke, students spoke, I spoke. Some local self-declared witches came and hexed Boston College, reminding us of the churchly habit of witch-burning. The next day the students began picketing the president's house, and the administration building was decorated at night with brilliant red graffiti (faint traces of which remain to this day, despite the costly use of modern technology to blast them away). The campus became a circus grounds, and television cameras were quick to arrive on the scene. The story was front page news in the Boston papers, duly reported in the *New York Times,* and recounted in a syndicated column which was published in major newspapers across the country. My case was receiving national, international, supernatural publicity, and the Jesuits could no longer hide behind their rosary beads.

The bureaucratic machinery began to grind. A special meeting of the university academic senate was held and a "faculty review committee" was elected to investigate the case. Since the committee was merely advisory to the president and since it was bound to "confidentiality," even a unanimous decision in my favor would not guarantee victory. When the academic year ended with no decision announced, it seemed that my fate was sealed.

The spring of 1969 had been an incredible time. From the roof of my apartment building, I could see the tower of Boston College's administration building, Gasson Hall. I recall having a strong intuition that there was some primary warfare going on, whose dimensions could not be reduced to the "issue" of academic freedom. It was an archetypal battle between principalities and powers, of which this "case" was a blatantly noticeable instance. In cruder and more immediate terms, I recognized that it was—and was more than —a war between "it" and me, and I willed to go all the way in this death battle. Perhaps the survival of "it" did not depend upon the outcome, but mine did. The practical/personal/political issue was simple. Under the insidious guise of "confidentiality" my teaching career was being destroyed. The university officials had refused to give any reasons publicly or to me privately for my firing, but the well-known phenomenon of grapevine innuendo would destroy my college teaching career.

Summer came, and since summer was the season when troublesome students were out of the way, the administration could be expected to behave in the way characteristic of university administrations. I would be quietly executed in my own absence. Such were my expectations when I arrived in June at a small college in Oregon to teach a summer course. Then the absurdly improbable happened. On the day of my arrival a telegram appeared in Oregon from the president of Boston College, informing me, without congratulations, that I had been granted promotion and tenure.

It was a strange victory. Apparently the book which had generated the hostility which led to my firing had generated the support which forced my rehiring. I now had the relative safety of a tenured university professor, subject of course to the possibility of harassment at any time in the future. But something had happened to the meaning of "professor," to the meaning of "university," to the meaning of "teaching." The "professors" from the various "fields" who had been my judges, the judges of my book, had themselves never written books, nor had they read or understood mine. Standing in negative judgment of my teaching, they were in fear of the students who had no use for their "teaching." I began to understand more about the prevailing "Beta consciousness" of academics, dwarfed by a system of "education" which made them unfree, uncourageous, and radically uneducated. Nor could I live under the delusion that this phenomenon of soul-shrinkage was peculiar· to this one university or to church-related universities or to those engaged in this particular field. Letters and conversations, especially with women, during and following the event, made it clear that this was a universal disease of "universities," which were microcosms reflecting the patriarchal world. I recognized that Boston College was not unusual. Perhaps, indeed, it lacked the more sophisticated means of oppression employed in the "great" universities, and there was even something like idealism that wove its way through the destruction and helped to make possible this absurd triumph.

It was the universalist quality of this personal "revelation" that was important. I began to understand more of the implications of the feminist insight that "the personal is political." The interconnections among the structures of oppression in a patriarchal society and the destructive dynamics which these structures generate in their victims became more and more visible. In other words, I understood more clearly the nature of the beast and the name of the demon: patriarchy.

The procession of consequences of *The Church and the Second Sex,* then, was a transforming process. So I moved into a more advanced class in a newly founded invisible counter-university, the Feminist Universe, whose students from all over the planet were beginning to discover each other.

As a result of the First Coming of *The Church and the Second Sex,* I had been hurled into instant fame as exposer of Christian misogyny—especially of the Roman Catholic variety—and champion of women's "equality" within the church. Armed with my quaint and esoteric scholarship and Celtic cunning, I faced on national television cleverly uncomprehending adversaries such as William F. Buckley and a string of think-alike clerics. I "lectured" to academic audiences and women's groups across the country about the sexism of the Christian tradition. Often in the late sixties I encountered hostility in women, not toward the patriarchs whose *misogynism* I exposed but toward me for exposing them.

By about 1970 this phenomenon of misplaced anger had almost disappeared. More and more people had caught up with *The Church and the Second Sex,* and the lines that formerly had elicited hostility brought forth cheers. But the "I" who was then standing before the friendly audiences and tossing out the familiar phrases was already disconnected from the words, already moving through a new time/ space. I often heard the old words as though a stranger were speaking them — some personage visiting from the past. My concern was no longer limited to "equality" in the church or anywhere else. I did not really care about unimaginative reform but instead began dreaming new dreams of a women's revolution. This was becoming a credible dream, because a community of sisterhood was coming into being, into be-ing. In the hearing/healing presence of these sisters I had grown ready to try writing/speaking New Words.[4]

---

[4] See *Beyond God the Father.*

Feminist Postchristian Introduction

A critical review of The Church and the Second Sex, *written from the perspective of 1975 A.F.* (Anno Feminarum)

During a recent archeological dig a curious volume entitled *The Church and the Second Sex* was unearthed. It appears to date from the year 1968 A.D., approximately seven woman-light years away/ ago. Because of its significant historical content and because it represents a period of critical reflection on the part of a species which is by now almost extinct, the species "Catholic Feminist," it seems important not only that it be made available in this time but also that it receive a serious critical review. In this piece, I shall attempt to do justice to the author in reviewing her book, judging it in its historical context, but I shall try not to overlook its limitations. I shall attempt to dialogue with her work chapter by chapter.

Before proceeding to an analysis of the specific content of each chapter, I shall make some general comments about language. The author frequently chooses to use the term "discrimination" to describe the predicament of women in a Christian culture. The choice of this term rather than a more accurate word such as "oppression," "obliteration," or "massacre" might seem to reveal an inclination to be cautious and generally "reformist." While this interpretation would be partially correct, I should point out that "discrimination" was the usual term employed by feminists of her time. She uses terms such as "misogynism" and "androcentrism" frequently. While I find these perfectly acceptable words, I note that she employs them often where I would be inclined to write "sexism," or "rapism." I suggest that the reader keep in mind that she did not have available to her the more adequate vocabulary and greater sensitivity to language which our feminist tradition has provided for us. This lack of tradition and precedent explains why she sometimes uses "man" and "he" as if these were generic terms. While I find this annoying,

I think that in fairness I should admit that in her circumstances I would have done no better.

Like Simone de Beauvoir, Daly uses the "objective" pronoun "they" to refer to women. It should be remembered that there did not yet exist a publicly expressed or expressable sense of bonding in sisterhood which would allow a feminist the psychological freedom to write "we" when referring to women. Moreover, no doubt Daly and de Beauvoir before her felt that a sense of respectable detachment and objectivity was conveyed by the use of the pronoun "they" to refer to women, especially if one were writing a scholarly work. One must consider the sense of isolation experienced by feminists in that bleak time, when even the use of the word "feminist" elicited patronizing smiles and pop-Freudian clichés from both women and men. In that climate, "they" must have felt quite fitting. Moreover, there certainly was no one to criticize an expression which we feminists now find inappropriately detached. Who at that time had ever heard of a woman-identified woman? A few bold women dared to say that women were "discriminated against" and that was a dangerous and apparently solitary point of view to express about "them."

There are other expressions that I find grating, even though I understand the background, for example, "chairman" (to refer to a woman). However, I think the point has been made, and I will try to refrain from alluding repetitiously in the course of this critique to the same or similar examples of semantic underdevelopment.

CHAPTER ONE

The Case Against the Church

This chapter (not to mention the book's title) reveals how strongly Daly was influenced by the French feminist philosopher Simone de Beauvoir. Unlike de Beauvoir, however, Daly expresses a hope, both here and throughout the book, for genuine change in the status of women in the church. In the preface of the original edition (deleted from this text) she had described as "ironic" the tension between the church and movements seeking to liberate women. Clearly she did not grasp the fact that it was not ironic but rather quite consistent with its principles that her church would oppose the liberation of women. It might seem odd that she apparently did not perceive this consistency, since she herself was the author of a major exposé of the long and consistent history of Christian misogynism. This baffling optimism can be understood if one is aware of the euphoria that prevailed among Catholics during the time of "Vatican Council II." So deceptive was this cloud of optimism that, despite the evidence which she herself amassed, Daly was unable to perceive that sexism was inherent in the symbol system of Christianity itself and that a primary function of Christianity in Western culture has been to legitimize sexism.

While recognizing that other cultural institutions were "discriminatory" (read: oppressive), Daly focused her attention upon the Judeo-Christian tradition. While she did recognize that other institutions in the West were themselves formed by and interrelated with the religious tradition to which she directed her criticism, she did not perceive the full import of this interrelatedness. Consequently, her concept of change coming from "outside" that religious tradition does not satisfy me, for she was not "outside" enough. Briefly, from within her time/space it was impossible to see the implications of the fact that her whole species was *possessed* by a planetary sexual caste system. Thus her vision had moved only partially outside patriarchy itself, and her visionary anger did not move her to take a qualitative leap into the new space and time of radical feminism as we know it.

Daly had to deal with the fact that de Beauvoir was an ex-Catholic. This would seem to explain the fact that she resorted to the device of "biographical" explanation for the French philosopher's "omission" of "certain dimensions" in her analysis of Catholicism. That is, she made a half-hearted attempt to explain de Beauvoir's apparent lack of hope for the church. Still, she had to agree with de Beauvoir's data (adding much more as a result of her own research), and she righteously concluded that "to attack her book on the basis of her life is to resort to *argumentum ad hominem*" (p. 57). It is amusing to note that Daly even quoted approvingly from a letter of Thomas Aquinas (whose misogynistic texts she dissects in a later chapter with cool ferocity) in which that medieval theologian wrote: "Remember the good things you hear, and do not consider who says them" (p. 57). So much for our author's use of Aquinas's "authority" to legitimize de Beauvoir's attack on Christianity.

With considerable skill, Daly brings together in this chapter the most significant texts of de Beauvoir relevant to Christianity, arranging them according to a few dominant themes and adding appropriate commentary. In general, she agrees with the French feminist, and for the most part rightly so. However, when she comes to the question of "transcendence through religion?" (pp. 66ff), Daly is not critical enough of the lyrical passages on Saint Teresa of Avila, whose situation de Beauvoir likens to that of great queens, "exalted by the power of social institutions above all sexual differentiation." Once again there is a curious ambivalence (to use one of her own favorite expressions) in the attitude of our author, who was *fully aware* of Teresa's sufferings from the church. In fact, in her second chapter she herself cites several poignant passages from Teresa's writings in which the saint expressed her anguish over the (church-imposed) chains that dragged her down because of her sex. How, then, could she so exuberantly echo de Beauvoir's unrealistic notion that "there is hardly any woman other than Saint Teresa who in total abandonment has herself lived out the situation of humanity" (p. 68)?

The final section of Chapter One, under the heading "Facing the problems," could be perplexing because of its self-contradicting combination of astuteness and "holding back." This syndrome is characteristic of the author in her last-ditch struggle to salvage Christianity in the face of her own evidence. She gives a concise summary of some relevant main points in de Beauvoir's existentialist philosophy, indicating substantial agreement with most of these. In my opinion, Daly was right to challenge the French existentialist's assumption that belief in God is inseparably linked with the idea of an *immutable* human nature. Today, in the light of feminist philosophy of Be-ing, we are aware of the deep connection between women's becoming and the unfolding of cosmic process—a process which some would still call "God."[1] But Daly's rebuttal of de Beauvoir's atheism is not vigorous enough, precisely because the only real alternative that she (and probably also de Beauvoir) could see to atheism was *Christian* faith. The author of *The Church and the Second Sex,* in my opinion, had not managed to move

[1] See *Beyond God the Father,* first chapter.

beyond this opposition of opposites: "Christian faith" versus "atheism." Consequently, she defends the indefensible.

"Has de Beauvoir omitted any significant data?" (p. 72) This question appears to be astute. But I think its real meaning was: "Isn't there something *good* about the church that de Beauvoir has not expanded upon?" This was, I believe, a desperate question, and Daly gives a desperate reply, finding a supposed clue to the "omitted" data in de Beauvoir's assertion that the church provided for Saint Teresa the needed condition for rising above the handicap of sex. This is indeed a convoluted reply when one considers that the church was a major cause of this "handicapped" condition of the female sex in the first place. Again, as Daly herself points out, Teresa was an exception, so her case says nothing to the situation of millions of women whose creativity was totally *erased*. What, then, is she trying to find in this search for "omitted" data? My informed guess is that she was aware of a depth of consciousness to which people became attuned through religious myth, even through oppressive religious myth. She knew that the patriarchal religions, including Christianity, conveyed a sense of transcendence. She valued this, and rightly so, but apparently she could not recognize a way to depth of consciousness, hope, and transcendence that would involve breaking out of Christianity. De Beauvoir's "atheistic" rejection of Christianity and Daly's desperate attempt to salvage it both stopped short. On the road ahead of them, not yet visible, was that point where the journeys of many women would bring insights together, so that postchristian feminist philosophy could spring forth.

Since I have already given some indication of the author's semantic handicaps, I will not repeat the same criticisms. However, I do feel compelled to point out a few revealing expressions that occur in this chapter. More than once she writes of her hopes for "purification" of "distortions of doctrine" in Christianity, tacitly assuming (1) that there is some true Christian doctrine underlying the "distortions"; (2) that Christian doctrine is not itself a distortion. There are also indications that she lacked consciousness of the political implications of grammar. For example, on page 70 I find the sentence: "He or she is the sum total of *his* works . . ." (italics mine). When the author does use both pronouns ("he or she") or writes of the "man-woman relationship," the masculine invariably precedes the feminine. This was, of course, the "accepted" style, and its use was not consciously political. But that is precisely the point. Moreover, Daly writes of the "seminal" elements in Christian doctrine as distinguished from its "oppressive" ideas (p. 73). Given the totally patriarchal character of Christianity, the use of the term "seminal" could have been used very appropriately, had it been employed to express the phallocentric nature of Christian doctrine. However, regretfully I must point out that this is not the sense of the text. "Seminal" is not used to mean male-centered, and indeed it is used in contrast with the word "oppressive."

Some of these symptoms of nonconsciousness of the politics of language reappear in later chapters. I shall try to refrain from overstressing them. Since I am attempting an in-depth study of this document in its historical context, it would be a serious failure on my part if I were to slip into mere carping pedantry that would betray the *intentions* of the author and discredit myself as a competent Dalyan scholar.

CHAPTER TWO

History: A Record of Contradictions

This is one of the book's most valuable chapters. The historical data has been meticulously researched. In many places Daly manifests a sense of irony, but in her overall view she is not ironic enough. The chapter title, for example, reveals her own amazement. It seems to me that the chapter would have been more accurately entitled: "History: A Record of Hypocrisy," or "History: A Record of Legitimized Sexism." But no. Daly was genuinely baffled by what she perceived as "a puzzling ambiguity if not an outright contradiction." The alleged conflict was between "Christian teachings on the worth of every human person and the oppressive, misogynistic ideas arising from cultural conditioning" (p. 74). In a certain sense, of course, and on a literal level, this could be seen as a contradiction, as can the contrast (also discussed in this chapter) between the symbolic glorification of "woman" and the real social oppression of women. However, it is significant that when discussing the second "tension of opposites" she is clear about the *hypocrisy* of the glorified "woman" idea and of how this functions to cloak social reality. In my judgment, the greater lucidity that characterizes her discussion of this more specific "contradiction" is due to the fact that she can allow herself to perceive this *particular* symbol as functioning to justify oppression and still remain a Christian, even Catholic, reformer. However, to admit the possibility that the "basic doctrine" of Christianity might be oppressive would be to put herself unequivocally outside its orbit—a genuinely threatening prospect, an unutterable, unthinkable thought in that time/space. Thus, she continues to make distinctions between this "basic doctrine" and the "oppressive ideas arising from social conditioning."

If Daly had let go of her distinction between this supposed hard core of Christian truth (never clearly defined) and the impurities from somewhere outside, she would have been rocketed into the postchristian era. In 1965–67 A.D. she was constructing a launching pad for a future space trip which she could not have foreseen clearly. It hardly seems appropriate for me to pass judgments upon an author who was not an astronaut before it was possible to become one. Rather, I am thankful for her labors. Speaking personally—and I hope this will not appear tasteless in a review of this nature—I must admit that if it were not for Daly's early work, I myself probably would never have tried on a feminist space suit.

But let us return to the subject at hand. The chapter begins with an analysis of biblical texts. The evidence brought forth from the Old Testament is devastating. Yet, in the very process of displaying the self-damning biblical texts, the author manifests her characteristic ambivalence by expressing her dismay at theologians and preachers who are unaware of "modern developments in biblical scholarship." Professorially, she adds: "Such misunderstanding of the Old Testament has done immeasurable harm" (p. 77). If I could take a journey back to her time, perhaps I could persuade her to consider the possibility that *understanding* the symbolic messages of the Old Testament only too well has caused immeasurable harm. I am tempted to imagine our conversation. "Professor Daly," I would say, "don't you realize that where myths are concerned the medium *is* the message? Don't you see that the efforts of biblical scholars to reinterpret texts, even though they may be correct within a certain restricted perspective, cannot change the overwhelmingly patriarchal character of the biblical tradition? Moreover, this 'modern' historical accuracy about detail has often been associated with an apologetic zeal that overlooks patriarchal religion's function of legitimating patriarchy. Consider, for example, the myth of Eve's birth from Adam. You accurately describe this as a 'hoax,' and you correctly point out that 'modern' interpretations of Genesis 'come too late for the millions of women who lived and died with the religious conviction of their divinely ordained inferiority and subordination' (p. 79). Now, I would say that this myth is not only a hoax, but a typical instance of what I call 'reversal' of biological and historical fact. Can't you pursue your own line of thought further and conclude that such reversal is a basic dynamic of patriarchal religion? This might lead you to a further conclusion, Professor Daly, namely, that within such a religious tradition it will always be too late, that mere reform and modernized scholarship will allow millions more to live and die simply with a more subtle and sophisticated conviction of their divinely ordained inferiority."

But I must not be carried away with this fantasy conversation. I will leave the professor at her blackboard explaining to her pupils the difference between the earlier creation story, the J document, and the later P document account. I shall let her mind her P's and J's until the time when a more revolutionary consciousness can emerge.

Daly does a competent analysis of Pauline texts. She was not unaware of the distinction between texts that her contemporaries attributed to "the real Paul" and those attributed to the "deutero-Pauline authors." I suspect, however, that she did not find this a distinction of consuming interest. At any rate she does not dwell upon it and generally writes simply about "Pauline texts." I find this reasonable since they had been known as such for two thousand years and had carried that awesome and oppressive authority. However, I must suppress my feelings of impatience when I read her desperate straw-grasping attempt to propose one Pauline text (Galatians 3:27–28) as an instance where "the dichotomy of fixed classes as dominant-subservient is transcended" (p. 84). The question that comes to my mind is: "What sense does it make to assert that *in Christ* 'there is neither male nor female'?" Wasn't "Christ" an exclusively male symbol, even though somewhat "feminized"? What on earth, then, could the text mean? But that is the point: it could not mean anything on earth, where there definitely were and are females and males and where that distinction has been overemphasized and distorted, especially in the church. If "in Christ" meant some unearthly place, then certainly Daly could never have been there since the symbol *says* "for men only."

The section on the patristic period obviously was painstakingly researched. Our author searched out the Latin texts and carefully verified her translations. One of her contemporary critics argued that she had been selective in exhuming only misogynistic texts from the so-called Fathers of the Church. His assumption was that there were some philogynistic texts to be found. Clearly, Daly wins hands down since no scholar of her time nor of any period since has been able to find such texts to refute her position.

When we come to the section on the Middle Ages, it becomes immediately evident that Daly is on very familiar territory. Her biographical data, found with the book, indicates that she had studied medieval philosophy and theology for some years. Perhaps this explains the peculiar zest and fascination with detail which characterizes her analysis of Thomas Aquinas. Having exposed the abysmal views on the subject of women held by the "Angelic Doctor" (as he was called in the Catholic tradition), she still maintains that the deep roots of his thought could have been liberating for women if their dynamics had not been blocked off by "outdated" biblical exegesis and biology and by the prevailing views of the culture. She did not acknowledge, of course, that "biblical exegesis" is inevitably "outdated." Moreover, her critique of medieval biology is, it seems to me, too restrained. Modestly, she affirms that the mother is "equally" active in the production of the child, instead of simply pointing out that the female is *more* active—a fact which patriarchal ideology simply reversed.

I think that I can detect in Daly's defense of Aquinas's "radically liberating principles" a quality different from her lip service to the single "liberating" Pauline text and even quite different from her general defense of "basic Christian doctrine." In the latter case, as I have pointed out, she seems to be avoiding the threat of a radical break from Christianity. But in her plea for Aquinas there is, it seems to me, a kind of positive passion (p. 95). It is my guess that what she adhered to in his thought—Thomistic scholar that she was —was his ontological sense, his intuition of being. Looking back from the vantage point of our present stage in history, I think it fair to say that she was struggling to find ontological roots for what we know today as feminist philosophy of Be-ing. In the better parts of Aquinas's work she found hints of what a philosophy of be-ing/becoming could begin to say. But, of course, as prepackaged in his categories, this ontological sense could *not* be radically liberating. The ontological process which Daly so ardently sought could only be found in the women's revolution, which had not yet surfaced. Consequently she took starvation rations from the best of the Christian philosophers. In her time, when sisterhood had not yet emerged, moving too far ahead would have meant venturing into an endless desert, into a state which an uncomprehending world would have called "madness" and treated as such. It is important for our historical sense, I think, that we try to comprehend this situation. Moreover, I empathize deeply with Daly's attempt to rescue ontology.

The chapter covers much interesting material. For example, there is information concerning the abbesses who wielded patriarchal power. The passages from Saint Teresa are also fascinating, and Daly's analysis of them makes it clear enough that Teresa suffered from sexism. At the same time, it hardly seems to me an appropriate compliment to proclaim that the saint "anticipated what biblical scholars would begin to suggest centuries later" (p. 100). In fact, it is more to the point that Teresa anticipated what feminists would say centuries later, but in language that would make feminist hair stand on end. In the texts cited by Daly she refers to the deity as her "Lord," "Judge," and "King." Moreover, she had a tendency to disassociate herself from women, saying, for example, that she "was not in the least like a woman." Daly surely must have found this disconcerting, but refrained from comment. Of course, she was seeing Teresa "in historical context" and perhaps was showing greater patience than I have manifested toward the Dalyan comments.

I am thankful for the author's research on the "early modern period." Her moving sketch of the efforts of nuns to break the bonds of the cloister and become active "in the world" has influenced my own writing on the concept of sisterhood, as well as the work of other feminists[2]. Since Daly was of Catholic background, her data is drawn primarily from the Catholic tradition. Personally, I do not

---

[2] For an important study of the history and problems of nuns in relation to feminism, see Janice G. Raymond, "Nuns and Women's Liberation," *Andover Newton Quarterly*, XII (March 1972 A.F.), pp. 201–212. See also the same author's work entitled "Nuns and Women's Liberation: A Study of the Effects of Patriarchy upon Roman Catholic Religious Communities of Women and an Alternative." Unpublished M. A. thesis, Andover Newton Theological School, Newton Centre, Massachusetts, 1971 A.F.

think that this detracts from the value of the work, except perhaps quantitatively since the Protestant "reformers'" treatment of women did not differ dramatically from the words and behavior of their Catholic counterparts. Indeed, this remarkable sameness makes the feminist critic of 1975 A.F. wonder to *what* significant social event the term "reformation" could possibly have referred.

I will conclude my remarks concerning this chapter by noting that the copious citations from what Daly refers to as "papal documents," particularly from the Popes Piuses, were at first misunderstood by me. Because of the bizarre content of these citations, their pomposity and internal inconsistency, I at first thought that they were from a body of satirical literature known in her time but lost to posterity. A second and more careful reading of the section convinced me that I had missed the point. Since I have considerable respect for Daly's scholarship, I take it on her authority not only that these documents, as well as their purported authors, did actually exist, but also that the documents were intended as straightforward, authoritative pronouncements and exercised great influence during her era.

CHAPTER THREE

Winds of Change

I found this chapter both puzzling and poignant. The author begins with a continued discussion of Popes, but this time the main subject is a personage named "Pope John." It amazes me that she speaks with unbridled enthusiasm about the writings attributed to this dignitary, using such expressions as "startling breakthrough" to describe them (p. 118). Indeed, the texts she cites seem to convey little more than some vague and grudging awareness that women are human. The enthusiasm of our author snatching at these crumbs tossed from on high speaks volumes about the desolation of the culture in which she struggled to survive. Combining these texts with a few more, garnered from the documents issued by the Second Vatican Council, she builds a case in support of the church's "growing recognition . . . of the equal rights of men and women" (p.

119ff.). She seems to become exuberant over things that the Vatican documents do *not* do. For example, this document "does *not* speak disparagingly of working mothers" (p. 120). Yet even this non-speech is precarious, it seems, for the document sternly proclaims that "children . . . need the care of their mothers at home." Again, Daly rejoices that Vatican II's Declaration on Christian Education *"has nothing to say* against coeducation" (p. 121, italics mine), even though she notes that it has regressive passages, such as those insisting that teachers "pay due regard to sex role differences." In sum, Daly is aware of what she calls the "three steps forward, one step backward" movement of the church in her time. She does not seem aware of the possibility that the real pattern of the dance may have been "one step forward, three steps backward."

There are indications, however, that Daly had a sense of foreboding when Pope John's successor, known as "Pope Paul," climbed into the papal throne and began making statements that could not be read as other than oppressive. Our author summons up her optimism and manages to say that this Pope Paul "has given some evidence of an evolution beyond the attitudes of the popes who *preceded* John (p. 121, italics mine). With evident depression, she notes some of his remarks and then moves on to another section of her chapter. For the benefit of the lay reader I should point out that this "Pope Paul" was the last of the popes whose name we find recorded in any of the sources. Since in 1975 A.F. there is little serious scholarly or popular discussion on the subject of popes, I simply offer this information for those with antiquarian curiosity and to illumine better the setting of Daly's labors.

Today, the arguments in some of the petitions sent by women theologians to the "Council fathers" appear hardly less strange than the documents of the "fathers" themselves. One of these women, for example, is mentioned by Daly as presenting reasoned arguments that "Canon 968, which limits ordination to men alone, is of human tradition rather than divine origin" (pp. 124–125). Apparently Catholics believed that some of their rules were written by men (males) and some were written by God. This belief posed some obscure, convoluted problems concerning who had written which. In any case, the primary focus of the "radical petitions" was the ordination of women to the priesthood, and, of course, none of the petitioners, any more than Daly herself, could see that the idea of "equality" within a patriarchal institution was doomed. In fairness, however, it should be pointed out that the vision of these "equal rights" feminists went further than that of anyone else in the religious world. Although their vision contained an ultimate contradiction, the idea of equality within patriarchy, that contradiction could not be seen until a certain distance from patriarchy had been attained and *it* could be seen *as a whole*. Their situation was comparable to that of pre-space age travelers who could see parts of the planet earth at different times but could not have that perspective of the whole which became possible for astronauts at a later age. These "equal rights" feminists had attained a genuinely respectworthy altitude in the jet age. Their demand for women priests was equivalent to a demand for entry into the ruling caste.

The same respect cannot be accorded to the "liberal" hierarchy who "supported" women. The one and only champion of women's rights whom Daly was able to exhume from the ranks of American bishops was a timid and inconsistent soul, one Archbishop Hallinan. Having proclaimed that the church should not continue to perpetuate female subservience and "the secondary place allotted to women in the past," Hallinan proposed as his major reform the idea that women could serve as "deaconesses"—a very secondary role, subservient to that of priest. This was, nevertheless, an unthinkably stellar role for women in the opinion of most of the hierarchy. No doubt this was a generous move for an Archbishop, and thus Hallinan was the all-American star that Daly's desperation drove her to exalt as "one notable exception" among the American bishops. Given this condition of sexual politics in the Catholic church, the women who proposed the ordination of women to the Catholic priesthood in the mid-sixties were indeed out of tune with their time. Their logic had brought some of them closer than they realized to the brink of the postchristian era.

In the section on "problems of Catholic married women," Daly deals with the oppressive Catholic stance on birth control. The quaint implication of the heading, of course, is that this would be a problem only for "married women." Given her Catholic identity, it is understandable that Daly offers no theoretical critique of the institution of marriage as oppressive in itself. Perhaps, however, her basic opinion on the subject can be inferred from her biographical notes, which indicate by omission that she herself had successfully avoided it. In any case, the section on "Catholic married women" deals cogently though briefly with birth control and the question of working mothers. She touches on the abortion issue. The brevity of her treatment of this subject should not be astonishing, since abortion was not an issue open for discussion even among radical Catholics in the mid-sixties A.D., when this chapter was written. What is surprising is that she mentions it at all and comes out on the side of recognizing moral ambiguity, actually even finding one bishop (Simons of Indore, India) who was willing to admit some personal sense of ambiguity about the problem.

The caption heading the next section, "Problems of the emerging sisters," may require a word of explanation to the contemporary reader who is, of course, accustomed to use the word "sister" to describe and/or address another feminist. "Sister," as used in this work, generally has a meaning roughly equivalent to "nun," that is, a female member of a Catholic religious order or congregation, usually a nonfeminist, even according to the standards of the period. A "sister" generally wore a veil and was thought to be a "bride of Christ," although what this could mean behaviorally was never clear. Although this may seem bizarre and confusing to the sisters in the women's movement, I can assure the reader that Daly was quite conventional in her use of the term. "Emerging sisters," then, means emerging from the cloister or convent. Again, perhaps some clarification is needed. A convent was a place where a group of women lived under the same roof in a "community" of isolation. Such places had rules which were male-created and structures which were hierarchical. In these respects a convent was totally different from a women's collective. Finally, I should point out that the seemingly incongruous fact that the "emerging sisters" mentioned by Daly have men's names (e.g. Luke, William, Charles) was basically due to the prevailing notion that men were the superior sex. Hence this dubious honor.

Hopefully the foregoing explanation will help to make more intelligible the content of this section. Daly contrasts the private remarks made by "younger and better educated sisters," indicating a need for "radical changes," with statements made by their leaders which were "not conspicuously progressive" (p. 136). Having read my explanation, the reader will understand that those chosen as "leaders" of the Catholic sisters of course had to attempt to please their male masters and so were not inclined to make radical statements or even to have radical thoughts. The "younger sisters" were low on the male-created totem pole, and they had to restrict their criticisms to private discussions, since there was no "equality" even among themselves. Although their immediate "superiors" were female, the pattern of "community" was copied from males. The convent bore some resemblance both to the patriarchal family and to the army. It was a mini-brotherhood, in which decisions were handed down from on high.

If some sisters in the women's movement in 1975 A.F. are amazed that women accepted such a regime, let me point out that options for females in that culture were few. For some, this may have been an escape from what could have been a far worse fate, burial in patriarchal marriage, even though this reason would not have been given consciously and explicitly. The other obvious option, living alone, which today can be seen as a liberated life-style, was dreaded by many, since they had been conditioned to believe that this would be a life of rejection, disgrace, and isolation. Since acceptance by men, rather than self-acceptance, was the norm, most women in the mid-sixties A.D. still felt that they were acceptable only if they became the property of husbands in marriage or else Brides of Christ, incorporated into a sort of Divine Harem.[3] Although Daly's biographical data does not indicate that she ever joined any of these Heavenly Harems, she did empathize with these "sisters" as sisters, probably because she saw in their situation some dim and distorted anticipation of a feminist future, which of course she herself could not clearly imagine either.

The nuns were in many ways worse off than religious monks, since their male superiors allowed them fewer freedoms. The system "encouraged" them, as it did other women, to have low self-esteem in the form of displaced or vicarious self-esteem. This explains Daly's description of the "emerging sisters" first emerging to fight for causes other than their own by participating in "civil rights" marches, for example (a pattern also discernible among other women). Having been conditioned to ascribe value only to male ideals and causes, their speaking out for liberation had to be for someone else's liberation. Only later, and partially as a result of this experience, did some begin to wonder about their own "civil rights."

These "progressive nuns," as Daly calls them, began in the 1960's A.D. to abandon their convents. Even in the process of doing this, they still saw themselves as loyal daughters of the church, who intended, as Daly wrote, "to serve the Church and world better" (p.

---

[3] Expression used by Janice Raymond.

137). This pattern of emergence was not totally dissimilar from that of other women, most of whom were imprisoned in marriage and/ or demeaning jobs. A significant number of women in that epoch, including such apparently submerged beings as the "sisters," were beginning to move together, without realizing it, into the emerging sisterhood of women.

The final section of the chapter, "Changes in fact," lists some events which appeared spectacular in that epoch, such as women "serving Mass" and "distributing Holy Communion." Daly's chronicle of the repressive measures against such activities is important for understanding women's history. Discussing the role of Protestantism in countering the conservative influence, she gives us insight into an important dialectic within Christianity. Understandably, she took an overly optimistic view of the Protestant influence, attributing to Protestantism a greater dissimilarity from the Catholic church than the facts warranted—the facts, that is, as perceived more clearly now, seven woman-light years removed from the scene.

CHAPTER FOUR

The Pedestal Peddlars

If I could dialogue with the author of *The Church and the Second Sex* today, I think we might have an enjoyable chat about this chapter. I might be tempted to tell her that some of her readers today must surely suspect that she had a unique talent for unearthing bizarre literature and then refuting it. I might point out that my contemporaries who have not studied the history of her time can be expected to wonder if she had access to some astonishing collections of rare books. But I think I can accurately anticipate her reply. "Rare books?" she would ask, astonished. "I found these in the local bookstores. They were representative of a whole genre of writing that was very common." And, given my historical knowledge of that period, I would be obliged in honesty to concede her point. But I must return to the concrete reality before me: the book itself.

Discussing the phallacies of the "eternal feminine" ideology, Daly does an acute analysis of one "Gertrud von le Fort." Von le Fort was comparable to a minor figure of more recent fame whom some readers will recall: Midge Decter. Like Decter, von le Fort was a thoroughly male-identified woman, praised and exalted by men, functioning as "the ultimate weapon in the hands of the boys."[4] Unlike Decter, however, the German author had a quality of perversity characteristic of the committed conservative which actually could inspire creative insight, if her words were wrenched out of their old semantic context, heard with new ears, and understood backward so that the meaning came out straight. For example, Daly cites von le Fort as saying: "The priesthood could not be confided to woman, for thereby the very meaning of woman in the Church would have been eliminated" (p. 150). As a Catholic Feminist, Daly was incensed at the statement, and understandably so. However, were she here now, listening with new ears, I think that she would have to concede that the statement is literally correct. The problem with the statement's author, of course, was that she wanted to *retain* "the very meaning of woman in the Church," that is, the oppression of women under the guise of "the eternal feminine" mystique. Daly wanted to do away with the oppression and keep the church, a contradiction which I have already discussed. I can only emphasize that for her to have seen the contradiction would have placed her in the now/here, which in her time would have meant *nowhere*.

I was genuinely pleased with Daly's analysis and refutation of male writers on the subject of women in the 1960's A.D. (for example, Bouyer, Arnold, Danniel, Oliver, Alberione) and her dissection of more ancient authors still popular in her time, such as Claudel and Teilhard de Chardin. Moreover, as I read on into her analysis of "the divine plan" and "Mary the model of all women," I chuckled and became caught up into the mood. Hopefully, this admission of personal reaction will not appear too self-indulgent to the reader. It is sometimes difficult for a grateful disciple to sustain the role of stern critic.

The plain fact is that I found little to disagree with in this chapter. I must say, however, that while Daly was not exactly incorrect in attributing the perpetuation of "Marian devotion" to a celibate clergy, I do find a tendency to overstress the difference between the

---

4 Phrase originated by Robin Morgan in her poem "The One That Got Away or The Woman Who Made It" in *Monster* (Vintage Books, New York: Random House, 1972, A.F.), p. 70.

male chauvinism of priests and that of married men or any other men who have sexual relationships with women. Thus she wrote, that "normal day to day relationships . . . alone can provide a realistic understanding of persons of the opposite sex" (p. 160). Understandably, she was particularly annoyed at the obtuseness of Catholic celibate clerics. Moreover, she could not have foreseen fully all of the questions which feminist thinkers of our now/here are raising about the notion of "normalcy." According to contemporary feminist analysis the "day to day relationships" between the sexes considered "normal" in sexist society—even since, or rather *especially* since, the so-called "sexual revolution"—are intolerably nonpersonal, oppressive, and dehumanizing. Indeed, so-called "personal relationships" within a sexist society are seldom productive of realistic understanding of "the other," but rather tend to perpetuate the vicious circle of stereotypes. Of course, Daly herself was by no means lacking in insight concerning this vicious circle. In fact, she had made this very point earlier in the book in her discussion of the patristic period, where she described the inferiority enforced upon women through socialization, which made females *seem* "naturally" defective (pp. 86–87). I wish it were possible to say to her: "Remember this insight and apply it *consistently* when analyzing your own culture. You *know* that the personal is political. Your own book displays this knowledge, even if the language in which it is expressed seems to me a bit archaic."

At the end of this chapter, our author points to the fading out of the myth of the "eternal feminine" in her time, despite the hopes that had been expressed by such authors as Berdyaev and Rilke for its future resurrection. I believe that she was correct in this opinion, as far as it went. She could not have foreseen that feminists of the future would begin to probe into a deeper past than that recorded in patriarchal history and to express hope for a more authentic rebirth than that of the male-made "eternal feminine."[5] She could not have guessed that in 1975 A.F. women would be speaking of a Second Coming of Women.

[5] See Elizabeth Gould Davis, *The First Sex* (Baltimore, Md.: Penguin Books, 1971 A.F.).

CHAPTER FIVE

The Demon of Sexual Prejudice: An Exercise in Exorcism

As I began to read this temptingly titled chapter, it struck me that "prejudice" is not a word that I myself would choose to describe the killing off of women's potential, the *gynocide* which is really the subject of this chapter. In short, I would choose or create a stronger word than "prejudice." Moreover, it struck me forcibly that once again the lead citation is from a *male*. This had crossed my mind when reading the second and fourth chapters, but now my discomfort had increased. "Why would Daly have adopted such an inappropriate tactic in a feminist work?" I muttered to myself querulously. But I caught myself immediately. "After all," I countered, "just how many feminist writings were available to her when she was writing this book in 1965–1967 A.D.?" The movement as we know it had not yet surfaced, and the nineteenth century "first wave" of feminism had been submerged, its writings buried in obscure corners of twentieth century libraries. Daly did, after all, unearth many of the twentieth century A.D. feminist sources, as well as the most influential oppressive texts from the long Judeo-Christian history. Were it not for her research and carefully noted bibliographical data, I would not have been aware of these resources. Nor would I have been moved to "discover" other foremothers, like Elizabeth Cady Stanton, Sojourner Truth, Matilda Joslyn Gage, or Virginia Woolf. So I will content myself with mentally inserting appropriate remarks from these and other great women at the beginnings of the male-headed chapters. I shall call this little game "Fill in the Blank," and I invite all readers to join me. Any number can play, but the game is particularly bewitching if there are seven (or multiples of seven) players.[6]

But I must proceed. In this chapter Daly discusses the mechanisms of "role psychology" in a way which I find refreshing. She never regresses to a merely intrapsychic perspective, but rather analyzes

---

[6] This numerological suggestion was made by Linda Barufaldi during a conversation in June, 1974 A.F.

the mechanisms of projection, introjection, and self-fulfilling prophecy as dynamics of a destructive socialization process. I am pleased that she never resorts to the device of "blaming the victim." She adeptly uses the sparse data available to her, indicating that there are connections between the imposition of passive self-images upon women and poor intellectual performance. Moreover, she makes the reader aware of the destruction of women's creativity by the anxieties which sexist society inflicts upon females who refuse to conform to self-stunting stereotypes. Unavailable to our author was the research of Matina Horner, well known among our contemporaries, which demonstrates that a "fear of success" has plagued women and hampered intellectual performance. Nevertheless, her "reading" of the problem was quite consistent with Horner's findings.

Although I am in basic agreement with this section, I sense an incompleteness, an absence of explication of Daly's remark that "it is very possible that genetic factors dispose boys to be more aggressive than girls" (p. 173). Within her context this statement seems almost like a grudging but honest admission of a possibly innate *liability* in females. *If* we *are* dealing with something "innate" here (and this is still unknown), I should be inclined to see it as an *asset* of women. Of course, the basic premise of this section is that the polarization of the sexes into "aggressive" as opposed to "passive" personalities is primarily the effect of socialization processes, which have created exaggerated and mutilating "psychological" differences between the sexes, having little or no causal basis in innate biological differences. Still, I would have liked some discussion here of the negative aspects of male "aggressivity." While I am sure that when Daly used the word "aggressive" she had in mind a healthy propensity for self-affirmation, desperately needed and to be encouraged in women, I myself tend to think also of less palatable meanings when I hear this term. I immediately envisage a complex web of meanings, implying *both* life-affirming and destructive tendencies. Of course, I am conscious of this complex network of meanings because in our time the horrors associated with *male* "aggressivity" are unavoidably obvious. One of the most haunting questions for feminists *now* is: Will the male propensity for aggressivity and violence (which I often call *rapism*)—whether completely the result of socialization or partially innate—result in the destruction of the human species? In our space/time, having witnessed a great upsurge in the number of rapes of our sisters, having recognized as manifestations of rapism the rape of southeast Asia, of racial minorities, and of the environment, and having retained a clear memory of the history of Watergate and the Nixionian God-fathers, feminists cannot possibly hear the word "aggressive" in a totally positive sense. I am not disagreeing with Daly's *intention* here, which I believe I understand quite well. She wanted women to affirm our great strength and largely untapped creative potential. But I want to point out dimensions of the problem of "aggressivity" which historical events have rendered too painfully obvious to ignore. As Adrienne Rich has written:

A man's world. But finished.
They themselves have sold it to the machines.[7]

As I read the section, "Effects upon the man-woman relationship," a few problems came to mind. I have already pointed out the importance of naming the female first. Thus the more proper expression would be "woman-man relationship," which would function to correct, or balance, what she herself calls the built-in bias of her culture. Even in our now/here, as we experience the growth of New Amazon culture, it is important to *counter* the culture-lag of those who have not entered the new time/space and who attempt to control thought through imposing old grammar and old words. We are, after all, still in a transitional stage.

If I could leap back into the past and confront the author on her own territory, I would casually raise some other questions about the section. After praising her work and admitting that the section is lucidly written and ahead of its time, I would then ask: "But why do you worry about elements of the 'Eternal Woman' myth as 'disastrous for marriage' (p. 174)? Why not discuss the possibility that marriage itself is a disaster? If you mean that the myth is destructive for personal relationships I could not agree more. But I wish you would put caution aside and stop talking in such *institutional* terms."

I would then pursue my critique in something like the following manner: "You were lucky to have found *one* psychoanalyst, this Lussier, who wrote something worth quoting to support your views, but you might have emphasized that he was an exception within his

[7] From "Waking in the Dark" in *Diving into the Wreck* (New York: W. W. Norton and Company, 1973 A.F.), p. 8.

profession. You *know* that not only clerics but also most analysts and therapists have promoted exactly the kind of nightmarish marital situations that you—and this Lussier—deplore."

If I thought I still had her attention, I would continue: "Now, about that quote from Betty Friedan on page 176: Why did you let the implied negative value judgment on homosexuality go by without serious questioning? I realize that this issue was not your primary focus of concern when you cited this passage. Rather, you were pleading the cause of married women who also have careers (which was Friedan's intention, as well). But why did you allow to go uncriticized the implication that homosexual preference is a sign of defect or failure on anyone's part? Negative judgments upon homosexuality stem from a patriarchal social system which has a vested interest in the nuclear family as the only 'legitimate' life-style. In a postpatriarchal culture, the labels 'homosexual' and 'heterosexual,' if retained at all, will be value-free."

It is my opinion that Daly would have listened to these views and considered them, were I able to make such a time trip into the past and make myself visible and audible. But unfortunately, voices from the future are harder to hear than those of the past. Here is her book, solid and visible before me. I have the distinct advantage of understanding her better than she could comprehend me.

Before I leave this chapter, I must say that the last section, "the task of exorcism," really pleased me. The author shows the phallacies of tokenism and points out that the way to exorcism is changing women's image by raising up our *own* images in our lives. It is unfortunate, however, that in the last paragraph she claims that this will not happen "until favorable conditions are not only allowed but also encouraged" (p. 178). I certainly do not know *who* will "allow" and "encourage" women to raise up our images if not women ourselves. And *who* will "remove impediments" and "foster" the right atmosphere, if not *us*? It is evident that she was still hoping for institutional, even churchly, encouragement. In 1975 A.F. we know that women must recapture our own energy, our own lives. We must do it ourselves.

CHAPTER SIX

Theological Roots of the Problem: Radical Surgery Required

I agree with the basic theme expressed in the beginning of this chapter, namely that the misogynism of Christian theology is deep-rooted and that merely removing symptoms will not cure the disease. Daly was on the right track here, I believe, and more recent history proved the soundness of her basic insight. Indeed, theological and other academic reformers, feeling the pressure from feminists such as our author herself, attempted to do exactly what she foresaw and warned against. They tried to remove symptoms of misogynism (read: sexism) on a superficial level while remaining fundamentally oppressive. Essentially this had been a "cover-up" tactic, successfully deceiving not only the listener or reader but also the speaker or writer. Not infrequently, "sensitized" authors, professors, and preachers have been careful to avoid the pseudogeneric "man," substituting such terms as "humankind," "humanity," or "people." Often they have also avoided the exclusive use of the pronoun "he" to refer to females and males, carefully adding "or she." Yet if one closely examines the content of what is being said, one frequently finds that it is subtly oppressive, calculated to confuse those easily satisfied with superficial grammatical reform. Some liberal theologians of the period following the First Coming of *The Church and the Second Sex* also attempted to make minor adjustments in the use of religious imagery. For example, they sometimes omitted the term "Father" when referring to Ultimate Reality, but they almost invariably compensated for this concession by stressing the unique importance of the God-Man, Jesus. Evidently some women were deceived by this "Band-Aid" treatment of Christianity's sexism. In contrast to this inadequate First (and Last) Aid, which could hide but not cure the disease of patriarchy, our author's approach— despite the fact that she was writing at an earlier time than these "faith healers" and despite her use of the conventional grammar of that earlier period—did move in the direction of radical healing.

Naturally, I vainly wish that it had been possible for her to move even further in that direction. She expressed the view that misogynism should be seen both as "symptom" and cause of "doctrinal disorders." As I was reading, it struck me as truly unfortunate that she explicitly chose to place *primary* emphasis upon the idea of antifeminism as a *symptom,* even though she did state that it was also at the origin of the "doctrinal disorders" which perpetuate it (p. 179). I cannot refrain from pointing out that "doctrine"*is* a disorder. I would say that sexism is the basic disorder, the cause of further disorders, and that we may count among its effects the existence and content of dogmatic "doctrines."

Yet a careful reading convinces me that Daly was moving in the direction of saying exactly this herself. She explicitly states that the cause-effect relationship between misogynism and distorted "doctrines" is not "one-way," that it is more accurately described as a "vicious circle" (p. 180). Moreover, even when she discusses antifeminism as a "symptom" having roots in "the problem of conceptualizations, images, and attitude concerning God" (p. 180ff), she shows that these "conceptualizations, images, and attitudes" are male-centered. Thus, even when she is allegedly writing of misogynism as a "symptom," the disorder of which it is a "symptom" turns out to be really a more deeply hidden form of misogynism, or at least androcentrism. Even when she writes of distortions in traditional notions of divinity which she describes as "quite distinct from vague identifications of God with the male sex," she says in the same breath that such warped ideas "may well be connected with these [male] identifications" (p. 181). Fortunately, in our time, the problem can be described more directly and unequivocally: I would say that *sexist* conceptualizations, images, and attitudes concerning God, spawned in a patriarchal society, tend to breed *more* sexist ideas and attitudes, and together these function to legitimate and perpetuate sexist institutions and behavior. Briefly, if God is male, then the male is God.

Daly rightly claims that such concepts as "divine immutability" and "divine omnipotence" function to justify misogynism. I would add that since these very notions of "divine attributes" originated in a patriarchal society, of course they do support the vested interests of such a society. Basic changelessness, or what she calls "the static world view," is essential to patriarchy, no matter how much the patriarchs may prattle about "progress," "revolution," and "change." This is inevitably so, because the only genuinely radical progress, revolution, and change would be the upheaval of patriarchy itself— movement *beyond* patriarchy. As for the idea of a unique, closed "revelation" in the past, which she discusses on page 184, that too is a product of the sexual caste system, and it functions to perpetuate that system, to keep it closed. I agree with Daly, then, that there is a vicious circle, that there are circles within circles, that misogynism breeds misogynism, but I think it is misleading to write of misogynism as a "symptom." Sexism *is* the disease, the planetary disease. It is also the demon she was trying to name.

The section entitled "Other theological developments required" made me uncomfortable. Daly wanted to see the church not merely as an institution but also as a movement in the world. This bifocal vision of course allowed her to perform a delicate balancing act— seeming to be both in and out of the church. Whatever she thought of the institution, she could still hopefully identify with the church *as movement.* This was a common enough approach in her time, and strange though it may seem to us in the now/here, it did not involve conscious or intentional dishonesty. Since I have some understanding of her situation, I realize that it was virtually impossible for her then to recognize the implications of the fact that the church was an oppressive social reality. If my voice could carry back into her world I would cry out as loud as possible: "Listen! When you can say 'No' to the institution you can begin to say a clearer and more effective 'Yes' to real movement in the world, your movement, the movement of your sisters—past, present, and future. Then you will really be able to talk about "Incarnation"—not some supposedly unique, male-deifying event locked forever in the past—but the incarnate movement of your sisters. Then you will think and speak about a Fall that matters, that is here and yet still on its way —a Fall into freedom."

But Daly was writing about traditional concepts and trying desperately to do something about them. Nor was she totally unsuccessful. It was her critique of the story of the Fall that led me to think of the women's revolution as a Fall into free space, beyond patriarchal good and evil. It seemed to me, as I meditated upon her obviously difficult struggle to undistort all the "doctrinal distortions," that I myself might as well continue to go all the way.

Our author writes that "the theology of marriage is in a state of transition, but the work is by no means completed" (p. 187). I hope that I will not seem overly ironic if I remark that it does now seem to have been completed. She adds that "the theology of the sacrament of Holy Orders has also suffered from a lack of balance" (p. 187). Since I am familiar with the sources available to her, I can honestly say that I couldn't agree more. Fortunately, that, too, is finished.

I do not mean to imply that I think Daly was completely wrong in hoping for a "development of doctrine," but I think the old words failed her. What had to occur was a qualitative leap beyond patriarchal "doctrine." When women enter feminist postchristian time/space, whatever might have been genuine in "doctrine" is not lost but rather transformed, wrenched out of the old context, as we are living, willing, thinking, *being* our own thoughts. If some reality to which a Christian doctrine was trying to point survives this leap into the postchristian context, that is all right, but what matters is that *we* survive and keep moving.

As I began to read the next section, "Needed: special attention to the problem," I felt genuine surprise to find the author at this point in the book now modestly writing of "women and the church" in a special section, since this is clearly the subject of her entire book. Since I know well that she was not an illogical person, I tried to find reasons for this seeming illogic. As I read over the material and thought about the environment in which it was produced, I understood the reasons. First, there *was* a special situation demanding her attention, namely the fact that some of her contemporaries and some theologians of an even earlier period had written books and articles about "the theology of woman." Daly had to show that while there was a real problem centering around "theology" and "women," the answer to it could not be a "theology of woman." Writings of this *genre* invariably were concerned mainly with perpetuating the "Eternal Feminine" stereotype while ignoring the problems of real women. She had to perform the delicate operation of refuting these, while at the same time stressing that there was indeed a special focus needed upon the subject of women and religion. Second, I think it did not seem as strange to her as it does to me that there would be a special section on women and the church in her book on women and the church, because she was affected by the intellectual climate in which she was immersed.

There was strong pressure from this environment which made her feel that the subject of her entire book still had to be seen in a "broader theological context." Understanding this atmosphere, I find the section understandable. In fact, I find it valuable, since in fact she gives here a strong, though cautiously worded, argument that this "broader theological context" was rooted in patriarchy and was therefore warped (read: sexist) at its roots. Moreover, her analysis of the ill logic involved in the "theology of woman" is not only very credible to such a critic as myself, but also useful, since this ideological monstrosity was later superseded in patriarchal universities by a similarly phallacious ideology, known as "the psychology of woman," to which her critique is applicable.[8]

Daly concludes the chapter by clearly indicating the obstacles to the development of a "liberating theological anthropology"—obstacles which still exist outside feminist now/here. Although I would not of course choose the expression "theological anthropology," I will not indulge in a lengthy quibble over her choice of an expression which surely was one of the better semantic options available for expressing her idea. Today we are creating feminist theory out of women's experience. This is, after all, what she was striving toward.

CHAPTER SEVEN

Toward Partnership: Some Modest Proposals

I have already commented upon the title of this chapter. Women discovering self-actualization in sisterhood in 1975 A.F. rarely talk of "partnership" with men, since this term seems to imply an unspeakable poverty of imagination, as if we could glimpse nothing more desirable than an equal piece of the patriarchal pie. Moreover, we know clearly that there can be no easy reconciliation or "cheap grace," that this is a time of struggle. From where I am, as I read this chapter, Daly appears unrealistic in her hopes for "dialogue and cooperation between men and women" (p. 195). She could not

---

[8] Our contemporary feminist psychologists have critiqued and refuted pseudo-psychology. See especially Phyllis Chesler, *Women and Madness* (New York: Doubleday, 1972 A.F.).

then have understood fully what we know through shared experience and through uncovering the histories of our foremothers
which were erased and reversed in patriarchal "history"—that sexist
socialization is unspeakably deep and self-perpetuating in the A.D.
time/space, that the rapism of males and of male institutions is not
easily unlearned. It is axiomatic among us that women and men are
not coming from the same place, that it is impossible to "dialogue"
on equal terms with the oppressor.

Although Daly's proposals for the eradication of "discrimination"
within the Catholic church were eminently reasonable within the
context of "reform," the hierarchy of the Catholic church was
eminently unwilling to listen to reason, continuing to oppress
women by enforcing the "feminine" footstool/pedestal role in-
doctrination. In 1974 A.D. Paul, the last pope, sensing vibrations of
feminist energy that penetrated back through the smog of A.D.
time, attempted to co-opt that energy by proposing that Mary was
the Model of the Liberated Woman. His document clearly revealed
that this "true" Woman's liberation consisted in standing behind
her Man/God. As a result of this document, some women laughed
so heartily that they shook themselves almost over the edge into
1974 Anno Feminarum. Other women, who had already reached
the edge, noted with interest this glaring manifestation of the
phenomenon of patriarchal reversal. Mary, remnant of the ancient
Mother Goddess of the prepatriarchal age, who had been do-
mesticated and enchained in Christian mythology, was being placed
on display—chains and all—as The Liberated Woman.

Our author's proposals received a different kind of attention from
leaders within the Protestant segments of Christianity, who were
more inclined to "listen to reason," offering women token opportunities which served to hide the nature of the monster Daly was
trying to reform—patriarchal religion. In apparent contrast to the
Catholic hierarchs' blatant insistence upon polarization of the human species into "feminine" and "masculine" roles, liberal Protestants used a tactic which I have named *false inclusion,* that is,
incorporation of some women into "masculine" roles. Although this
gave some the impression that there was a great difference between
Catholic and Protestant Christianity in relation to "the problem" of
women, the fact is that in their basic behavior patterns the Godfathers "on both sides" were on the same side, drearily alike.

Daly correctly sensed that some of her more modest proposals for Catholicism would grudgingly be granted and that a more adequate test of Catholic sincerity about "equality" would be the issue of women priests. Hence there is a rather lengthy section devoted to this subject. If by a stretch, or rather a shrinkage, of my imagination I were to accept her basic premise that "reform" of the Catholic church might have been possible and desirable, I would have to agree with this priority as well as with her arguments. Yet I cannot easily overcome my sense of dismay that the integrity of her position required such an expenditure of energy in the refutation of bigots who deserved no reply. Feminists of our time, of course, are careful about wastage of energy. We have learned from our study of history that "dialoguing" with the mindless ideologists of patriarchal religion is useless bloodshed, timeshed, spiritshed.[9] We have learned to use a kind of power which I have named *power of absence,* which is possible because we are *present* to each other.

I think that a key to the apparent puzzle of why Daly kept trying can be found in her response to the argument that "the priest represents Christ and therefore must be male." She countered this by claiming that such a statement "betrays a distorted understanding of the meaning of Christ . . . giving prior importance to his maleness rather than to his humanity" (p. 199). I am afraid that it was Daly, and not the conservatives, who had missed the point about the Christ symbol. She was trying to transcend the untranscendable, that is, the message of male supremacy contained in the symbolic medium itself. That did not work, as history has shown.

At the same time, our author was prophetic, without realizing the full implications of what she was saying, when she wrote that "the very suggestion that the same individual could be the bearer of these two images ["woman" and "priest"] is a declaration that an age has ended and another has begun" (pp. 206–207). If my reading is accurate, the age which she perceived—at least on some level of consciousness—as moving toward its end was the patriarchal epoch. But the implications of this insight were too overwhelming to be understood all at once, in an era in which no recognizable "cognitive minority" was there to support a vision that would run

---

[9] "Timeshed" and "spiritshed" are new words created by Virginia Woolf. See her book *Three Guineas* (New York: Harcourt, Brace, and World, 1938 A.F.), p. 64.

totally counter to the prevailing world—view. She saw hierarchies disappearing, priestly caste disappearing, but she did not yet foresee the bonding of women in sisterhood, an exodus community that would leave behind the destroyers to die of their own internal ailments.

The reader of this review has already been partially prepared for the content of the next section, which is on "the nun." The assessment here of the predicament of nuns seems to me essentially accurate. Of course, the idea of the "emerging nun" was destined to self-destruct, since "emerging" would seem to have its logical consequence in ceasing to be a "nun." Daly's discussion of the advantages which the nuns had "in the past" over married women contains a statement that some sisters in the women's movement might find quaint. I refer to the statement that "she paid the price of isolation from the male" (p. 211). Of course, I think that Daly was right in isolating "isolation" as a major difficulty, but we now realize that the more essential problem for all women in all "states of life" has been isolation from each other. The fact of living under the same roof, whether harem roof, convent roof, apartment building roof, or suburban split-level roof, has not guaranteed any real bonding among women. The invisible walls between women, constructed of economic and emotional dependency upon men, divided consciousness, self-hatred, and horizontal hostility, had been made so thick that genuine and effective bonding was extremely difficult not only in the past that preceded Daly's era, but also in the past which was her era.

The last section of the chapter assures us that the "reformed, democratized church of the future is not yet here" (p. 213). Indeed, it wasn't there, and it isn't here either. While this fact was "painfully obvious" to our author, it is no less obvious but far less painful to me. In her hope that the "old order" would be overcome by the church, which she vainly wished would become "God's avant-garde," Daly overlooked the fact that the church and churchly inveterately have been the rear guard of the old order.

Her hope extended to institutions other than the church, but her analysis of these also often reveals that the wealth of experience which the process of the feminist revolution has brought to us was unavailable to her. For example, she writes that "single-sex educational institutions . . . should wherever possible evolve into, or be replaced by, coeducational institutions" (p. 215). This might puzzle those who are working today toward the creation of feminist universities. Once again, I must point out that understanding the author's historical situation helps resolve the puzzle. The isolation of women in nonfeminist colleges (*all* women's colleges) was appalling to her, since these reinforced feminine stereotypes. Struggling against this, she and her contemporaries looked to coeducation as the answer. Implicit in this "solution," of course, was the idea of "equality" as the feminist goal. Subsequent experience demonstrated that "equality" in fact did not happen in the so-called coeducational institutions, which feminists now generally perceive as subeducational. The "normal day to day encounters" were not infrequently rape in one form or another (physical or mental), especially following the "sexual revolution." The instances when male members of the university "community" did work together with female members nonexploitatively were not frequent enough to affect the general atmosphere or to alter the normal functioning of sexual politics. Not only were administrators and professors by and large sexist (even if not "intentionally" so), but the curriculum content also was hopelessly androcentric. Today, we are experimenting with new forms of woman-centered, woman-controlled studies which make it possible to learn our own history and think our own thoughts. Of course, since 1975 A.F. is still a transitional time, our methods of surviving subeducation are shifting and diverse. Our programs, courses, and centers are separate spaces created on the boundary of these "educational" institutions. It is through living "on the boundary" that women gather energy to use the resources worth using at these institutions and to create our own resources.

Daly touches upon other institutions, such as the "field" of medicine, politics, and the media. She could not have foreseen the women's health revolution that began with Self Help clinics, in which women are recapturing control of our own bodies, relearning and adding to the wisdom of our foremothers who were healers and therefore burned as witches. She could not have foreseen the collective indecent exposures of the political "system" and the legal profession, epitomized in the Watergate affair, which radicalized our sisters' understanding of politics and inspired our redefinition of "politics." Nor could she have foreseen the escalated obscenity of the media, particularly of the non-newscasters, "talk show" moderators, and advertisers, whose nocturnal emissions and diurnal ejaculations penetrate our television screens, landing half-noticed before the glazed stares of their viewers in a hundred million "living" rooms. An increased understanding of the media's functioning in sexist society has inspired a more cautious assessment of its possibilities by feminists today.

Appropriately, the chapter concludes with a remark about "the mounting suspicion in the minds of many that Christianity—particularly as it is embodied in the Catholic church—is the inevitable enemy of human progress (p. 219). It is my suspicion that this was Daly's *own* suspicion—though perhaps not yet fully acknowledged by herself—and that it was mounting.

CONCLUSION

The Second Sex and the Seeds of Transcendence

I sighed when I read this title, asking myself if she really *had* to choose the word "seeds." It struck me as curiously fitting that the lead citation was from Joan of Arc. Joan had at least made a partial escape from patriarchy (as had Daly, in her own way). Joan's escape was significant enough to require that the church kill her (and later make her a "Christian saint"—the ultimate conquest of her independence), but it was indeed *partial,* since her stature was reduced to that of the Virgin-Warrior who aids men to fulfill men's goals. The ambiguous and partial quality of Joan's escape is suggested by the content of the lead citation itself: "I do best by obeying and serving my sovereign Lord—that is, God" (p. 220). It seems that Joan was able to defy the earthly "lords" because of an ultimate—and ultimately masochistic—dependence upon the superlatively sadistic Lord-God who willed her torture and death.

Of course, Daly's attention was focused not upon this ultimate "obeying and serving" but upon Joan's escape from the earthly masters. However, as I read the title of the conclusion and this citation together, it did concern me that the "seeds of transcendence" might subintentionally have been envisaged (either by Daly or by her readers) as this sovereign Lord's product. In that case, the Second Sex, dreaming of transcendence, would find itself forever supine on the Procrustean bed of "the Sovereign Lord." (It is no accident that some of our sisters today have chosen to name their feminist newspaper "Off Our Backs.")

It may be objected that I am seeing too much in the imagery here, which was, after all, the ordinary language of Christians. But the problem, as I see it, is that Daly herself was not in a situation which could enable her to examine this imagery closely enough. Nor, to my knowledge, was anyone else of her time. However, the most important point of her book's conclusion is not its archaic imagery but rather her affirmation that "the world is moving" (p. 220). The difference between de Beauvoir and herself, as she perceived it, was a difference between despair and hope. While I am not so sure that de Beauvoir was totally despairing, I am convinced that Daly's hope was real, although it was not focused clearly enough. Like de Beauvoir, she expressed the wish that "men and women can learn to 'set their pride beyond the sexual differentiation'" (p. 223). The time had not yet arrived when women would learn to set our pride not only beyond but also *in* the sexual differentiation—not in the differentiation as defined by the patriarchs ("the eternal feminine"), but as defined by *us. This* pride, we now know, is rooted in Amazon power.

Feminist Postchristian Conclusion to the Feminist Postchristian Introduction

As critic, what have I managed to say of this work? It has made me alternately exasperated and joyful. The biographical data accessible to me concerning the author indicates that she was not an overly modest person, so I don't think she would mind my saying that she helped to build a tradition in which I now participate. I would be less than just if I failed to acknowledge this. I have found the work worth studying at this time, and I recommend it to scholars who wish to understand the process of the feminist movement.

I realize that a review of the kind I have undertaken may invite an onslaught of criticism from all sides. Some may rush to accuse me of asserting myself as the world's leading Dalyan scholar and disciple. I can only assure these critics that I approached this task with timidity; yet it did seem that I had been called, both by training and circumstances, to take on this work.

I realize, too, that others may criticize me for "attacking" a feminist, for even though her work dates from another period, the fact that her book has been brought into the limelight again may make it appear to be in "competition" with my own. I can only repeat that I feel no unsisterly sense of competition, but rather only gratitude for her influence over my own formative years.

Let me make it perfectly clear that I can foresee some of the comments that may appear in reviews of this review, or at the very least in the conversations of my critics. Perhaps in this time of paper shortage I can prevent some unnecessary use of these resources by anticipating what some will feel compelled to say:

"Daly has now gone off the deep end."
　　　　　　—LIBERAL CATHOLIC

"I saw this coming in 1968."
　　　　　　—CONSERVATIVE CATHOLIC

"Unscholarly, abrasive, slick."
　　　　　　—BOSSTOWN COLLEGE ADMINISTRATOR

"Ladies, this is a broadside."
　　　　　　—TOKEN WOMAN, *U.W.I.H.O.B.*[10]

"She misunderstands both Daly and Saint Paul."
　　　　　　—RADICAL CATHOLIC

"I fear that she will not be taken seriously by the male theological establishment."
　　　　　　—CATHOLIC FEMINIST

"Her problem has progressed from a simple case of penis envy to a rare and convoluted delusory form of castration anxiety."
　　　　　　—EMINENT PSYCHOLOGIST

"Despite her disclaimers, she still *belongs* to the Judeo-Christian tradition."
　　　　　　—LIBERAL PROTESTANT PROFESSOR

"She should join the Unitarian Universalists."
　　　　　　—UNITARIAN UNIVERSALIST

[10] Meaning: "Ultimate weapon in the hands of the boys." See Robin Morgan's poem, "The One That Got Away," in *Monster,* p. 70.

"Tasteless."
—ANONYMOUS

"Stunning!"
—MYSELF

I will conclude this conclusion simply by stating that whatever the response or nonresponse of others may be, I have enjoyed this discussion with the 1968 A.D. Daly. Perhaps others will find it profitable. I hope so, because the hope that a time/space seven woman-light years ahead of *now* will come into be-ing depends upon our patient efforts to build up a feminist tradition.

This hope will be fulfilled only if women continue to make qualitative leaps in living our transcendence. A short-circuited hope of transcendence has caused many to remain inside churches, and patriarchal religion sometimes has seemed to satisfy the hunger for transcendence. The problem has been that both the hunger and the satisfaction generated within such religions have to a great extent alienated women from our deepest aspirations. Spinning in vicious circles of false needs and false consciousness, women caught on the patriarchal wheel have not been able to experience women's own experience.

I suggest that what women require is *ludic cerebration,* the free play of intuition in our own space, giving rise to thinking that is vigorous, informed, multidimensional, independent, creative, tough. Ludic cerebration is thinking out of experience. I do not mean the experience of dredging out All That Was Wrong with Mother or of instant intimacy in group encounters or of waiting at the doctoral dispensary or of self-lobotomization in order to publish, perish, and then be promoted. I mean the experience of be-ing. *Be-ing* is the verb that says the dimensions of depth in all verbs, such an intuiting, reasoning, loving, imaging, making, acting, as well as the couraging, hoping, and playing that are always there when one is really living.

It may be that some new things happen within patriarchy, but one thing essentially stays the same: women are always marginal beings. From this vantage point of the margin it is possible to look at what is between the margins with the lucidity of The Compleat Outsider. To change metaphors: the systems within the System do not appear so radically different from each other to those excluded by all. Hope for a qualitative leap lies in *us* by reason of that deviance from the "norm" which was first imposed but which can also be *chosen* on our own terms. This means that there has to be a shift from "acceptable" female deviance (characterized by triviality, diffuseness, dependence upon others for self-definition, low self-esteem, powerlessness) to deviance which may be unacceptable to others but which is acceptable to the self and *is* self-acceptance.

For women concerned with philosophical/theological questions, it seems to me, this implies the necessity of some sort of choice. One either tries to avoid "acceptable" deviance ("normal" female idiocy) by becoming accepted as a male-identified professional, or else one tries to make the qualitative leap toward self-acceptable deviance as ludic cerebrator, questioner of everything, madwoman, and witch.[11]

I do mean witch. The heretic who rejects the idols of patriarchy and therefore refuses to bow down before the God"Method"is the blasphemous creatrix of her own thoughts. She is finding her life and intends not to lose it.

The witch that smoulders within feminist philosophical and theological questioners can blaze forth. In spite of our Ph.D.'s (our disease of degrees), it is possible to refuse intellectual servitude and the degrading "honors" that are its rewards. To borrow from Nazim Hikmet (courtesy of Roger Garoudy):

> If I do not burn,
> If you do not burn,
> If we do not burn,
> How shall the shadows
> Become light?

The witch that smolders within every woman who cared and dared enough to become a theologian or philosopher in the first place seems to be crying out these days: "Light my fire!" The qualitative leap of those flames of spiritual imagination and cerebral fantasy can be a new dawn. I hope that we won't trade *this* birthright (the right to give birth to ourselves) for a mess of professional respectability.

Virginia Woolf knew of the need for a feminist tradition, when she wrote of her hope for the eventual arrival of Shakespeare's

---

[11] Another way of expressing "questioner of everything" is to say "Nonquestioner"—an expression which I frequently use to convey the fact that women's most important questions are treated as nonquestions by those in patriarchal A.D. time, especially academics. See *Beyond God the Father*, Introduction.

sister.[12] I hope for the arrival also of the sisters of Plato, of Aristotle, of Kant, of Nietzsche: sisters who will not merely "equal" them, but do something different, something immeasurably more. I dream of these, my sisters, as drawing from the vision of our past and future foremothers, waking the human species to glimpse still further stars.

[12] See *A Room of One's Own* (Harbinger Books, New York: Harcourt, Brace, and World, 1929 A.F.), pp. 48–50, 117–18.

CHAPTER ONE

The Case Against the Church

'Christian ideology has contributed no little to the oppression of woman'

Simone de Beauvoir

Those engaged in the struggle for the equality of the sexes have often seen the Catholic Church as an enemy. This view is to a large extent justified, for Catholic teaching has prolonged a traditional view of woman which at the same time idealizes and humiliates her. It is precisely this ambivalence, characteristic of so many Catholic utterances about women, which those committed to improving the legal, professional and economic condition of women find deplorable.

Proponents of equality charge that there is inexcusable hypocrisy in a species of ecclesiastical propaganda which pretends to put woman on a pedestal but which in reality prevents her from genuine self-fulfillment and from active, adult-size participation in society. They point out that symbolic idealization tends to dupe women into satisfaction with the narrow role imposed upon them. Made to feel guilty or 'unnatural' if they rebel, many have been condemned to a restricted or mutilated existence in the name of religion. Moreover, the Church has been described as a pressure group exercising influence on the practical level, through whatever press media and political, religious and social organizations it controls, to prevent changes which would improve the condition of women. Thus it is maintained, with supporting documentation, that

'wherever the Catholic Church is strongly implanted, in the countries where it is the state religion or simply the dominant religion, the hierarchy has always persisted in maintaining woman

53

in her traditional situation of inferiority, and in opposing every liberal reform capable of improving her condition in the family and in society.'[1]

So effective has the conservative pressure and propaganda been, that this idealizing ideology is accepted and perpetuated not only by countless members of the clergy, but indeed by many women. Fascinated by an exalted symbol of 'Woman', they are not disposed to understand the distress imposed upon countless real, existing women.

In the light of this state of affairs the Catholic Church appears to many as the last stronghold of anachronism and prejudice, refusing to adapt its structures to the condition of modern women, still preaching to them the passive virtues of obedience, submission and meekness, while seeming to refuse or ignore the profound aspirations of half the human race to liberty and full personhood.

It is true, of course, that many Catholic women in America and other advanced countries do not suffer explicitly from any of this, and accordingly they are not aware of any real problem. To reach and convince such persons, recent writers of feminist polemic have amassed an impressive body of historical facts. These demonstrate that in the recent past Catholic bodies have opposed the right of women to vote and to an adequate education; and that in some regions they still uphold legislation that will keep married women in what can only be called a condition of servile economic and legal dependence. Other evidence supports the claim that in all countries in which the Catholic Church is the state religion or the privileged religion—e.g. Italy, Spain, Portugal—the infidelity of a woman is severely punished (in some cases, by imprisonment) whereas the man is punished only if he installs a concubine in the home. In these countries, moreover, the Church promotes the totalitarian family: the father has *patria potestas* over the children, even if there is a legal separation due to his own wrong-doing, and he has the administration of the goods of the household. Ecclesias-

[1] Andrée Michel and Geneviève Texier, *La condition de la française d'aujourd-'hui* (Genève: Editions Gonthier, 1964), t. II, p. 26.

tical pressure against birth control fits naturally within this context of oppression. In the poverty-stricken south of Italy, it is shown, it is not rare for a woman to have twenty children. The reduction of the woman to the condition of biological beast, the spread of delinquency and prostitution coincident with the multiplication of offspring who cannot be adequately provided for—critics impute these in large measure to the policy of the Church which even today, it is charged, continues to combat the legitimate aspirations of women, justifying this by archaic ideology, making a fetish of 'nature', while ignoring the vocation of the individual to dominate 'nature'.[1]

When it is objected that ecclesiastical attitudes in the advanced countries deviate significantly from this 'traditional' pattern, the contemporary critics often counter by saying that any moderation is not indicative of official attitudes, but is instead necessitated by a cultural milieu hostile to the 'traditional' mentality. But this counter-argument is hasty and unconvincing. While it is impossible honestly to maintain that it is false, nevertheless a criticism which does not go further is simplistic and therefore unsatisfactory. It is better to recognize that, since the Church is immersed in a wide variety of social situations, inevitably there are various patterns of interaction. The more progressive milieu produces a more progressive Church. While this may be seen as an enforced compromise, it would on the other hand be naive to imagine this modification of the Church as the stretching of a rubber band which will automatically snap back to 'normal' when the pressure is removed. There is no compelling reason to preclude the possibility that a progression is involved. The day-to-day and country-by-country experience of the Church is educational, and it brings about evolution of its doctrine. However slowly, surely the Church learns somewhat from 'the world', and eventually progressive thinking does have some influence upon the upper regions of its ponderous organism. If pessimism on this score was plausible before Vatican II, it is no longer a completely realistic attitude.

On balance, if some of the contemporary criticism of the

[1] *Ibid.*, II, pp. 26–40.

Church's stance on women is over-simplified and unsympathetic, it is also in large measure supported by indisputable facts. The very minimum required by intellectual honesty and good faith is that the questions thus raised be faced by all without defensiveness, rancor, or dissimulation. There is mounting evidence of a growing awareness among Catholics that there is a problem. It is one thing, however, to know that a problem exists and something else to face it. Moreover, it is essential to any worthwhile discussion to establish the nature of the problem, even though its complexity may not allow a very easy formulation.

The second sex

The problematic of woman's general situation has, in fact, been expounded by the French existentialist philosopher, Simone de Beauvoir, in her famous two-volume work, *The Second Sex*—unquestionably the most vigorous and comprehensive as well as influential study of the subject yet produced. No other work of this *genre* has approached it in scope and level of philosophical reflection. A wealth of research in history, anthropology, biology, psychology, philosophy and theology went into its making. While few people agree with all of its theses, no important work on the subject written in the past two decades has been unaffected by it. Even works intended to 'answer' it are in large part derivative. As a French Jesuit scholar put it: 'Even where she has been contradicted and, on certain points, refuted, her influence has left its mark and prevents one from reposing in the comfort of ready-made ideas.'[1] So pre-eminent is de Beauvoir's analysis that no one today who is seriously concerned about the problem can afford to ignore it.

In Simone de Beauvoir's study, no special section is devoted to the role of the Church in conditioning women. However, a vigorous criticism of Catholic ideology and practice is to be found disseminated throughout its pages. Written by an atheist who is an adherent of the existentialist philosophy of Jean-Paul

---

[1] Xavier Tilliette, S.J., 'Le féminisme et les problèmes de la femme', *Etudes*, mai, 1965, p. 670.

Sartre, this analysis is characterized by a clinical detachment which may sometimes shock the sensibilities of the reader who is a Christian. Yet it is sometimes a wholesome thing to be shocked into awareness. One would do well to follow the advice of Thomas Aquinas to a student who wanted to become a scholar: 'Remember the good things that you hear, and do not consider who says them.'

On the other hand it is true that biographical information about an author may be the source of insights as to why he sees things as he does. Thus we know from her memoirs that Simone de Beauvoir cannot be considered a totally neutral 'outsider' as far as the Church is concerned. Brought up by a pious Catholic mother and an unbelieving father, she undoubtedly experienced conflicting influences from a very young age. She has vividly conveyed in her memoirs that she had been a pious little girl and that her early and decisive loss of faith was not the indifferent drifting of an indecisive personality. Having experienced Christianity—in a given milieu, to be sure—she whole-heartedly rejected it.[1] If certain dimensions are left out of her analysis, biographical data may help to explain the omission. However, such facts do not provide a criterion for judging what she has written. To attack her book on the basis of her life is to resort to *argumentum ad hominem*.

When the numerous passages in *The Second Sex* which deal with Christianity in general and the Catholic Church in particular are collected and examined, it becomes evident that there are various conceivable ways in which these could be organized. We shall strive for clarity by bringing into focus the relatively few major themes touching the Church which recur in the work and which are directly relevant to this study.

Oppression and deception

The first of de Beauvoir's themes to be considered is the following: the Christian religion has been an instrument of the oppression of women. In the Middle Ages,

[1] Simone de Beauvoir, *Memoirs of a Dutiful Daughter* (Harmondsworth, Middlesex: Penguin Books, 1963), especially pp. 134–40.

'the canon law admitted no other matrimonial regime than the dowry scheme, which made woman legally incompetent and powerless. Not only did the masculine occupations remain closed to her, but she was forbidden to make depositions in court, and her testimony was not recognized as having weight.'[1]

Moreover, her worst enemies were the clerics.[2] Even though modern society, at least in the predominantly non-Catholic countries, has emancipated women from the shackles of oppressive legislation, the Church has only reluctantly gone along with this amelioration of her legal status. In fact, 'the Church is notably hostile to all measures likely to help in woman's emancipation'. Why does the Church want to keep women down? Because in their dependent condition they are a 'powerful trump' in its hand. 'There must be religion for women; and there must be women, "true women", to perpetuate religion.'[3]

To de Beauvoir, this oppression is masked by deception. This has always been the case to some extent, but of course it has become more necessary in recent years, for modern secular society will no longer tolerate the oppressive legislation of the past. Thus: 'In modern civilization . . . religion seems much less an instrument of constraint than an instrument of deception.'[4] One form which this deception takes is the distraction of woman's attention from present injustice to promises of rewards in an afterlife. 'But, above all, it [religion] confirms the social order, it justifies her resignation, by giving her the hope of a better future in a sexless heaven.'[5] Thus, her situation is that of one who has been duped: 'The passivity enforced upon woman is sanctified. . . . There is no need to *do* anything to save her soul, it is enough to *live* in obedience.'[6] This passi-

[1]Simone de Beauvoir, *The Second Sex*, translated by H. M. Parshley (London: Jonathan Cape, 1953; New York: Alfred A. Knopf, Inc., 1953), p. 98. The remaining footnote references in this chapter are to the Knopf edition.
[2]P. 104.
[3]P. 624.
[4]P. 621.
[5]P. 624.
[6]P. 622.

vity, compensated for by daydreams of rewards in the next life, is, in fact, a curse:

'The curse that is upon woman as vassal consists . . . in the fact that she is not permitted to do anything; so she persists in the vain pursuit of her true being through narcissism, love, or religion. When she is productive, active, she regains her transcendence; in her projects she concretely affirms her status as subject; in connection with the aims she pursues, with the money and the rights she takes possession of, she makes trial of and senses her responsibility.'[1]

The enforced passive role, then, according to de Beauvoir, is mutilating; and women have been encouraged to acquiesce in it through the inculcation of a pie-in-the-sky mentality fostered by the Church. Prevented from full personal development through genuine participation in the affairs of society, they have not achieved full adulthood. Moreover, the Catholic male may soothe his bad conscience over depriving woman of her autonomy through a specious sort of reasoning. This is conveyed forcefully in the section on the poet, Claudel:

'It has been said that the earthly calling of woman is in no way destructive of her supernatural autonomy; but, inversely, in recognizing this, the Catholic feels authorized to maintain in this world the prerogatives of the male. Venerating woman *in God,* men treat her in this world as a servant, even holding that the more one demands complete submission of her, the more surely one will advance her along the road of her salvation.'[2]

De Beauvoir maintains that religion has deceived woman in another, though closely related, way. Besides diverting woman's attention to bright rewards in a future life, Christianity creates the delusion of equality already attained.

'Woman is asked in the name of God not so much to accept her inferiority as to believe that, thanks to him, she is the equal of the lordly male: even the temptation to revolt is suppressed by the claim that the injustice is overcome. Woman is no longer denied

[1] Pp. 679–80.
[2] P. 231.

transcendence, since she is to consecrate her immanence to God; the worth of souls is to be weighed only in heaven and not according to their accomplishments on earth.'[1]

This 'equality' which women have attained through Christianity is in fact insubstantial. On the one hand, there is ample evidence that woman is despised as a sexual being. Yet, at the same time she is exalted in an unrealistic way. De Beauvoir maintains that this pseudo-exaltation is a result of guilt feelings:

'It is Christianity which invests woman anew with frightening prestige: fear of the other sex is one of the forms assumed by the anguish of man's uneasy conscience.'[2]

Another element besides fear arising from bad conscience also helps to account for this glorification: man's will to subject her is ambiguous.

'By complete possession and control woman would be abased to the rank of a thing; but man aspires to clothe in his own dignity whatever he conquers and possesses.'[3]

Her 'exaltation' is therefore ultimately the glorification of man. In short, the pseudo-equality conferred upon woman by Christian ideology is not a genuine acceptance of her as person and partner.

De Beauvoir is by no means naive enough to lay all the blame upon the Church. There are many other convergent influences, but the role of religion is powerful in the crippling process and as a result:

'the fact is that the traditional woman is a bamboozled conscious being and a practitioner of bamboozlement; she attempts to disguise her dependence from herself, which is a way of consenting to it'.[4]

She may be vaguely aware that something is wrong with her situation, but the myth of equality already attained, which is promoted in Christianity, contributes to the paralysis of her will to strive for genuine equality.

[1]P. 621.
[2]P. 167.
[3]P. 80.
[4]P. 709.

In consequence, women's efforts at creative intellectual work are hampered. Of course, some do see through the myths. A few women writers strive to expose the problem and in so doing, render a great service. Usually, however,

'they are still too concerned with serving this cause to assume the disinterested attitude towards the universe that opens the widest horizons. . . . Woman exhausts her courage dissipating mirages and she stops in terror at the threshold of reality.'[1]

That is, even gifted women who have broken through the myths are handicapped; their capacity for objectivity and creativity is partially worn out in the struggle to break the webs of delusion. 'Women do not contest the human situation, because they have hardly begun to assume it.'[2]

Dogma versus women

A second theme relevant to our subject in de Beauvoir's work is that the Church by its doctrine implicitly conveys the idea that women are naturally inferior. In pagan religions of antiquity, the mother-goddess was worshipped. Judaism and Christianity represent a reaction against this. 'It was as Mother that woman was fearsome; it is in maternity that she must be transfigured and enslaved.'[3] This enslavement was accomplished symbolically in the cult of the Virgin Mother of God, who is glorified only in accepting the subordinate role assigned to her.

'For the first time in human history the mother kneels before her son; she freely accepts her inferiority. This is the supreme masculine victory, consummated in the cult of the Virgin—it is the rehabilitation of woman through the accomplishment of her defeat.'[4]

The point is that women are encouraged to identify with this image of Mary, and to do so has devastating effects. Speaking of the servile condition of women in the Catholic countries, de Beauvoir says: 'And that flows in large part from women's

[1] P. 710.
[2] P. 711.
[3] P. 171.
[4] *Ibid.*

own attitude: the cult of the Virgin, confession, and the rest lead them towards masochism."[1] In this way, de Beauvoir sees Catholic dogma as contributing to the conditioning of women to adore and serve man.

Harmful moral teaching

A third element in de Beauvoir's analysis is the harmfulness of certain aspects of moral doctrine. That Orthodox Jews in their morning prayers thank God 'that he did not make me a woman', and that Plato seems to have uttered a similar prayer can be understood as expressions of the *de facto* situation. However, a *de facto* situation is subject to change. Thus:

> 'The males could not enjoy this privilege fully unless they believed it to be founded on the absolute and the eternal; they sought to make the fact of their supremacy into a right ... (Among other structures) the religions invented by men reflect this wish for domination. In the legends of Eve and Pandora men have taken up arms against women. They have made use of philosophy and theology. . . .'[2]

There are, according to our author, two major sources of the misogynistic cast of Catholic moral theology: Hebrew tradition and Greek philosophy. In regard to the former she asserts: 'Through St Paul the Jewish tradition, savagely antifeminist, was affirmed.' As for Greek philosophy, this lent special support to the idea of feminine inferiority. The Aristotelian idea of fixed 'natures', as well as its view of woman as having only a minor role in procreation, that of merely supplying the matter whereas the male supplied the form, was taken over by St Thomas Aquinas. Thus woman's place is fixed by the 'nature' which she has. This idea served the patriarchal institutions which the Church perpetuates and reflects: the male could lay claim to his posterity by claiming a major role in procreation. The idea of woman's special sinfulness, stemming from commonly held interpretations of the Bible, combined with a notion of her inferior 'nature', affirmed in Aristotelian philosophy, thus

[1]P. 290n.
[2]P. xxii.

made it seem that the sociological fact of woman's subordination was inscribed in the heavens.

De Beauvoir maintains that Christian antifeminism has always been linked to antisexuality. In fact, 'in a religion that holds the flesh accursed, woman becomes the devil's most fearsome temptation'. Perhaps one might have thought that this should work both ways, since women can also be tempted by men. Not at all.

'And, of course, since woman remains always the Other, it is not held that reciprocally male and female are both flesh; the flesh that is for the Christian the hostile *Other* is precisely woman. In her the Christian finds incarnated the temptations of the world, the flesh and the devil. All the Fathers of the Church insist on the idea that she led Adam into sin.'[1]

Moreover, 'since the Middle Ages, the fact of having a body has been considered, in woman, an ignominy'.[2] This view is reflected in the idea of maternity as unclean. The religious ceremony of 'churching' after childbirth is a remnant of earlier rites of purification.

The fact that the Church serves a patriarchal society is said to be at the root of its moral attitudes toward women, for 'oppression of women has its cause in the will to perpetuate the family and to keep the patrimony intact'.[3] Hence, the Church perpetuates a double standard of morality. 'When woman becomes man's property, he wants her to be virgin and he requires complete fidelity under threats of extreme penalties.'[4]

One result of the 'honest' woman's enslavement to the family was the spread of prostitution.

'Christianity poured out its scorn upon them [prostitutes] but accepted them as a necessary evil. Both St Augustine and St Thomas asserted that the suppression of prostitution would mean the disruption of society by debauch.'[5]

[1] P. 167.
[2] P. 168.
[3] P. 89.
[4] P. 83.
[5] P. 102.

Prostitution illustrates the hypocrisy of the double standard. It is the male's demand that creates the supply, yet he suffers no disgrace as a result. Man is measured by other standards besides sexuality, and the respectable official remains such whether he frequents brothels or not. Woman, having been reduced to the condition of a venereal being, 'stakes her moral value in the contingent realm of sexuality'.[1]

De Beauvoir finds hypocrisy and even unconscious sadism in Christian attitudes toward abortion.

'It is remarkable that the Church at times authorizes the killing of adult men, as in war or in connection with legal executions; it reserves an uncompromising humanitarianism for man in the fetal condition.'[2]

Ironically, it is very often the husband or lover who demands abortion as a solution. Yet the Church supports legislation against this, so that frequently abortion is done illegally under unhygienic conditions in which the woman suffers enormously and is subjected to the possibility of ruined health for the rest of her life. Particularly harmful to women is the Church's opposition to contraception. When contraceptives are not widely available, abortion is

'the only recourse for women unwilling to bring into the world children doomed to misery and death. Contraception and legal abortion would permit woman to undertake her maternities in freedom. As things are, woman's fecundity is decided in part voluntarily, in part by chance.'[3]

According to this analysis there is a basic enmity between much traditional Christian moral teaching and the personal aspirations of women. Reduced to the condition of slavery to the species, instruments of reproduction, they cannot transcend their situation:

'The fundamental fact that from the beginning of history doomed woman to domestic work and prevented her taking part in the

[1]P. 614.
[2]P. 486.
[3]P. 492.

shaping of the world was her enslavement to the generative function.'[1]

Obviously, the Church is not to blame for this basic biological fact. De Beauvoir's point is that the Church is helping to perpetuate the enslavement after science has made liberation possible. This it has done by forbidding to her the most effective means of preventing repeated, unwanted maternity. Moreover, insofar as its moral teaching suggests that gainful employment by married women is suspect, it is perpetuating her servility in yet another way, for:

'It is through gainful employment that woman has traversed most of the distance that separated her from the male; and nothing else can guarantee her liberty in practice. Once she ceases to be a parasite, the system based on her dependence crumbles; between her and the universe there is no longer any need for a masculine mediator.'[2]

Exclusion from the hierarchy

Analysis of de Beauvoir's work reveals a fourth major point of criticism of the Church. This is that the Church, by excluding women from the hierarchy, contributes significantly to the process of inculcating inferiority feelings and causes psychological confusion.

'God's representatives on earth: the pope, the bishop (whose ring one kisses), the priest who says Mass, he who preaches, he before whom one kneels in the secrecy of the confessional—all these are men. . . . The Catholic religion among others exerts a most confused influence upon the young girl.'[3]

The effect of this is to imbue the girl with a sense of *specific* inferiority. It is futile for her to aspire to such an exalted role no matter how great her talents and piety.

The exclusion of women from the hierarchy has psychological

[1]P. 117.
[2]P. 679.
[3]P. 290.

meaning distinct from her exclusion from other authoritative groups. It is linked with an idea of divinity as male:

> 'On her knees, breathing the odor of incense, the young girl abandons herself to the gaze of God and the angels: a masculine gaze.'[1]

This attitude is reinforced by the fact that God is called Father, that Christ is male, that the angels, though they are pure spirits, have masculine names. The effects of this are to be seen in many pious women and alleged female mystics:

> 'We encounter this inextricable confusion between man and God in many devotees. The confessor in particular occupies an ambiguous place between earth and heaven. He listens with mortal ears when the penitent bares her soul, but his gaze envelops her in a supernatural light; he is a man of God, he is God present in human form.'[2]

So the tendency to equate the male sex with the divine is encouraged. It is true that there are pious men, some of whom have been excluded from seminaries for various reasons, who do not become priests. However, theirs is not at all the same case; their exclusion is individual. Moreover, the point is not at all that a few women may have the desire to become priests which cannot be fulfilled; it is, rather, that Catholic women, by the fact of the exclusion of *all* women from such a role, are conditioned to believe that they have an irremediably inferior nature. This conditioning leads to a devastating mutilation. Seemingly to them the only way to triumph over this debased nature of theirs is docility before the male, who serves as the only intermediary between themselves and a masculine God.

Transcendence through religion?

An adequate consideration of de Beauvoir's critique must include a fifth point. This is her treatment of the fact that women can achieve transcendence through religion. In view of all she has written on the harmful aspects of religion, that she should recognize this is perhaps astonishing. On the whole her

[1]P. 290.
[2]P. 671.

work mercilessly draws a picture of typical religious women—especially those purported to have been mystics—as neurotic, over-emotional, narcissistic. She describes in detail the repulsive ascetical practices of some female saints. The reader is reminded that St Angela of Foligno drank with delight the water in which she had just washed lepers' hands and feet. There was Margaret Mary Alacoque, who cleaned up the vomit of a patient with her tongue and filled her mouth with the excrement of a man sick with diarrhoea. 'Jesus rewarded her when she held her lips pressed against his Sacred Heart for three hours.'[1] Moreover: 'She was the one who offered to the adoration of the faithful the great red clot, surrounded with flaming darts of love.'[2] There is ample evidence of the sado-masochistic fantasies of female mystics brooding over the lacerated body of Christ.

But de Beauvoir admits at least one clear exception to all this religious neuroticism—St Teresa of Avila. Although St Teresa's writings also have an erotic vocabulary, nevertheless unlike the lesser mystics she is not a hysteric, and she is not the slave of her nerves and her hormones.

'The truth is, as she herself understood, that the value of a mystical experience is measured not according to the way in which it is subjectively felt, but according to its objective influence. The ecstatic phenomena are almost the same in St Teresa and in Margaret Mary Alacoque, but their messages are of very diverse interest. St Teresa poses in a most intellectual fashion the dramatic problem of the relation between the individual and the transcendent Being; she lived out, as a woman, an experience whose meaning goes far beyond the fact of her sex; she must be ranked with Suso and St John of the Cross. But she is a striking exception.'[3]

What is interesting here is that de Beauvoir recognizes the validity of St Teresa's experience and that she recognizes her as an exceptional woman—almost unique (although she admits

[1]P. 676.
[2]P. 677.
[3]P. 674.

that a few others, notably Catherine of Siena, approach her stature in some respects). Teresa is credited with achieving transcendence.

Of central interest in the passages on St Teresa is the reason given for her ability to transcend the limitations imposed upon her sex. It is partially revealed in the following passage:

> 'The women who have accomplished works comparable to those of men are those exalted by the power of social institutions above all sexual differentiation.... The proportion of queens who had great reigns is infinitely above that of great kings. Religion works the same transformation: Catherine of Siena, St Teresa, quite beyond any physiological consideration, were sainted souls; the life they led, secular and mystic, their acts, and their writings rose to heights that few men have ever reached.'[1]

The point is that the Church as an institution can provide the needed condition for a St Teresa to rise above the handicap of her sex. As institution, therefore, the Church can play the same liberating role for some of its adherents as the structure of royal government for feminine monarchs.

Is there nothing else to explain St Teresa? De Beauvoir, in discussing her uniqueness, seems to suggest that there is:

> 'There is hardly any woman other than St Teresa who in total abandonment has herself lived out the situation of humanity; we have seen why. Taking her stand beyond the earthly hierarchies, she felt, like St John of the Cross, no reassuring ceiling over her head. There were for both the same darkness, the same flashes of light, in the self the same nothingness, in God the same plenitude. When at last it will be possible for every human being thus to set his pride beyond the sexual differentiation, in the laborious glory of free existence, then only will woman be able to identify her personal history, her problems, her doubts, her hopes, with those of humanity; then only will she be able to seek in her life and her works to reveal the whole of reality and not merely her personal self. As long as she still has to struggle to become a human being, she cannot become a creator.'[2]

[1]P. 130.
[2]P. 714.

This astonishingly lyrical passage in a clinical and unrelentingly critical work reiterates the idea that here was a unique case of a woman who was a free person, who 'lived out the situation of humanity' more totally, perhaps, than the greatest of monarchs. As for the psychological leverage which produced this phenomenon, de Beauvoir does not explain further. The one indisputable fact is that Teresa of Avila was a Christian mystic.

Facing the problems

It is by no means a simple task to make a fair criticism of de Beauvoir's pronouncements concerning the role of the Church in perpetuating the inferior condition of women. No one is more ready than she to grant that there are many other factors which, together with religion, have worked against women. That the Church is by no means made to bear the whole burden of guilt is evident. It is seen as one factor in the complex context of patriarchal structures, of which it is both product and perpetuator. Rather than being *the* cause of woman's unfortunate condition, religion appears rather as a superstructure, as an instrument of oppression and deception appropriate to a culture with given thought-patterns. This by no means lessens the poignancy of de Beauvoir's observations, but it does suggest that the charge made against her, that she exaggerates the role of the Church, is not well-founded.

It has been claimed that since Simone de Beauvoir's writings presuppose a certain philosophical attitude, that of the atheistic existentialism of Jean-Paul Sartre, her interpretation of the facts should be rejected *a priori* by a Christian. On this basis, a naive and pietistic rebuttal of her thesis runs something like this: 'An atheist cannot really understand the doctrine and practice of the Church.' Unfortunately this sort of defensive stance, understandable though it may be, rests upon a highly questionable hypothesis. It simplistically assumes that non-Christians can have no valid insights concerning the expressions of belief and the behavior of Christians. Implicit in this attitude is the idea that the Church is a congregation of disembodied spirits, living on a wholly 'supernatural' plane, whose 'official' utterances and behavior are totally beyond the scope of merely psychological or sociological analysis. In fact, however, Christians are human beings, subject to the same kinds of failings as other people, and often owe a debt of gratitude to non-believers for their criticisms. Non-believers are an aid in the continual struggle to purify Christian doctrine of its inevitable admixture of nonsense and Christian practice of the tendency to hypocrisy and injustice. A certain callousness to the harmful effects of some ideas and situations, cloaked by the supranaturalist justification that 'it will all come out right at the last judgment', has led to —one might almost say 'necessitated'—violent reactions.

Simone de Beauvoir's atheistic existentialism does of course embody several salient ideas that are particularly relevant to her treatment of the problem of women. First, according to this philosophy, which is one of despair, there is only this life and what one makes of oneself in this life. Given such a perspective, the failure to develop what human talents one has—to lead the life of the escapist, and thus the life of the typical woman as de Beauvoir sees her—has the dimensions of high tragedy. Since the compensations of an after-life are denied, present injustice is seen and felt in all its poignancy. It is futile to speak about what a person might have done or might have been. He or she is the sum total of his works and nothing more. A second, closely related point is that since there is no God who might have a 'plan' for this world, there are no fixed essences. There is no fixed 'human nature'. Thirdly, it follows that one is not born man or woman; one becomes thus. This is not to deny biological differences. What it means is that the characteristic attitudes of men and women are acquired; they are cultural, the results of conditioning. Thus, 'masculinity' and 'femininity' are the effects of historical processes. What is called 'femininity' is really only a situation of fact in a given culture. It is not definitely grounded either in biology or in a mysterious feminine essence. Fourthly, the masculine-feminine opposition is alienating. Woman, as 'the Other', is exploited, duped. . . . In order to be liberated, she must first become conscious of her situation. She will then cease to be imprisoned in the false values of 'femininity', in a pseudo-nature. Once conscious of her real situation, she can be free to become whatever she makes of herself.

There is no cheap and easy answer to these basic elements in de Beauvoir's philosophical position. In regard to the first point: to answer this life-view simply by superimposing belief in an afterlife upon the tragedy of the human situation on earth (with reference to the tragedy of woman's situation in particular) is to miss the point of the modern atheist's protest. De Beauvoir claims that such a belief is itself alienating: it distracts from the need to face the harmfulness of the given situation. Thus the 'cure' perpetuates the illness. Religious thinkers increasingly recognize that there is meaning and value in this atheistic criticism of Christian belief. Faith in an afterlife can indeed be used as a psychological gimmick which helps to distract attention from present injustice.

In regard to the point about fixed essences: in the face of modern evolutionary theory, it is extremely difficult to uphold the idea of a fixed human nature, which is supposedly grasped by a process of abstraction, nor does there seem to be any justification for clinging to a medieval theory of knowledge. However, many contemporary Christian thinkers would deny Sartre's thesis (adopted by de Beauvoir) that belief in the existence of God is inseparably linked with the assertion that there is an immutable human nature. Believing Christians also see man as an evolving being. Moreover, even if it is legitimate to speak of a human 'nature', this does not imply possession of an exhaustive or even exact knowledge of this 'nature' through some mysterious process of abstraction of essences. Man's knowledge of man is also continually evolving.

As to whether one is born or becomes man or woman, dogmatic assertions about an unchanging feminine essence do not find anything like general acceptance among those who follow developments in modern philosophy and in the social sciences and psychology. In fact, our awareness of the profound and subtle effects of conditioning upon the human personality is continually increasing. There is an impressive stock of evidence in support of de Beauvoir on this point, and despite the tenacious hold of the 'eternal feminine' upon the popular mind, the concept of woman is changing, whether one is existentialist or not.

Finally, the fact that woman has been exploited and that the fixed images of masculine and feminine have been used to further her exploitation is indeed demonstrable, as de Beauvoir among others has shown. There is nothing in all this to justify a refusal of the wealth of insight which her work brings to the problem.

What, then, can the Christian who is truly sensitive to the problem of women and the Church offer as an adequate response in the dialogue initiated by de Beauvoir?

As we have suggested, it will not be fruitful to begin with an opposition of philosophical or theological 'principles' to her position. This offers too easy a way of avoiding the real issues. Indeed, many who are not adherents of Sartre's atheistic existentialism agree in large measure with de Beauvoir's analysis of woman's situation. Since human knowledge does not begin with 'principles' but with experience, the most fruitful approach will begin with an effort honestly to answer the question: 'To what extent is this interpretation of Christianity's role in the oppression of women in accord with the data of experience, that is, with historical fact?' This approach will entail an examination of sources—scripture, the writings of the Fathers and of theologians, and papal statements.

It is often the case that disagreement with a critic bears less upon what he has actually said than upon what he has failed to say. Therefore, one should ask a further question: has de Beauvoir omitted any significant data? There is a suggestion (probably an unwitting one) that she has, in the passages on St Teresa, for whom, de Beauvoir says, the Church provided the needed condition for rising above the handicap of her sex. What are the implications of this? Why does de Beauvoir not develop this theme? It must be asked whether her analysis has brought into its perspective all of the important dimensions.

Before closing this chapter there is one other matter deserving consideration. It seems essential to this writer that we recognize that religious doctrine and practice are not in fact static, but rather are continually evolving. This is in large measure the effect of developments in the physical and social sciences, and in psychology, mixed with the influences of changing social conditions. While there have been harmful distortions of doctrine and practice, it is not necessary that these remain with us. A constant purification of doctrine and reform of practice are not only possible but necessary. The insight necessary to effect this evolution comes from human experience, and especially from the challenge of encounter with opposed viewpoints. There are, clearly, promising elements already present in Christian thought which can be sources of further development toward a more personalist conception of the man-woman relationship on all levels. These seminal elements must be distinguished from the oppressive, life-destroying ideas with which they have been confused, and by which they are in danger of being choked off. The distinction having been made, there remains the necessity of seeking to bring about, insofar as our own historically conditioned insights enable us, conditions in which a genuinely life-fostering evolution can take place. For the thinker need not be a helpless spectator of the course of history. There is both place and need for creative thought and action.

It is probable that Simone de Beauvoir's psychological detachment from religious belief is a reason for both the vigor and clarity of her criticism of the Church's role in the oppression of women, and for its limitations. Others must continue to explore the problem, especially those who can accept the value of her insights and who are existentially aware of the meaning of faith, and thereby able to move forward with hope. Such an exploration is intended in the following chapters.

CHAPTER TWO

History: A Record of Contradictions

'To pretend that Christianity was intended to stereotype existing forms of government and society, and protect them against change, is to reduce it to the level of Islamism or Brahminism.'

John Stuart Mill

A study of Christianity's documents concerning women reveals a puzzling ambiguity if not an outright contradiction. Most observable is the conflict between the Christian teachings on the worth of every human person and the oppressive, misogynistic ideas arising from cultural conditioning. If the latter do not contradict they at least obscure the basic doctrine. Intimately bound up with this dialectic there is another tension, between a pseudo-glorification of 'woman' and degrading teachings and practices concerning real women. The second tension of opposites is an effect of the first. Its existence betrays an uneasy awareness that 'something is out of joint', and it reflects an inauthentic response to this awareness. The symbolic glorification of 'woman' arose as a substitute for recognition of full personhood and equal rights. So we may say that the record of Christianity in regard to women is a record of contradictions.

1. SCRIPTURE

The Bible manifests the unfortunate—often miserable—condition of women in ancient times. The authors of both the Old and the New Testaments were men of their times, and it would be naïve to think that they were free of the prejudices of

74

their epochs. It is therefore a most dubious process to construct an idea of 'feminine nature' or of 'God's plan for women' from biblical texts. As one theologian expressed it: 'Let us be careful not to transcribe into terms of nature that which is written in terms of history.'[1]

An example will illustrate this point. The New Testament gave advice to women (and to slaves) which would help them to bear the subhuman (by today's standards) conditions imposed upon them. It would be foolish to erect, on this basis, a picture of 'immutable' feminine qualities and virtues. Thus, although obedience was required of women and slaves, there is nothing about obedience which makes it intrinsically more appropriate for women than for men. The idea of taking feminine 'types' from the Bible as models for modern women may be an exercise for the imagination, but it is difficult to justify as a method. Any rigid abstraction of types from history implies a basic fallacy.

Old Testament

The Bible contains much to jolt the modern woman, who is accustomed to think of herself as an autonomous person. In the writings of the Old Testament women emerge as subjugated and inferior beings. Although the wife of an Israelite was not on the level of a slave, and however much better off she was than wives in other near-eastern nations, it is indicative of her inferior condition that the wife addressed her husband as a slave addressed his master, or a subject his king.

According to Fr Roland de Vaux:

'The Decalogue includes a man's wife among his possessions, along with his house and land, his male and female slaves, his ox and his ass (Ex 20:17; Dt 5:21). Her husband can repudiate her, but she cannot claim a divorce; all her life she remains a minor. The wife does not inherit from her husband, nor daughters from

---

[1] Louis-Marie Orrieux, O.P., 'Vocation de la femme: recherche biblique', *La femme; nature et vocation. Recherches et débats* (Paris: Librairie Arthème Fayard), cahier n. 45, décembre, 1963, p. 147.

their father, except when there is no male heir. (Nb 27:8). A vow
made by a girl or married woman needs, to be valid, the consent
of father or husband and if this consent is withheld, the vow is
null and void (Nb 30:4-17).'[1]

Whereas misconduct on the part of the wife was severely
punished, infidelity on the part of the man was punished only
if he violated the rights of another man by taking a married
woman as his accomplice. In the rabbinical age, the school of
Shammai permitted a husband to get a divorce only on the
grounds of adultery and misconduct. However, some teachers
of the more liberal school of Hillel would accept even the most
trivial excuse. If the husband charged that his wife had cooked
a dish badly, or if he simply preferred another woman, he could
repudiate his wife. Even earlier than this it was written in
Sirach 25:26: 'If thy wife does not obey thee at a signal and a
glance, separate from her.'

Respect for the woman increased once she became a mother,
especially if she produced males, since these were, of course,
more highly valued. A man could, indeed, sell his daughter as
well as his slaves. If a couple did not have children, it was
assumed to be the fault of the wife. Briefly, although Hebrew
women were honored as parents and often treated with kindness,
their social and legal status was that of subordinate beings. It is
understandable that Hebrew males prayed: 'I thank thee, Lord,
that thou hast not created me a woman.' From the point of view
of the modern woman, the situation of women in the ancient
Semitic world—and, indeed, in the ancient world in general—
has the dimensions of a nightmare.

Christian authors through the centuries have made much of
the Genesis accounts of the creation of Eve and the geographical
location of the rib. This, together with her role as temptress
in the story of the Fall, supposedly established beyond doubt
woman's immutable inferiority, which was not merely physical
but also intellectual and moral. So pervasive was this interpretation that through the ages the antifeminist tradition has justified

[1] Roland de Vaux, *Ancient Israel, its Life and Institutions*, translated by
John McHugh (New York: McGraw Hill Book Co., 1961), p. 39.

itself on the basis of the origin and activities of the 'first mother' of all mankind. In a somewhat more sophisticated and disguised vein this is continued, even today, particularly by preachers and theologians who are unaware of developments in modern biblical scholarship. Such misunderstanding of the Old Testament has caused immeasurable harm.

Most of the usage of Old Testament texts to support sex prejudice reveals a total failure not only to grasp the fact of the evolution of human consciousness in general but also to understand the fact and meaning of the evolution of thought in the Old Testament itself. The foundation upon which the case for the subordination of woman is built lies in the older of the two accounts of creation. The earlier creation story (J document), found in Genesis 2, has been stressed as a basis for Christian thinking about women, while the P document account, found in Genesis 1—written several centuries later—has not been stressed, nor have its implications been understood.

Contemporary scriptural exegetes of all faiths, having the tools of scholarship at their disposal, as well as insights of psychology and anthropology, are enabled to look critically at the first chapters of Genesis. The two creation accounts, which differ greatly from each other, have been carefully scrutinized. The later creation story gives no hint that woman was brought into being as an afterthought. On the contrary, it stresses an original sexual duality and describes God's act of giving dominion to both. The plural is used, indicating their common authority to rule: 'And God said, Let us make mankind in our image and likeness, and let them have dominion . . .' (Gen 1:26). The following verse says: 'God created man in his image. In the image of God he created him. Male and female he created them' (Gen 1:27). This is understood by exegetes to mean that the image of God is in the human person, whether man or woman. Moreover, the plural is used in the following:

> 'Then God blessed them and said to them, "Be fruitful and multiply, fill the earth and subdue it. Have dominion over the fish of the sea, the birds of the air, the cattle and all the animals that crawl on the earth" ' (Gen 1:28).

Thus, the burdens of reproduction are not specially associated with the woman, nor is there any indication that 'technical' or 'professional' work should be proper to the man.

It is the earlier (J) creation account, found in the second chapter, which has been the source—or excuse—for many of the disparaging theories about women. The intention of the author of this account seems to have been to express the creation of mankind as involving two stages. As Gerhard von Rad explains the J view:

> 'The creation of woman is very far removed from that of man, for it is the last and most mysterious of all kindnesses that Yahweh wished to bestow upon the man. God designed a help for him, to be "corresponding to him"—she was to be like him, and at the same time not identical with him, but rather his counterpart, his complement.'[1]

Contemporary scholars, such as McKenzie,[2] reject the idea that the story of the later creation of Eve intends to teach the subordination of woman. Rather, it is maintained that what is being conveyed is her original equality. Moreover, the old arguments for feminine inferiority which were based on the use of the word translated 'helper' to describe Eve do not stand up against linguistic studies, which demonstrate that the original word employed does not carry any implication of subordination.[3] Today, both the Genesis accounts, whatever their relative merits, are understood to teach that man and woman are of the same nature and dignity and that they have a common mission to rule the earth.

All of this does not change the fact that for thousands of years theologians and preachers have dourly been grinding out assurances of divine approval of woman's secondary place in the universe, 'as known from scripture'. Thus, Pope Paul's recent

---

[1] Gerhard von Rad, *Old Testament Theology*, I, trans. by D. M. G. Stalker (New York: Harper and Brothers, 1962), p. 149.

[2] John L. McKenzie, S.J., *The Two-Edged Sword* (Milwaukee: Bruce, 1956), p. 95.

[3] Pastor André Dumas, 'Biblical Anthropology and the Participation of Women in the Ministry of the Church', in *Concerning the Ordination of Women* (Geneva: World Council of Churches, 1964), p. 30.

statement to Italian women that 'perfect equality in their nature and dignity, and therefore in rights, is assured to them from the first page of sacred scripture' comes too late for the millions of women who lived and died with the 'religious' conviction of their divinely ordained inferiority and subordination. A psychoanalyst has written: 'The biblical story of Eve's birth is the hoax of the millenia.'[1] Unfortunately, the theologians who grimly pontificated about Mother Eve down through the centuries displayed little sense of irony and humor.

Humorless also have been the misogynistic tirades occasioned by the mythical account of the Fall. It should be observed that in the biblical story, as continued in Genesis 3, the woman's subordination to man—a sociological fact recognized by the author—is not the result of nature but rather of sin. Noteworthy also is the fact that the 'division of labor' theme is placed in the context of the effects of the Fall. The man is now associated with the task of conquering nature. The woman is seen only in the context of the burdens involved in reproduction. Isolated in fixed sex 'roles', they are no longer partners in all things. There is no indication that things must always be this way, since in fact this division is not inscribed in 'nature' but rather is the result of sin. What this suggests is that men and women, in striving to overcome the effects of sin, should evolve toward that real partnership on all levels which is required if the image of God is to be realized in them.

New Testament

In the New Testament it is significant that the statements which reflect the antifeminism of the times are never those of Christ. There is no recorded speech of Jesus concerning women 'as such'. What is very striking is his behavior toward them. In the passages describing the relationship of Jesus with various women, one characteristic stands out starkly: they emerge as persons, for they are treated as persons, often in such contrast with prevailing custom as to astonish onlookers. The behavior

[1] Theodor Reik, *The Creation of Woman* (New York: George Braziller, Inc., 1960), p. 124.

of Jesus toward the Samaritan woman puzzled even his disciples, who were surprised that he would speak to her in public (John 4:27). Then there was his defense of the adulterous woman, who according to the law of Moses should have been stoned (John 8:1-11). There was the case of the prostitute whose many sins he forgave because she had loved much (Luke 7:36-50). In the Gospel narratives the close friendship of Jesus with certain women is manifested in the context of the crucifixion and resurrection. What stands out is the fact that these, his friends, he saw as persons, to whom he gave the supreme yet simple gift of his brotherhood.

The contemporary social inferiority of women was, indeed, reflected in the New Testament. Although the seeds of emancipation were present in the Christian message, their full implications were not evident to the first century authors. The most strikingly antifeminist passages are, of course, in the Pauline texts, which are all too familiar to Catholic women, who have heard them cited approvingly *ad nauseam*. We now know it is important to understand that Paul was greatly preoccupied with *order* in society and in Christian assemblies in particular. In modern parlance, it seemed necessary to sustain a good 'image' of the Church. Thus it appeared to him an important consideration that women should not have too predominant a place in Christian assemblies, that they should not 'speak' too much or unveil their heads. This would have caused scandal and ridicule of the new sect, which already had to face accusations of immorality and effeminacy. In ancient Corinth, as one scholar has pointed out, for a woman to go out unveiled would be to behave like a prostitute.[1] Paul was concerned with protecting the new Church against scandal. Thus he repeatedly insisted upon 'correct' sexual behavior, including the subjection of wives at meetings. Once this is understood, it becomes evident that it is a perversion to use Pauline texts, which should be interpreted within their own social context, to support the claim that even today, in a totally different society, women should be subject.

[1] Pastor André Dumas, *op. cit.*, p. 28.

Paul looked for theological justification for the prevailing customs, such as the custom that women should wear veils. This partially accounts for his reference to Genesis 2 in I Corinthians 11:7ff, which he interprets to mean that woman is for man and not the contrary. We have here the idea that man is the 'image and glory of God', whereas woman is 'the glory of man'. Then there is his biased statement which has been quoted with relish by preachers ever since: 'For man was not made from woman, but woman from man. Neither was man created for woman, but woman for man.' Modern scripture scholars do not, of course, agree with this interpretation of Genesis. Moreover, Paul himself evidently noticed that there was something wrong and corrected himself immediately afterward: 'Nevertheless, in the Lord woman is not independent of man nor man of woman; for as woman was made from man, so man is now born of woman. And all things are from God.' However, the damage was done. For two thousand years women have endured sermons on the 'glory of man' theme, and we still receive a yearly harvest of theological essays and books dealing with the 'theology of femininity', which rely heavily upon the 'symbolism of the veil' and 'God's plan for women' as made known through Paul.

A similar procedure of using the then current interpretation of Genesis to buttress convention is seen in another text, which is no longer generally thought to have been written by Paul, although it surely was written under the influence of the Pauline tradition:

'[I desire] also that women should adorn themselves modestly and sensibly in seemly apparel, not with braided hair or gold or pearls or costly attire but by good deeds, as befits women who profess religion. Let a woman learn in silence with all submissiveness. I permit no woman to teach or to have authority over men; she is to keep silent. For Adam was formed first, then Eve; and Adam was not deceived, but the woman was deceived and became a transgressor. Yet woman will be saved through bearing children, if she continues in faith and love and holiness, with modesty' (I Timothy 2:9-15).

The author tries to support the androcentric attitudes and practices of his times by reference to Genesis. The fact is, of course, that there is no evidence that God made woman subordinate or that the social facts of the past should be prolonged and erected into an immutable destiny.

It is interesting to observe that those who have been fond of quoting such texts down through the ages to keep women 'in their place' have been obliged to adapt their interpretations. For example, that famous 'I permit no woman to teach' was used in the past against women who attempted to teach the catechism. It was later used by some to support prohibitions against their taking theological degrees. Today, women do take such degrees and do in fact teach theology. The same text, however, is still used by some writers to support their exclusion from the hierarchy, although it has been refuted. Moreover, it is evident that a certain selectivity is operative in the use of such texts on the subject of women. Few of those who cite this passage in justification of women's traditional silence would, for example, go so far as to argue that women should not braid their hair, nor wear gold or pearls or expensive clothing. To go to this extent would be considered absurd. On the other hand, many still cite Paul's words to support the custom of women covering their heads in Church. Such inconsistencies demonstrate the unreliability of the process of applying culturally conditioned texts within changed and changing social contexts.

One of the most frequently quoted texts is, of course, the following:

> 'Wives, be subject to your husbands, as to the Lord. For the husband is the head of the wife as Christ is the head of the Church, his body, and is himself its Saviour. As the Church is subject to Christ, so let wives also be subject in everything to their husbands' (Eph 5:22-24).

An Anglican scholar has pointed out that great caution must be used in understanding this analogy:

'Woman certainly did not derive her being from man, nor does she derive her significance from him.'[1]

The same author explains that

'rejection of the wife's subordination does not invalidate the analogy, but simply requires a revision of the terms in which its ethical and personal implications are expressed. Thus, because marriage is a relation of mutual and not unilateral love, the exemplary love of Christ for the Church stands as a pattern to be imitated by the wife no less than the husband; indeed, the full moral and theological significance of their *henosis* only emerges when the notion of male headship is discarded in favor of a higher conception of sexual order.'[2]

It is to be hoped that this development of the Pauline conception, which reveals a humanist, personalist attitude toward the man-woman relationship, will eventually prevail in Christian thinking.

We are now in a position to see that the widespread habit of the clergy of perpetuating the oppressive Pauline ideas is hardly justifiable. There is perversity involved in the prolongation of doctrines and practices in an age in which they can be seen as faulty and harmful—which is quite a different matter from their expression in a milieu in which they appeared justifiable. These texts have been used over the centuries as a guarantee of divine approval for the transformation of woman's subordinate status from a contingent fact into an immutable norm of the feminine condition. They have been cited to enhance the position of those who have tried to keep women from the right to education, to legal and economic equality, and to access to the professions. The irresponsible use of these texts continues today.

The equal dignity and rights of all human beings as persons is of the essence of the Christian message. In the writings of Paul himself there are anticipations of a development toward realization of the full implications of this equality. We have seen

---

[1] D. S. Bailey, *The Man-Woman Relation in Christian Thought* (London: Longmans Green, and Co., 1959), p. 302.
[2] *Ibid.*, p. 303.

that after the harshly androcentric text in I Corinthians, he
attempts to compensate somewhat:

'Nevertheless, in the Lord woman is not independent of man nor
man of woman; for as woman was made from man, so man is now
born of woman. And all things are from God' (I Cor 11:11-12).

Moreover, the dichotomy of fixed classes as dominant-
subservient is transcended:

'For as many of you as were baptized into Christ have put on
Christ. There is neither Jew nor Greek, there is neither slave nor
free, there is neither male nor female; for you are all one in Christ
Jesus' (Gal 3:27-28).

As one theologian has pointed out:

'This does not mean that the kingdom of heaven has to do with
non-sexed beings. Paul is enumerating the relationships of domination: these are radically denounced by the Gospel, in the sense
that man no more has the right to impose his will to power upon
woman than does a class or a race upon another class or another
race.'[1]

It is not surprising that Paul did not see the full implications
of this transcendence. There is an unresolved tension between
the personalist Christian message and the restrictions and com-
promises imposed by the historical situation. It would be naïve
to think that Paul foresaw social evolution. For him, transcendence would come soon enough—in the next life. The inconsistency and ambivalence of his words concerning women
could only be recognized at a later time, as a result of historical
processes. Those who have benefitted from the insights of a
later age have the task of distinguishing elements which are
sociological in origin from the life-fostering, personalist elements
which pertain essentially to the Christian message.

[1] Louis-Marie Orrieux, O.P., *op. cit.*, p. 142.

2. THE PATRISTIC PERIOD

An examination of the writings of the Church Fathers brings vividly into sight the fact that there is, indeed, a problem of women and the Church. The following statement of Jerome strikes the modern reader as weird:

> 'As long as woman is for birth and children, she is different from man as body is from soul. But when she wishes to serve Christ more than the world, then she will cease to be a woman and will be called man (*vir*).'[1]

A similar idea is expressed by Ambrose, who remarks that

> 'she who does not believe is a woman and should be designated by the name of her sex, whereas she who believes progresses to perfect manhood, to the measure of the adulthood of Christ. She then dispenses with the name of her sex, the seductiveness of youth, the garrulousness of old age.'[2]

These strange utterances can be understood only if one realizes the lowness of women in the commonly held view. The characteristics which the Fathers considered to be typically feminine include fickleness and shallowness,[3] as well as garrulousness and weakness,[4] slowness of understanding,[5] and instability of mind.[6] For the most part, the attitude was one of puzzlement over the seemingly incongruous fact of woman's existence. Augustine summed up the general idea in saying that he did not see in what way it could be said that woman was made for a help for man, if the work of child-bearing be excluded.[7]

---

[1] PL 26, 567. *Comm. in epist. ad Ephes.*, III, 5.
[2] PL 15, 1844. *Expos. evang. sec. Lucam*, lib. X, n. 161.
[3] John Chrysostom, PG, 61, 316. *In epist. I ad Cor.*, cap. 14, v. 35., *Homilia* XXXVII.
[4] John Chrysostom, PG, 62, 544–5. *In epist. I ad Tim.*, cap. 2, v. 11. *Homilia* IX.
[5] Cyril of Alexandria, PL 74, 691. *In Joannis evang.*, lib. XII, xx, 15.
[6] Gregory the Great, PL 76, 453. *Moral.*, lib. XXVIII, cap. 3.
[7] PL 34, 395–6. *De Genesi ad litteram* IX, cap. 5.

Clement of Alexandria was also evidently baffled. Although he was somewhat more liberal than Augustine and concluded that men and women have the same nature, he inconsistently upheld masculine superiority.[1]

In Genesis the Fathers found an 'explanation' of woman's inferiority which served as a guarantee of divine approval for perpetuating the situation which made her inferior. John Chrysostom thought it followed from the later creation of Eve that God gave the more necessary and more honorable role to man, the more petty and the less honorable to woman.[2] Ambrosiaster remarks that woman is inferior to man, since she is only a portion of him.[3] Thus there was an uncritical acceptance of the androcentric myth of Eve's creation. Linked to this was their refusal, in varying degrees of inflexibility, to grant that woman is the image of God, an attitude in large measure inspired by Paul's first epistle to the Corinthians. Ambrosiaster states baldly that man is made to the image of God, but not woman.[4] Augustine wrote that only man is the image and glory of God. Since the believing woman, who is co-heiress of grace, cannot lay aside her sex, she is restored to the image of God only where there is no sex, that is, in the spirit.[5]

Together with the biblical account, the Fathers were confronted with an image of woman produced by oppressive conditions which were universal. In contrast to their modern counterparts, women in the early centuries of the Christian era—and, in fact, throughout nearly all of the Christian era—had a girlhood of strict seclusion and of minimal education which prepared them for the life of mindless subordinates. This was followed by an early marriage which effectively cut them off for the rest of their lives from the possibility of autonomous action. Valued chiefly for their reproductive organs, which also inspired horror, and despised for their ignorance, they were denied full personhood. Their inferiority was a fact; it appeared to be

---

[1] PG 8, 1271–5. *Stromatum*, lib. IV, cap. 8.
[2] PG 51, 231. *Quales ducendae sint uxores*, 4.
[3] PL 17, 240. *Commentaria in epist. ad Corinth. primam.*
[4] *Ibid.*
[5] PL 42, 1003–5. *De Trinitate* XII, 7.

'natural'. Thus, experience apparently supported the rib story, just as the myth itself helped 'explain' the common experience of women as incomplete and lesser humans. The vicious circle persisted, for the very emancipation which would prove that women were not 'naturally' defective was denied them in the name of that defectiveness which was claimed to be natural and divinely ordained. Thus, Augustine taught that the order of things subjugates woman to man.[1] Jerome wrote that it is contrary to the order of nature, or of law, that women should speak in the assembly of men.[2] He maintained that the man should be commanded to love his wife, whereas the woman should fear her husband:

> 'For love befits the man; fear befits the woman. As for the slave, not only fear is befitting him, but also trembling.'[3]

Thus the 'ideal' marital situation proposed by Jerome—an 'ideal' suited to encourage such perversities as the sado-masochistic couple—appears highly abnormal to the modern person. It is significant that he was unable to find an adequate difference between the roles of wife and slave other than the fact that the fear of the latter should be so strong as to be accompanied by trembling.

The presumed defectiveness of woman extended also, and perhaps especially, into the moral sphere. The primary grievance against her was her supposed guilt in the Fall. The violence of some of the tirades on this subject has psychoanalytic implications. Tertullian, for example, wrote for the edification of his contemporaries:

> 'Do you not know that you are Eve? ... You are the devil's gateway. ... How easily you destroyed man, the image of God. Because of the death which you brought upon us, even the Son of God had to die.'[4]

Clement of Alexandria taught that it is shameful for woman

---

[1] PL 34, 204. *De Genesi contra Manich.* II, 11.
[2] PL 30, 794. *Expos. in epist. I ad Cor.*, cap. 14.
[3] PL 26, 570. *Comm. in epist. ad Ephes.* III, 5.
[4] PL 1, 1418b-19a. *De cultu feminarum, libri duo* I, 1.

to think of what nature she has.[1] Augustine cynically complained
that man, who was of superior intelligence, couldn't have been
seduced, and so the woman, who was small of intellect, was
given to him.[2] The logical inconsistencies implied in this seem
to have escaped him: this dull-witted creature could hardly
have been too responsible. Moreover, she was clever enough to
seduce man, which the ingenious devil could not do. Why did
that paragon of intelligence and virtue succumb so easily? It
is all too evident that logic is not operative in such invective,
which neurotically projects all guilt upon the woman. For the
Fathers, woman is a temptress of whom men should beware.
That the problem might be reciprocal is not even considered.

There were attempts to balance the alleged guilt-laden condition of the female sex, but these, unfortunately, did not take the
form of an admission of guilt shared by the sexes. Instead, Eve
was balanced off by Mary. Thus, for example, Origen remarks
that as sin came from the woman so does the beginning of
salvation.[3] Augustine wrote that woman is honored in Mary.[4]
He claimed that since man (homo) fell through the female sex,
he was restored through the female sex. 'Through the woman,
death; through the woman, life.'[5] This type of compensation
produced an ambivalent image of woman. Mary was glorified,
but she was unique. Women in the concrete did not shake off
their bad reputation and continued to bear most of the burden
of blame. The sort of polemic, therefore, which attempts to
cover the antifeminism of the Fathers by pointing to their glorification of Mary ignores the important point that this did not
improve their doctrine about concrete, living women. In fact
there is every reason to suspect that this compensation unconsciously served as a means to relieve any possible guilt feelings about injustice to the other sex.

In the mentality of the Fathers, woman and sexuality were
identified. Their horror of sex was also a horror of woman.

---

[1] PG 8, 430. *Paedagogi* II, 2 (end).
[2] PL 34, 452. *De Genesi ad litteram* XI, 42.
[3] PG 13, 1819 C. *In Lucam homilia* VIII.
[4] PL 40, 186. *De fide et symbolo*, 4.
[5] PL 38, 1108. *Sermo* 232, 2.

There is no evidence that they realized the projection mechanisms involved in this misogynistic attitude. In fact, male guilt feelings over sex and hyper-susceptibility to sexual stimulation and suggestion were transferred to 'the other', the 'guilty' sex. The idea of a special guilt attached to the female sex gave support to the double moral standard which prevailed. For example, in cases of adultery, the wife had to take back her unfaithful husband, but if the wife was unfaithful, she could be rejected.

Even in the face of such oppressive conditions a few women managed to attain stature. Jerome admitted that many women were better than their husbands.[1] But more significant is the fact that the existence of exceptions, no matter how numerous, did not change the generalizations about feminine 'nature'. Hence the strange ambivalence which we have noted.

On the whole, then, the Fathers display a strongly disparaging attitude toward women, at times even a fierce misogynism. There is the recurrent theme that by faith a woman transcends the limitations imposed by her sex. It would never occur to the Fathers to say the same of a man. When woman achieves this transcendence which is, of course, not due to her own efforts but is a 'supernatural' gift, she is given the compliment of being called 'man' (*vir*). Thus there is an assumption that all that is of dignity and value in human nature is proper to the male sex. There is an identification of 'male' and 'human'. Even the woman who was elevated by grace retained her abominable nature. No matter what praise the Fathers may have accorded to individuals, it is not possible to conclude that in their doctrine women are recognized as fully human.

Some individual women were, of course, honored and respected in the patristic age. Moreover, women exercised a role in the Church's ministry. The widows had the duty of instructing female converts for baptism, but they never constituted an order of the ministry. The office of deaconess is referred to in scripture (e.g. Romans 16:1), and Pliny the Younger refers to them in one of his letters. Other documents give more de-

[1] PL 26, 536. *Comm. in epist. ad Ephes.*, III, 5.

tailed information.[1] It appears that at first the widows ranked higher and that later they ceded first place to the deaconesses, who took over their functions. Whereas the widows did not receive ordination and 'imposition of hands',[2] deaconesses did, and the latter were part of the ecclesiastical hierarchy.[3] In the West especially, their functions were severely restricted because of their sex, and they existed only until the end of the sixth century, when baptism of adults became rare, leaving the widows with virtually no function. In the East, their powers were often more extended, and there is evidence that they lasted several centuries longer in some of the Churches. There is no small irony in the fact that during an age in which opinion of women was so low, some of them were, in fact, members of the hierarchy, whereas in a later and more enlightened age, when the Church itself is urging them to take a more active part in public life, they are completely excluded from the hierarchy.

3. THE MIDDLE AGES

Theological opinion of women was hardly better in the Middle Ages, although some of the fierceness of tone was mitigated. The twelfth century theologian, Peter the Lombard, whose *Sentences* became a standard textbook to be commented upon by teachers of theology, went so far as to write that woman is sensuality itself, which is well signified by woman, since in woman this naturally prevails.[4] Bonaventure repeated many of the standard ideas. He thought that the image of God is realized more in man than in woman, not in its primary meaning, but in an accidental way.[5] He repeats the old idea that

[1] Cf. the article 'Diaconesses', in *Dictionnaire de théologie catholique* (hereafter referred to as DTC), t. IV, col. 685–703.
[2] *Apostolic Constitutions* VIII, 25.
[3] *Ibid.*, VIII, 19, 20.
[4] PL 191, 1633. *Collectanea in epist. D. Pauli in epist. ad Cor.*, cap. XI, 8–10.
[5] *Comm. in Sec. Librum Sententiarum Petri Lombardi* (Quaracchi edition), dist. XVI, art. 2, q. 2.

woman signifies the 'inferior part' of the soul; man, the 'superior part'.[1]

What was new in the picture in the Middle Ages was the assimilation into theology of Aristotelianism, which provided the conceptual tools for fixing woman's place in the universe and which, ironically, could have been used to free her. In the writings of Thomas Aquinas, which later came to have a place of unique pre-eminence in the Church, Aristotelian thought was wedded to the standard biblical interpretations, so that the seeming weight of 'science' was added to that of authority. Thus, following Aristotle, Aquinas held that the female is defective as regards her individual nature. He wrote that she is, in fact, a misbegotten male, for the active force in the male seed tends to the production of a perfect likeness in the masculine sex. Her existence is due to some defect in the active force (that of the father), or to some material indisposition, or even to some external influence, such as that of the south wind, which is moist. He adds that, as regards human nature in general, woman is not misbegotten, but is included in nature's intention as directed to the work of generation.[2] She has, then, a reason for being— that is, she is needed in the work of generation. It seems that this really is all she is good for, 'since a man can be more efficiently helped by another man in other works'.[3]

It would be a mistake, however, to conclude that Thomas thought woman has a major or even an equal role, even in her one specialty, i.e. reproduction. He wrote:

'Father and mother are loved as principles of our natural origin. Now the father is principle in a more excellent way than the mother, because he is the active principle, while the mother is a passive and material principle. Consequently, strictly speaking, the father is to be loved more.'[4]

---

[1] Ibid., dist. XVIII, art. 1, q. 1.
[2] Summa Theologiae, I, 92, 1, ad 1. Albert the Great also wrote that woman is misbegotten: in II P. Sum. Theol. (Borgnet), tract. 13, q. 80, membrum 1.
[3] Thomas Aquinas, Summa Theologiae, I, 92, 1 c.
[4] Ibid., II–II, 26, 10 c.

He continues:

> 'In the begetting of man, the mother supplies the formless matter of the body; and the latter receives its form through the formative power that is in the semen of the father. And though this power cannot create the rational soul, yet it disposes the matter of the body to receive that form.'[1]

Thus, the role of the woman in generation is purely passive; she merely provides the matter, whereas the father disposes this for the form. This view of woman as a purely passive principle which merely provides the 'matter' of the offspring is, of course, linked to an entirely outdated and false biology: that the mother is, in fact, equally 'active' in the production of the child was unknown in the thirteenth century.

This idea of women as 'naturally' defective, together with the commonly accepted exegesis of the texts concerning woman in Genesis and the Pauline epistles, and the given social situation of women in a condition of subjection are three factors whose influence can be detected in Thomas's arguments supporting the traditional androcentric views. Thus, in regard to marriage, he judged that, although there is proportional equality between man and wife, there is not strict equality; neither in regard to the conjugal act, in which that which is nobler is due to the man, nor in regard to the order of the home, in which the woman is ruled and the man rules.[2] Moreover, the exclusion of women from Holy Orders is upheld on the basis that a sacrament is a sign, and that in the female sex no eminence of degree can be signified, since the woman has the state of subjection.[3] There is no probability at all that Thomas was able to see this 'state of subjection' as merely the result of social conditioning, of a situation which could change. He believed that social inferiority was required by woman's 'natural' intellectual inferiority: 'So by such a kind of subjection woman is naturally subject to man, because in man the discretion of reason predominates.'[4] This, he thought, would have been the case even

---

[1] *Ibid.*, II-II, 26, 10, ad 1.
[2] *Ibid.*, Suppl., 64, 3 c.
[3] *Ibid.*, Suppl., 39, 1 c.
[4] *Ibid.*, I, 92, 1, ad 2.

if sin had not occurred, i.e. even before the Fall. Thus, in Thomas's view, the question of woman's autonomy is hopelessly closed. The best she could hope for, even in the best of worlds, would be a kind of eternal childhood, in which she would be subject to man 'for her own benefit'.

The puzzlement which characterized patristic thought on women is again starkly evident in Thomas's writings. This is all the more striking because his thought is worked out in an ordered synthesis; it is not a collection of disconnected snatches of rhetoric, as is sometimes the case with the Fathers. The very existence of women seems to have been an awkward snag in the orderly universe which he envisaged. For the modern reader, it is startling to read the question posed in the *Summa Theologiae*: 'Whether woman should have been made in the first production of things?'[1] The very existence of the question is significant. Although Thomas argues that human bi-sexuality should have been 'from the beginning', his whole mode of argument reveals a naïvely androcentric mentality which assigns what is properly human to the male and views sexual union as merely 'carnal'. Woman is seen as a sort of anomaly.

The anomaly of woman had nevertheless to be assimilated into the system. A striking ambiguity, which looks very much like a contradiction, resulted. It was necessary to admit, for example, that the image of God is found both in man and in woman, for this Thomas recognized to be the teaching of Genesis. Yet Paul had said that 'woman is the glory of man', and indicated that she was not the image of God. Thomas concludes that

'in a secondary sense the image of God is found in man, and not in woman: for man is the beginning and end of woman; as God is the beginning and end of every creature.'[2]

The degrading idea that 'man is the beginning and end of woman' is reinforced by the parallel: man: woman; God: creature. Besides the intrinsic unacceptableness of this idea

[1] *Ibid.*, I, 92, 1 c.
[2] *Ibid.*, I, 93, 4, ad 1.

there is an extreme difficulty in reconciling it with the assertion in the same paragraph that the image of God in its principal meaning (i.e. the intellectual nature) is found in both man and woman. If woman has an intellectual nature, then her end cannot be man, for intellectuality is the radical source of autonomous personhood.

The tension between irreconcilable ideas is also apparent from Thomas's teaching on the rational soul which, he holds, is not transmitted by the reproductive process but rather is directly infused by God.[1] Therefore, the form which constitutes the individual, whether male or female, as a human person is not derived from the father, but is directly from God. Thomas has made it clear, moreover, that in his opinion

'there is no other substantial form in man besides the intellectual soul; and that the soul, as it virtually contains the sensitive and nutritive souls, so does it virtually contain all inferior forms, and itself alone does whatever the imperfect forms do in other things.'[2]

What is more, he strongly maintains that intellectual understanding is not by means of any bodily organ; rather it is an operation which is *per se* apart from the body.[3] Similarly, the operation of the will is also performed without a corporeal organ.[4]

It is abundantly clear, therefore, that even according to Thomas's own principles, the alleged defectiveness of women, both as to their role in generation and considered as products of the generative process, becomes extremely difficult to uphold. Indeed, in the light of these principles it becomes impossible to uphold. According to Thomas, it is the intellectual soul which makes the human person to be the image of God.[5] This is neither caused by the male, nor is it essentially different in man and woman.

We said earlier that there is a striking difference between Thomas and the Fathers. The latter often manifest an un-

[1] *Ibid.*, I, 118, 2 c.
[2] *Ibid.*, I, 76, 4 c.
[3] *Ibid.*, I, 75, 2 c.
[4] *Ibid.*, I, 77, 5 c.
[5] *Ibid.*, I, 93, 6 c.

resolved tension between their idea of woman in her 'nature' and woman with grace, to such an extent that when she has grace, she no longer is called 'woman', but 'man'. Thus, there is an identification of 'male' and 'human', which is overcome to some extent by grace. Thomas, of course, shares the feeling that women as such are not quite human. However, leaving all questions of grace aside, there is indecision in his thought on the level of nature itself. For Thomas, possession of an intellectual soul is natural and essential to men and women. In the light of this radical natural equality, it makes little sense to say that man is the principle and end of woman. Why, then, does he say it?

The discord between the philosophical anthropology of Thomas and his androcentric statements is due to the then commonly accepted biblical exegesis, Aristotelian biology, and the prevailing image and social status of women. The deep roots of Thomas's thought—his philosophical conceptions of the body-soul relationship, of intellect, of will, of the person, and his theological ideas of the image of God in the human being and of man's last end—clearly support the genuine equality of men and women with all of its theoretical and practical consequences. In opposition to the outdated exegesis and biology which he accepted, these Thomistic principles are radically on the side of feminism. Thomas himself could not see—or would not permit himself to see—the implications of these principles in regard to women. And we have seen why: the logical conclusions he might have drawn would at that time have appeared contrary to faith and contemporary experience.

Today, fidelity to truth and justice requires that thinkers who are aware of these implications make them explicit, rather than parroting as 'Thomistic doctrine' harmful and untenable ideas which Thomas surely would not propose, were he alive today.

Despite medieval theories, there were some cases of powerful women in the Middle Ages. Nuns, especially, had a certain autonomy, which even St Thomas recognized. It is one of the ironies of history that there were abbesses who legitimately exercised great power, far beyond what is accorded to religious women today. They were 'persons constituted in ecclesiastical dignity' who had 'the administration of ecclesiastical affairs and pre-eminence of grade'.[1] In fact, abbesses had power of jurisdiction. Like bishops and abbots, they wore the mitre and cross and carried the staff.

The abbesses of St Cecilia in Cologne had the power of jurisdiction and of suspension over clerics.[2] The abbesses of Conversano, in Italy, ruled a Cistercian abbey and its neighbouring parishes and wielded enormous power. This was symbolized in a ceremony of homage in which the newly consecrated abbess, with mitre and cross, was seated before the external door, under a baldachin. Each member of the clergy under her jurisdiction passed before her, prostrating himself and kissing her hand.[3] The homage ceremony was modified in 1709, and the last abbess of Conversano died in 1809.

Another interesting instance was that of the abbesses of Las Huelgas, near the city of Burgos in Spain. The abbess of Las Huelgas was

'dame, superior, prelate, legitimate administrator, spiritual and temporal, of the said royal monastery and of its hospital, as well as of the convents, churches, and hermitages of its filiation, of the villages and places of its jurisdiction, of the manors and vassalages, by virtue of Apostolic bulls and concessions, with plenary, exclusive jurisdiction, quasi-episcopal, *nullius diocesis,* and with royal privileges: a double jurisdiction exercised in peaceful possession, as is publicly known.'[4]

The powers of this jurisdiction included giving legal judgment, just as bishops did, in criminal and civil cases and in cases concerning benefices; the power of giving dimissories for ordinations; the power of giving licenses for preaching, for confessing, for exercising care of souls, for entering religious life; the power

---

[1] Article 'Abbesses', in DTC, t. I, col. 18.
[2] Elizabeth Schüssler, *Der vergessener Partner* (Düsseldorf: Patmos, 1964), p. 89.
[3] Article, 'Abbesses', DTC, col. 21.
[4] *Ibid.*, col. 20.

of acknowledging abbesses, of imposing censures, and of con-
voking synods.[1]

Although attempts have been made to explain away most of
this as not really constituting spiritual jurisdiction, such attempts
have not been completely successful. Thus it is suggested that
the abbesses could have convoked synods through a vicar as
intermediary, since according to canonists women are not able
to convoke synods.[2] However, there is no convincing evidence
offered that there were such intermediaries.

In addition to cases such as those we have mentioned, there
were also double orders, in which both monks and nuns were
ruled by an abbess.[3]

Besides the abbesses, there were other great individual women
in the secular world. There were such outstanding rulers as
Clotilde and Blanche of Castille, and learned women like
Eleanor of Aquitaine and Blanche of Navarre. There were great
saints: Catherine of Siena wielded enormous influence in her
milieu, and the story of Joan of Arc has no parallel. However,
it would be absurd to judge the general condition of women
by such examples. The naïve idea of those who say that 'true
ability will always prove itself', and point to such extraordinary
cases, simply ignores the fact that countless women were completely stifled by an environment which worked against the
development and expression of their talents.

The prevailing low status of women was fixed by law and
custom. By canon law a husband was entitled to beat his wife.
Canon law allowed only the dowry system for matrimony, and
under this system women were defenseless. Moreover, since
they were legally incompetent, they were not considered fit to
give testimony in court. In general, they were considered as
man's property. Since for feudal lords marriages were a way of
gaining property, women were pawns in the game of acquiring
wealth. The Church's complicated marriage laws offered ample
opportunity for trickery and abuse. Thus, while the history of

---

[1] *Ibid.*, col. 21.
[2] *Ibid.*
[3] Cf. Schüssler, *op. cit.*, p. 91.

the Middle Ages reveals a few glorious feminine personalities, that side of the scales is extremely outbalanced by the masses of mute and anonymous victims of hypocrisy and oppression.

4. BEGINNINGS OF THE MODERN PERIOD

'The very thought that I am a woman is enough to make my wings droop.'[1] This remark, which was made by Teresa of Avila, suggests that the situation of women was not yet greatly improved in the sixteenth century. Why would a person of such intelligence and greatness have such a low conception of her own sex? Perhaps it is not too surprising when one realizes that some preachers of the time, as well as fathers of families, considered it wrong for women even to learn to read and write.[2] In such an atmosphere, it must have been difficult for a woman to have much esteem for herself and other members of her sex. In fact, Teresa's words often reflect, perhaps unconsciously, the attitudes of her milieu. She speaks frequently of the 'weaknesses' of women. The following remark is revealing:

'During the very sorest trials that I have suffered in this life, I do not recall having uttered such expressions, for I am not in the least like a woman in these matters but have a stout heart.'[3]

The implicit assumption is that real courage is normal only for men. Moreover, more than one admirer of Teresa made remarks similar to that of John of Salinas: 'She is a man.'[4] It is thought-provoking that this great woman and her friends, when they tried to express the nature of her uniqueness, spontaneously had recourse to expressions which disassociated her from her own sex.

Teresa's writings abound with passages in which she ex-

[1] Life, Ch. X. The Complete Works of St Teresa of Jesus. Translated and edited by E. Allison Peers (London: Sheed and Ward, 1949), vol. I, p. 61.
[2] Dominique Deneuville, Sainte Thérèse d'Avila et la femme (Paris: Editions du Chalet, 1964), p. 40. This enlightening work gives many useful references to St Theresa's works in French translations.
[3] Spiritual Relations, III. Peers edition, vol. I, p. 317.
[4] Cited in Deneuville, op. cit., p. 113.

presses a terrible uneasiness over the handicaps imposed upon her sex. She writes of the obstacle of sex, which prevents her from preaching.[1] Irony as well as anguish are reflected in the following passage, most of which, significantly, was deleted from her manuscript but later restored:

'When thou wert in the world, Lord, thou didst not despise women, but didst always help them and show them great compassion. Thou didst find more faith and no less love in them than in men. . . . We can do nothing in public that is of any use to thee, nor dare we speak of some of the truths over which we weep in secret, lest thou shouldst not hear this, our just petition. Yet, Lord, I cannot believe this of thy goodness and righteousness, for thou art a righteous Judge, not like judges in the world, who, being after all, men and sons of Adam, refuse to consider any woman's virtue as above suspicion. Yes, my King, but the day will come when all will be known. I am not speaking on my account, for the whole world is already aware of my wickedness, and I am glad that it should become known; but, when I see what the times are like, I feel it is not right to repel spirits which are virtuous and brave, even though they be the spirits of women.'[2]

Teresa suffered greatly from her awareness of the ignorance imposed upon her sex. She refers to this ignorance many times, and indicates that she is fully aware of its harmful consequences. Her suffering on this account was all the more acute and lasting, because she clearly saw the value of learning. The following passage gives an indication of the intensity of her anguish:

'O Lord, do thou remember how much we have to suffer on this road through lack of knowledge! The worst of it is that, as we do not realize we need to know more than we think about thee, we cannot ask those who know; indeed we have not even any idea what there is for us to ask them. So we suffer terrible trials because we do not understand ourselves; and we worry over what is not bad at all, but good, and think it very wrong.'[3]

Years of experience and observation caused Teresa to modify

---

[1] *Interior Castle*, VI, vi. Peers ed., vol. II, p. 298.
[2] *Way of Perfection*, Ch. III. Peers ed., vol. II, p. 13.
[3] *Interior Castle*, IV, i. Peers ed., vol. II, pp. 233–44.

any tendency to delusions about masculine perfection. After describing certain exalted spiritual experiences, she says:

> 'The Lord gives these favors far more to women than to men: I have heard the saintly Fray Peter of Alcantara say that, and I have also observed it myself. He would say that women made much more progress on this road than men, and gave excellent reasons for this, which there is no point in my repeating here, all in favor of women.'[1]

She noted the blind underestimation of women which caused parents to regret the birth of daughters:

> 'It is certainly a matter for deep regret that mortals, not knowing what is best for them, and being wholly ignorant of the judgments of God, do not realize what great blessings can come from having daughters or what great harm can come from having sons, and, unwilling, apparently, to leave the matter to him who understands everything and is the creator of us all, worry themselves to death about what ought to make them glad.'[2]

Apparently, as a consequence of mystical experience, Teresa's understanding rose above the common interpretation of Pauline texts concerning women, which she had at first accepted:

> 'It had seemed to me that, considering what Saint Paul says about women keeping at home (I have recently been reminded of this and I had already heard of it), this might be God's will. He (the Lord) said to me: "Tell them they are not to be guided by one part of scripture alone, but to look at others; ask them if they suppose they will be able to tie my hands." '[3]

Thus Teresa's understanding—like that of Catherine of Siena, who recorded in her Diary a similar experience—transcended the theology of her times and anticipated what biblical scholars would begin to suggest centuries later.

During the centuries following the Middle Ages theological opinion concerning women did not change radically. Cardinal Cajetan (1469-1534), a famous commentator on the writings

---

[1] *Life*, Ch. XL. Peers ed., vol. I, p. 293.
[2] *Book of the Foundations*, Ch. 20. Peers ed., vol. III, p. 98.
[3] *Spiritual Relations: Favors of God*, XIX. Peers ed., vol. I, p. 344.

of Thomas Aquinas and one of the leading theologians of his time, expressed almost total agreement with Thomas' views about women. His usual comment on these passages was: 'All of this is evident' (Omnia patent). He did, however, deviate slightly from the Master's doctrine by expressing the opinion that there are many works which can be expected to be done better by a woman than by a man.[1]

Ignatius of Loyola (1491-1556), founder of the Jesuits, thought he saw a similarity between women and Satan: 'The enemy conducts himself as a woman. He is a weakling before a show of strength, and a tyrant if he has his will.'[2]

Especially revealing were (and still are) reasons given for the exclusion of women from holy orders. The Spanish Dominican, Dominic Soto (1494-1560) reflected sixteenth century opinion in his treatment of this subject: he held that the female sex is a natural impediment to the reception of Holy Orders. The ladies were not alone in this category, however, for he also listed hermaphrodites inclining to this sex, monsters, and the perpetually demented. Having given the usual arguments based upon texts of Paul, he added that even the light of nature shows that it would be absurd for women to be promoted to consecrate and to hear confessions, for even if there are some who are prudent, that sex manifests a certain poverty of reason and softness of mind.[3]

Consistent with such an opinion of woman was a doctrine of marriage which perpetuated her situation of helpless subordination and legal impotence. Thus Soto posed the questions of whether it is licit for a man to 'put away' his wife because of fornication and because of adultery, and answered affirmatively to both. Significantly, the question of whether a wife could 'put away' her husband for such offenses was not even raised.[4]

Francis de Sales (1567-1622), a liberal for his age, wrote some

---

[1] Commentarium in I partem summae theologiae S. Thomae Aquinatis, q. 92, a. 1.

[2] Spiritual Exercises, 'Rules for the Discernment of Spirits', First week, Rule 12.

[3] In Quartum Sententiarum Commentarii, d. 25, q. 1, a. 2.

[4] Ibid., d. 36, q. 1, a. 1 and 3.

'advice for married people' which reflected the mentality of
the times.[1] Addressing himself to husbands, he told them that
the weaknesses and infirmities of body and mind of their wives
should not provoke disdain, but rather a sweet and loving compassion, since God made them that way

> 'so that, since they depend upon you, you will receive from them
> more honor and respect, and so that you will have them for com-
> panions in such a way that you will nevertheless be their chiefs
> and superiors.'

While both husbands and wives are told to love tenderly and
cordially, the wife's love for her husband should be 'respectful
and full of reverence'. In creation woman was taken from man's
side, under his arm, 'to show that she should be under the
hand and guidance of her husband'. The intellectual superiority
of the male is taken for granted in these passages. De Sales'
remarks on marital fidelity suggest by their choice of wording
a moral superiority of the male as well. He wrote: 'Husbands,
if you want your wives to be faithful to you, make them see the
lesson by your example.' These passages reveal that the androcentric assumptions of the Fathers and medieval theologians
had been preserved intact. In fact, the tone of unctuous con-
descension does not disguise, but rather reinforces these
assumptions (the *compassion* of the husband is balanced by a
corresponding *reverence* on the part of the wife). An essentially
alienating and de-personalizing form of man-woman relationship is exalted as the Christian ideal.

Although there was no basic change in theory concerning
women during the early modern period, an important movement began which, although it most directly affected religious
women, had a wider significance. The sixteenth and seventeenth centuries witnessed the beginnings of the dramatic
struggle of religious women to free themselves of the cloister.
In the Middle Ages it had become an accepted fact that once

---

[1] *Introduction à la vie dévote* (Paris: Editions Fernand Roches, 1930), t. II,
troisième partie, ch. 38.

a woman became a nun, she was to be enclosed in the convent for life. In 1289, Boniface VIII had imposed strict enclosure upon all religious women. The Council of Trent renewed the constitution of Boniface with a few alterations, and soon afterward, Pius V issued decrees that all religious women must accept solemn vows and the cloister. This Church legislation reflected a strong distrust of feminine competence and morals. The attitudes which it reflected were strongly entrenched, and revolutionaries who saw the need for change were strongly opposed.

Now a number of courageous women struggled to break the old patterns. Among these was Angela Merici (1474-1540), founder of the Ursulines, whose ideas were daring and novel for the times. According to her idea, the Ursulines were not to be bound by cloister, nor to have a habit nor a common life. Their only vow was to be a vow of chastity. They were to live a life of consecrated virginity while laboring as apostles in the world. Unfortunately, ecclesiastical authorities were not ready to understand these changes. After Angela's death, the authorities—especially Charles Borromeo, Cardinal of Milan—gradually managed to force her company back into the old monastic forms, insisting upon cloister, religious habit, and the like. The founder's plans were defeated. A similar fate was imposed upon the plans of Francis de Sales and Jeanne de Chantal for their Sisters of the Visitation. Vincent de Paul's Daughters of Charity were more successful in accomplishing innovations.[1]

Undoubtedly, the most daring of the innovators was Mary Ward (1585-1645), who founded the 'English Ladies'. She intended that her group would work 'in the world', conducting schools for girls. They would be like the Jesuits, but would not be subjected to them, as to a 'First Order'. Rather, they were to be governed directly by women responsible solely to the pope, independently of bishops and of men's orders. Also

[1] A historical study of these attempts is to be found in James R. Cain, *The Influence of the Cloister on the Apostolate of Congregations of Religious Women*. Excerpt from a doctoral dissertation in canon law, Lateran University (Rome: 1965), pp. 1-58.

daring for the time were Mary Ward's ideas on the education of girls. A strong advocate of the emancipation of women, she planned to teach girls Latin and other secular subjects which heretofore had been reserved largely to men. She insisted that

> 'there is no such difference between men and women that women may not do great things, as we have seen by the example of many saints. . . . For what think you of this word, "but women"? As if we were in all things inferior to some other creature which I suppose to be man! . . . And if they would not make us believe we can do nothing, and that we are but women, we might do great matters.'[1]

At the same time, Mary Ward accepted part of the traditional teaching concerning woman's 'place', which her modern counterparts are challenging in the second half of the twentieth century. She was willing to accept the submission of wives to their husbands, that men are head of the Church, that women could not administer the sacraments or preach in public Churches. It would have been extremely difficult to question these points in the seventeenth century, when women were still considered unfit to study Latin or to teach very small boys. She was, however, a great revolutionary within the context of her times, struggling to free women to develop and use their talents in the service of the Church.

For her pains, Mary Ward was rewarded with persecution by clerical enemies. One of the chief among these was William Harrison, Archpriest of England, who together with some colleagues wrote to Pope Gregory XV in 1621, trying to get the congregation dissolved, since they were doing work 'unfitting for women'. What were the exact reasons given for opposition to this dedicated group? The first objection of Mary Ward's enemies was that women had never before taken upon themselves an apostolic office—an objection which revealed a strange ignorance of the early years of Christianity—and this was no time to begin. Describing the characteristics of women, the

[1] Mother M. Margarita O'Connor I.B.V.M., *That Incomparable Woman* (Montreal: Palm Publishers, 1962).

archpriest reflected the opinions prevalent in the Church: since that sex is 'soft, fickle, deceitful, inconstant, erroneous, always desiring novelty, liable to a thousand dangers', the Church Fathers had cried out against them. Harrison's second objection was that while the group professed to be religious, they did not submit to cloister, as required. Third, they presumed too much authority, and spoke too freely on spiritual matters. This, of course, was claimed to be against the teaching of Paul, who in I Corinthians 14:34-5, had said that women should be silent in the churches. Another objection was that they would teach erroneously and lead others into heresy. Moreover, it was maintained that the women would cause scandal by frequenting the homes of people and travelling freely. Finally, these ladies because of their apostolic work were the subject of ridicule.[1] So much for the clerical refutations of Mary Ward's efforts. These did not, of course, represent the opinions of all of the clergy. The Jesuits, for example, were divided on the subject.

Mary Ward appealed to Pope Urban VIII in an audience in 1624, and he had her case reviewed by a board of cardinals. They did not come to a definite decision, but apparently agreed with each other against the possibility of 'the power of women to do aught of good to any but themselves in a life consecrated to God.'[2] Finally in 1629 a decree of suppression was issued. Mary regarded this as a spurious document, and instructed her members to disregard it. In retaliation, three ecclesiastics from the Holy Office arrested her in Munich in 1630 as a heretic and a schismatic; she was imprisoned in a Poor Clare convent, under extremely unhealthful conditions, until released by a decree of Pope Urban.

The official Bull of suppression was signed by Urban in 1631. The wording of the Bull eloquently reveals the ecclesiastical mentality. It said, among other things,

'certain women, taking the name of Jesuitesses, assembled and living together, built colleges, and appointed superiors and a Gen-

[1] Cited in Cain, *op. cit.*, p. 42.
[2] O'Connor, *op. cit.*, p. 87.

eral, assumed a peculiar habit without the approbation of the Holy See ... carried out works by no means suiting the weakness of their sex, womanly modesty, virginal purity ... works which men most experienced in the knowledge of the sacred scriptures undertake with difficulty, and not without great caution.'[1]

The crawl of progress continued, however. The institute survived as a 'new institute', with modified regulations, but in the mid-eighteenth century it was again under fire. Benedict XIV issued a Bull (*Quamvis justo*), which stated that the new Institute of English Virgins was 'kindly tolerated', but that they must not recognize Mary Ward as their founder. Finally, papal approbation was given in 1877 under Pius IX, the vigorous original plan having been modified. Not until the present century was Mary Ward reinstated as founder.

What is the significance of this case? It illustrates tension and opposition between those who hold ecclesiastical authority —the guardians of the traditional androcentric structures—and those who try to bring women out of their condition of imposed inferiority and immaturity. The arguments used by William Harrison and the cardinals against Mary Ward are not unfamiliar to twentieth century Catholics. The basic contest has not changed: she and her followers struggled for the right to teach catechism and Latin, and were rebuked as trying to do what is unfitting for women and against the teaching of Paul. While since then, assuredly, much territory has been gained, today the same arguments are given to justify the enormous obstacles to autonomy and equality which still remain. Vestiges of the cloister still impede religious women today, hampering their personal and intellectual development in subtle ways, and thus indirectly selling short those whom they teach and with whom they have contact. Obstructive masculine legislation has contributed greatly toward perpetuating the basis which exists in fact for the caricature of 'the good Sisters'.

---

[1] *Ibid.*, pp. 115–16.

5. EMANCIPATION AND PAPAL DOCUMENTS

It was not Catholic ideology but the industrial revolution which led to feminine emancipation. The eighteenth, nineteenth and twentieth century theologians continued to justify the traditional subordinate and legally helpless situation of married women. Cardinal Gousset (1792-1866) held that the administration of property belonged to the husband alone. He could sell or dispose of it as he wished, without the agreement of his wife.[1] The latter was expected to follow him wherever he should decide to go, even to a foreign country, and to submit to him in all things.[2] Indeed, the education permitted to young girls hardly equipped them for anything better than the life of mindless subjects. The clergy who concerned themselves with their spiritual direction generally encouraged only the passive virtues, and discouraged anything more than a modest intellectual ambition. A typical example was the work of the Abbé Juilles, who in the middle of the nineteenth century wrote a book of advice for girls, in which he counseled them to develop the virtues of humility, charity, and purity, but overlooked such virtues as courage and ambition. He encouraged them to apply themselves to Christian teaching on a modest level, but not to aspire to the level of scientific knowledge.[3]

The official Catholic reaction in the nineteenth and twentieth centuries to the modern movement toward feminine emancipation manifested the persistence of the conflict between the Christian concept of women as persons, made to the image of God, and the notion of them as inferior, derivative beings. The first pope to confront the movement was Leo XIII. Against the socialists, whom he saw as threatening the stability of marriage, he defended 'paternal authority'. As for the husband-wife relationship, he re-affirmed the subjection of the female:

---

[1] *Théologie morale* (Paris: Jacques Lecoffre et cie, 1858), I, p. 315.
[2] *Ibid.*, II, p. 605.
[3] *La jeune fille chrétienne dans le monde* (Paris: Ambrose Bray, 1861).

'Wherefore as the Apostle admonishes: "As Christ is the head of the Church, so is the husband the head of the wife"; and just as the Church is subject to Christ, who cherishes it with most chaste and lasting love, so it is becoming that women also should be subject to their husbands, and by them in turn be loved with faithful and constant affection.'[1]

This, of course, implies a limited view of woman's 'nature,' which he briefly expresses in another document:

'Women, again, are not suited for certain occupations; a woman is by nature fitted for home work, and it is that which is best adapted at once to preserve her modesty and to promote the good bringing up of children and the well-being of the family.'[2]

In his encyclical on Christian marriage, Leo asserted:

'The husband is the chief of the family and the head of the wife. The woman, because she is flesh of his flesh and bone of his bone, must be subject to her husband and obey him; not, indeed, as a servant, but as a companion, so that her obedience shall be wanting in neither honor nor dignity.'[3]

The implied interpretation of Genesis is unacceptable by the standards of modern biblical scholarship. Moreover, there is an intrinsic inconsistency within the statement itself. The riddle of how someone who is subject can truly be considered as a companion did not, it seems, appear as a problem to Leo. A comparable one-sidedness can also be seen in his treatment of divorce, which was viewed as an unqualified evil. He even claimed that by divorce,

'the dignity of womanhood is lessened and brought low, and women run the risk of being deserted after having ministered to the pleasures of men.'[4]

The other side of the picture was simply ignored; the fact that many women desired nothing more than to be freed definitively

---

[1] Encyclical Letter, *Quod Apostolici Muneris*, 28 December, 1878.
[2] Encyclical Letter, *Rerum Novarum*, 15 May, 1891.
[3] Encyclical Letter, *Arcanum Divinae*, 10 February, 1880.
[4] *Ibid.*

from partners who exploited their wives' inability to obtain a divorce under existing laws was tacitly passed over.

Although Benedict XV, in 1919, pronounced in favor of votes for women, this did not represent any sweeping change in the official outlook concerning women themselves. It was thought by many Catholics that women's votes would support conservative and religious parties. It would be naïve to suppose that this consideration did not affect official attitudes.

One of the great struggles in the effort to achieve adulthood for women has been the striving for an equal education. Resistance to this striving can be seen in the words of Pius XI, who wrote in 1929, in his encyclical on the Christian education of youth:

'False also and harmful to Christian education is the so-called method of "coeducation". This too, by many of its supporters, is founded upon naturalism and the denial of original sin; but by all, upon a deplorable confusion of ideas that mistakes a leveling promiscuity and equality for the legitimate association of the sexes. The creator has ordained and disposed perfect union of the sexes only in matrimony and, with varying degrees of contact, in the family and in society. Besides there is not in nature itself, which fashions the two quite different in organism, in temperament, in abilities, anything to suggest that there can be or ought to be promiscuity, and much less equality, in the training of the two sexes.'[1]

From the last words it appears that Pius XI was even more horrified at the idea of equality than of promiscuity. It is noteworthy that he linked coeducation with equality and therefore opposed it. Separate and 'different' education is, in fact, one of the surest ways of supporting the illusion that women are inferior in ability. In proclaiming that the 'differences' should be 'maintained and encouraged',[2] Pius XI unconsciously conceded that these differences are not as natural in origin as he would want to believe.

In his encyclical on Christian marriage Pius XI, citing Paul, repeated the familiar ideas on the 'order' of domestic society:

[1] Encyclical Letter, *Divini Illius Magistri*, 31 December, 1929.
[2] *Ibid.*

'This order includes both the primacy of the husband with regard to the wife and children, the ready subjection of the wife and her willing obedience.'[1]

His hostility to feminine emancipation is hardly disguised. He attacks those 'false teachers' who say that 'the rights of husband and wife are equal', and who say that there should be emancipation 'in the ruling of the domestic society, in the administration of family affairs, and in the rearing of children', and that this liberty should be 'social, economic, and physiological'.[2] Through loaded wording, psychological pressure is brought to bear against women who would want to improve their situation. He wrote, for example, that according to the doctrine of the 'false teachers', the married woman should, 'to the neglect of these [her family] be able to follow her own bent and devote herself to business and even public affairs'.[3] The whole tone and context suggests that anyone who does devote herself to business or public affairs is suspected of doing this to the detriment of her family. This is suggested also by omission, since there is no hint of the possibility that by such activity the woman could become a more well-rounded person and therefore a better wife and mother. It is noteworthy, furthermore, that Pius's choice of language unconsciously refuted the 'feminine nature' hypothesis upon which he elsewhere relied so heavily. It is the admission of such an ambitious 'bent' in women which reveals the shakiness of his views about 'the natural disposition and temperament of the female sex'.

'True emancipation', according to Pius XI, will not involve 'false liberty and unnatural equality with the husband'.[4] He referred to equality in dignity, and then effectively negated this by affirming the necessity of 'a certain inequality'.[5] It is abundantly obvious that he favored the traditional androcentric situation; yet the pressure of social evolution forced him to use

[1] Encyclical Letter, *Casti Connubii*, 31 December, 1930.
[2] *Ibid.*
[3] *Ibid.*
[4] *Ibid.*
[5] *Ibid.*

expressions which have just enough ambiguity to leave the door open a crack for regrettable but unavoidable social change. Thus, he wrote:

> 'Again, this subjection of wife to husband in its degree and manner may vary according to the different conditions of persons, place, and time.'[1]

This prepared the way for an evolution of doctrine, but at the price of an ambiguity which could be interpreted in a manner that would militate against progress as long as the social situation and mores would allow. In the numerous passages of this type, the pendulum swings between the strong affirmation of a supposedly essential order, and a cautious admission of possible deviations from this. The following passage also illustrates this point:

> 'It is part of the office of the public authority to adapt the civil rights of the wife to modern needs and requirements, keeping in view what the natural disposition and temperament of the female sex, good morality, and the welfare of the family demands, and provided always that the essential order of the domestic society remain intact.'[2]

It is significant that in this process of adaptation it was the 'public authority' which was said to adapt the rights of the wife. All this was to be decided for her. There was no suggestion of a democratic process in which she might claim her rights or actively further social change in her own favor.

The copious utterances of Pius XII manifest the same resistance to change, often descending into detail with great explicitness. He insisted upon male headship in marriage.[3] As for married women entering the fields of work and public life:

> 'It is doubtful that such a condition is the social ideal for the married woman.'

However, he went on in the same text to claim that providence

---

[1] *Ibid.*
[2] *Ibid.*
[3] *Address to Married Couples*, 10 September, 1941.

gives to the Christian family the power 'to avoid the perils which are doubtless hidden in [such a state]'. He praised

'the sacrifice of a mother who, for special motives, must, beyond her domestic duties, also work to provide with hard daily toil for the upkeep of her family'.

His advice to such working women:

'During the hours and days which you can dedicate entirely to your dear ones, add zealous attention to redoubled love.'[1]

The text reveals the same indecision we have seen in the writings of Pius XI between a supposed 'ideal' situation (that of a bygone agricultural society) and the facts of modern life. It is notable that work is seen by Pius XII solely as an obligation taken on for the family, and not at all as a means of self-expression or as a contribution to society. Moreover, stress is laid on the double duty of the working wife, without a balancing reference to the duties or attitudes of husbands.

In one of his widely published addresses, the ambivalence of Pius XII's attitude is revealed in modes of expression that appear comical some twenty-odd years later. Having bemoaned the fact that women have been breaking out of bondage to the home, he could conclude:

'Your entry into public life has come about suddenly, as an effect of the social events of which we are being spectators; that does not matter! You are called to take part in it.'[2]

A key concept in the whole adjustment to modern society was 'spiritual motherhood', an easily manipulated concept which permitted some expansion of the traditional role but with limitations.

'Every woman is destined to be a mother, mother in the physical sense of the word, or in a more spiritual and higher but no less real meaning.'[3]

---

[1] *Address to Newlyweds*, 25 February, 1944.
[2] *Address to Women of Catholic Action*, 21 October, 1945.
[3] *Ibid.*

Just how restrictive and unrealistic this conception is becomes clear in the next passage:

> 'The creator has disposed to this end the entire being of woman, her organism, and even more her spirit, and above all her exquisite sensibility. So that a true woman cannot see and fully understand all the problems of human life otherwise than under the family aspect.'[1]

Many women find a discrepancy between this exclusive identification with the maternal role and their own experience of themselves, and find this identification with one role alienating. Pius takes care of such cases by using the expression 'true woman', implying that anyone who does not fit the stereotype is not what she should be.

While Pius XII seemed capable of viewing the work of a married woman as legitimate only insofar as it was a necessity imposed upon her to help support the family, his view of the man's work is, significantly, very different:

> 'For if by elevating himself creditably and honestly in society by means of his profession and labor, the man confers esteem and security on his wife and children—since the pride of children is their father—the man must not forget how much he contributes to a happy domestic life if, in every circumstance, he shows, in his own heart as well as in his exterior behaviour and speech, regard and respect for his wife, the mother of his children.'[2]

Missing entirely is any thought that esteem in society as a reward for her own professional excellence is a good to be prized by the woman as well. For Pius XII she remained the purely relational being, who receives esteem from society because of her maternal role. Absent too is any recognition of the fact that this condition of dependence upon another for one's self-image can be alienating.

Since the mental framework evidenced in Pius XII's writings is one in which women are envisioned as totally 'other', it is not

[1] *Ibid.*
[2] *Address to Newlyweds,* 8 April, 1942.

surprising that he showed little sensitivity for their problems and personal aspirations. The following statement is revealing:

'A cradle consecrates the mother of the family; and more cradles sanctify and glorify her before her husband and children, before Church and homeland. The mother who complains because a new child presses against her bosom seeking nourishment at her breast is foolish, ignorant of herself, and unhappy.'[1]

There is in the context no suggestion of sympathetic understanding or of compassion for another's situation. The possibility that the woman is overburdened and exhausted by repeated pregnancies is not considered. To quote again:

'Even the pains that, since original sin, a mother has to suffer to give birth to her child only draw tighter the bond that binds them: she loves it the more, the more pain it has cost her.'[2]

Such statements could well lead one to agree with Simone de Beauvoir's idea that there is an unconscious sadism at the root of certain moral attitudes concerning women. At the very least, there is in evidence an insensitivity and one-sidedness which is astonishing.

Pius XII perpetuated the custom of giving a double meaning to 'equality'. Having granted the equality of women with men 'in their personal dignity as children of God', he repeats the familiar jargon which serves to nullify the practical implications of real equality. Thus he wrote of 'the indestructible spiritual and physical qualities, whose order cannot be deranged without nature herself moving to re-establish it', affirming that 'these peculiar characteristics which distinguish the two sexes reveal themselves so clearly to the eyes of all', that only obstinate blindness or doctrinairism could disregard them.[3] The difficulty with this is, of course, that not only physical qualities but also 'spiritual' ones are presumed to be linked universally and exclusively to members of one sex. It is precisely this bridge from the biological differentiation to the level of personality

---

[1] *Address to Women of Catholic Action*, 26 October, 1941.
[2] *Address to Obstetricians*, 29 October, 1951.
[3] *Address to Women of Catholic Action*, 21 October, 1945.

differences which responsible thinkers today who are aware of the role of cultural conditioning would regard as highly problematic, and as anything but clear 'to the eyes of all'.

Pius XII's specific allusions to the alleged 'spiritual' differences reveal the unreliability and traditional bias of his assumptions. Thus:

> 'This effective collaboration in social and political life in no way alters the special character of the normal action of woman. Associating herself with man in his work in the area of civil institutions, she will apply herself principally to tasks which call for tact, delicate feelings, and maternal instinct, rather than administrative rigidity.'[1]

The expression, 'associating with man in *his* work', sustains the image of her as relational and subordinate. The text suggests, moreover, that she should be kept out of responsible administrative posts. This is confirmed by a statement in the same context about

> 'the sensibility and delicacy of feeling peculiar to woman, which might tempt her to be swayed by emotions and thus blur the clearness and breadth of her view and be detrimental to the calm consideration of future consequences,'

although it is conceded that these qualities are

> 'of valuable help in bringing to light needs, aspirations, and dangers in the domestic, welfare, and religious fields.'[2]

Having discouraged women from posts requiring 'administrative rigidity', Pius XII attempted in the same text, in a most unrealistic way, to point out compensatory factors:

> 'Only woman will know, for example, how, without detriment to efficacy, to temper with kindness the repression of loose morals; only she will know how to preserve from humiliation and educate in decency and in the religious and civil virtues delinquent youth;

[1] *Ibid.*
[2] *Ibid.*

only she will be able to render fruitful service in the rehabilitation of discharged prisoners and of delinquent girls.'[1]

Why would 'only she' be able to do these things? The works described could be done by competent professional psychologists, men or women. Pius XII seems to have been anxious, indeed too anxious, to find a 'role' for women in line with 'spiritual motherhood'. The unreliability of this conception is as evident from exaggerated praise of supposed specifically female talents as from the more negative statements.

The idea that the fixed sexual stereotypes might be the effect of social conditioning was not given serious consideration by Pius XII or his predecessors. All of the alleged specifically feminine characteristics are seen as rooted unalterably in feminine 'nature'. Yet it was impossible consistently to uphold such a view, and like his predecessor, Pius XII unwittingly refutes it. This is seen, for example, in his emotional description of the daughter of the working mother:

'Used to seeing her mother always absent and the home dismal in its abandonment, she will find no attraction in it, she will not feel the slightest inclination for domestic occupations, and she will be unable to understand their nobleness and beauty or desire to devote herself to them some day as a wife and mother.'

Moreover, she

'will want to emancipate herself as early as possible and, according to a truly sad expression, "live her own life".'[2]

So the alleged natural bent to domesticity is after all suspiciously subject to rapid change.

Even aside from specific instances of unwitting self-refutation, the whole tactic of these recent popes has been self-refuting. To paraphrase one of Shakespeare's famous lines, it seems the gentlemen did protest too much. If women's subordination were really so 'natural', it would not be necessary to insist so

[1] *Ibid.*
[2] *Ibid.*

strongly upon it. It would seem that people would not have to be told authoritatively to behave 'naturally'. The opposition of these popes to birth control, which becomes ever more acutely embarrassing to a Church endeavouring to face up to the necessity of change, was also rooted in a rigid and inadequate conception of 'nature'.

Hopefully, Church leaders will profit from the mistakes of the past, and not continue to repeat them.

CHAPTER THREE

Winds of Change

'Are there some of you who don't like girl servers?
Please tell us why you don't like them. We can't
think of any good reason.'

Rita Martin
Third Grade

With the death of Pius XII the Catholic Church acquired as
pope a man entirely different from his predecessors in temperament and stamp of mind. With Pope John XXIII came opened
windows and an on-rushing *aggiornamento* which lasted
throughout his brief reign. It has become abundantly clear,
despite a few discouraging setbacks, that the Church cannot
return to its condition before the advent of Pope John and
Vatican II.

It is not surprising that one of the signs of new life in the
Church is an increasing awareness of the need to take an objective and reappraising look at the situation of women. The first
startling breakthrough on the ideological level came from Pope
John himself, in the encyclical *Pacem in Terris* of 1963. He
wrote:

'Since women are becoming ever more conscious of their human
dignity, they will not tolerate being treated as mere material instruments, but demand rights befitting a human person both in
domestic and in public life.'[1]

Further on, he states:

'Thus in very many human beings the inferiority complex which
endured for hundreds and thousands of years is disappearing,

[1] Pope John XXIII, *Pacem in Terris*. Encyclical of 11 April, 1963, n. 41.

118

while in others there is an attenuation and gradual fading of the corresponding superiority complex which had its roots in social-economic privileges, sex, or political standing.'[1]

In another passage, Pope John says:

'Human beings have the right to choose freely the state of life which they prefer, and therefore the right to set up a family, with equal rights and duties for man and woman, and also the right to follow a vocation to the priesthood or the religious life.'[2]

What is most striking in Pope John's words is the sympathetic and positive attitude they convey. Unlike his predecessors, he frankly described change in terms of the gradual fading of inferiority and superiority complexes, and he did not speak regretfully of it. Missing is the usual disparagement of feminine emancipation which one had grown accustomed to expect from papal writings. The customary double-talk has been dropped. To those who are familiar with the writings of John's predecessors, it is no less than astonishing to read the reference to 'equal rights and duties for man and woman', unaccompanied by any nullifying statement about the need for 'a certain inequality'.

The spirit of Pope John is discernible in some statements concerning women in Vatican II's Pastoral Constitution on the Church in the Modern World. This document affirms without any hint of disapproval the following fact:

'Where they have not yet won it, women claim for themselves an equity with men before the law and in fact.'[3]

This constitution gave evidence of the Church's growing recognition of the need for genuine practical realization of the equal rights of men and women:

'Nevertheless, with respect to the fundamental rights of the person, every type of discrimination, whether social or cultural,

---

[1] *Ibid.*, n. 43.
[2] *Ibid.*, n. 15.
[3] *Pastoral Constitution on the Church in the Modern World (Gaudium et Spes)*, Introductory Statement, n. 9. All quotations from Council Documents are taken from *The Documents of Vatican II*, edited by Walter M. Abbott, S.J. (New York: America Press, 1966).

whether based on sex, race, color, social condition, language, or religion, is to be overcome and eradicated as contrary to God's intent. For in truth it must still be regretted that fundamental personal rights are not yet being universally honored. Such is the case of a woman who is denied the right and freedom to choose a husband, to embrace a state of life, or to acquire an education or cultural benefits equal to those recognized for men.'[1]

In treating marriage, the constitution transcends the biologism of an older theology and adopts a more personalist attitude. It also seems to transcend the old canonical distinction between the primary and secondary ends of marriage that was so hampering to the development of a profound theology of marriage. Moreover, it does not explicitly condemn artificial contraception, but appears to leave the door open for further consideration. It also avoids the familiar jargon about the subordination of women. It does not speak disparagingly of working mothers, although the following passage is ambivalent enough to be given either a conservative or a liberal interpretation:

'The children, especially the younger among them, need the care of their mother at home. This domestic role of hers must be safely preserved, though the legitimate social progress of women should not be underrated on that account.'[2]

The Church in the Modern World has its weaknesses. It does not attempt to clarify what might be meant by 'legitimate social progress', for example. In the chapter on culture, this passage occurs:

'Women are now employed in almost every area of life. It is appropriate that they should be able to assume their full proper role in accordance with their own nature. Everyone should acknowledge and favor the proper and necessary participation of women in cultural life.'[3]

Whatever women's 'proper role' and 'own nature' may be is left in the dark. A hard-headed, progressive statement would not

---

[1] *Ibid.*, n. 29.
[2] *Ibid.*, n. 52.
[3] *Ibid.*, n. 60.

be phrased so loosely. However, the ambiguity can work both ways.

Vatican II's Declaration on Christian Education, moreover, has nothing to say against coeducation, which suggests that a long road has been traveled since the days of Pius XI. It is true that there are regressive overtones in the passage about teachers, admonishing them that

'they should pay due regard in every educational activity to sexual differences and to the special role which divine providence allots to each sex in family life and in society.'[1]

However, the vagueness and impracticability of the statement render it innocuous.

Finally, the Decree on the Apostolate of the Laity makes a positive affirmation concerning women:

'Since in our times women have an ever more active share in the whole life of society, it is very important that they participate more widely also in the various fields of the Church's apostolate.'[2]

Overall, Vatican II did not have much to say concerning women specifically. Under the circumstances and at that point in history this may have been better than saying too much; from the liberal's point of view, a minimum of official statements is usually preferable to too many. It is also true that the modifications attached to some of the statements give the impression of 'three steps forward, one step backward'. Yet this can hardly be described as anything other than progress.

Pope Paul has appeared to try to maintain an openness to progress on the question of women, and has given some evidence of an evolution beyond the attitudes of the popes who preceded John. Addressing members of the Italian Women's Center during their jubilee celebration in 1965, he congratulated them for preparing themselves and others for new public duties. Saying that the social processes which assure women of their rights and obligations are not yet completed and that women should explore and formulate the principles which

[1] *Declaration on Christian Education (Gravissimum Educationis)*, n. 8.
[2] *Decree on the Apostolate of the Laity (Apostolicam Actuositatem)*, n. 9.

underlie true feminism, he also stated:

> 'You should remind women that perfect equality in their nature and dignity, and therefore in rights, is assured to them from the first page of the sacred scriptures'.[1]

On the one hand it can be regarded as encouraging that Pope Paul spoke of 'perfect equality in rights', without qualification; on the other hand, the statement is weak in that he fails to be specific about the implications of this 'equality'.

Even less encouraging was Pope Paul's much-publicized address of 1966 to delegates of the Italian Society of Obstetrics and Gynecology. In it the Pope stressed the symbolism of woman and was strikingly imprecise, as the following statement illustrates:

> 'For us she is the creature most docile for any formation and suitable, therefore, for all cultural and social functions and particularly for those which are most congenial to her moral and spiritual sensitivity.'[2]

One might wonder how such a 'docile' creature could be suitable for 'all cultural functions'. For many the great irony lay in the fact that this address was the vehicle chosen by the Pope to announce that the thought and norm of the Church on birth control had not changed. One of the many puzzling problems raised by the address was this: how can women possibly exercise 'equal rights' in society if they are prohibited from practicing birth control—the means necessary to free them from unwanted and excessively numerous pregnancies?

Still other actions taken by Pope Paul have reinforced the impression that he does not recognize the implications of women's equality. His rigid opposition to the legalization of divorce in Italy was disheartening. Pope Paul's stance had particular significance for the women of Italy, a country where society is extremely permissive in regard to infidelity on the part of the husband and extremely strict in regard to the same

---

[1] Pope Paul VI, *Address to Italian Women's Center*, 30 May, 1965. Cited in *La documentation catholique*, t. LXII, n. 1450, 20 juin, 1965, col. 1065.
[2] Pope Paul VI, *Address to Delegates of the Italian Society of Obstetrics and Gynecology*, 29 October, 1966.

failing on the part of the wife. This general social attitude is reflected in Italian law, which is far more lenient toward the male, and which keeps married women in a state of subjection and dependence. The degrading situation of Italian women is deplorable by the standards of more advanced countries. It is the Church alone which prevents divorce legislation and other reforms. The Pope's statement that divorce is a 'sign of pernicious moral decadence' rings hollow to those familiar with the condition of sexual morality in Italy, where application of the double standard is flagrant. Moreover, such a statement increases the credibility gap when it is juxtaposed with his abstract statements concerning the equality of women.

Nevertheless, it is evident from the above passages that an evolution has taken place in the official ideology. This is seen not only in positive statements but in the omission of old formulae which expressed resistance to change. It is also evident that the old prejudices have far from disappeared from official Catholic thought and practice.

Beginnings of ferment

While the statements of recent popes and of the Council are important, they are not more significant than a number of other evidences of change in outlook. In fact, the ferment concerning women in the Church began to manifest itself in a variety of ways shortly after the opening of the Council. Discrimination against women, which formerly would have passed unnoticed except by a few, received careful scrutiny in the press. An example is the case of the woman journalist who, because of her sex, was physically prevented from approaching the altar railing to receive Holy Communion at a Council Mass during the second session of Vatican II. (During the first session, women journalists had not even been allowed to attend the Council Mass, a restriction which moved their male colleagues to send in a petition on their behalf.) The event was significant in at least two ways. First, it showed the persistence of a strange mentality which seems to regard half the human race as not quite human. Second, the widespread criticism of this incident showed that the attitude it betrays is generally recognized by the modern world as antiquated, odd, and offensive.

Another indication of the change was the appearance of petitions sent to the Council Fathers by women, requesting that the Council reconsider the traditionally subordinate situation of women in the Church in the light of modern scholarship, of science, and of contemporary conditions. These petitions contained cogent arguments against the inferior role which the Church assigns to women. Notable was the petition of Dr Gertrud Heinzelmann, a Swiss lawyer, demonstrating that the teaching of St Thomas Aquinas concerning women, which is still implicitly the official doctrine of the Church, is entirely outdated. Based upon an Aristotelian biological theory of generation now known to be false and upon biblical interpretations no longer acceptable by standards of modern scriptural exegesis, the Thomistic teaching is shown as containing much that is offensive and debasing. Dr Heinzelmann pointed out that while Thomism contains principles from which conclusions favorable to women could have been drawn, St Thomas himself was not consistent in applying them. Her conclusion was that his theory has contributed to the hampering of half of humanity in its development, activity, and expression.[1]

Three German women theologians also presented petitions to the Council. One of these, Iris Müller, described the hardship imposed upon her as a result of her conversion to Catholicism, for she had completed her studies for the Evangelical ministry prior to her conversion and now, as a Catholic, could not fulfill a comparable role. Written in collaboration with Ida Raming, her petition analyzes the various traditional arguments for the exclusion of women from the priesthood, and in an objective manner points out the defectiveness and inconclusiveness of these time-honored arguments. Another theologian, Josefa Münch, petitioned for changes in canon law, setting forth reasoned grounds for holding that Canon 968,

---

[1] Gertrud Heinzelmann, 'Women and the Council—Hopes and Expectations', in *Wir schweigen nicht länger!* (*We Won't Keep Silence Any Longer*), edited by Gertrud Heinzelmann (Zurich: Interfeminas Verlag, 1965), pp. 79-99.

which limits ordination to men alone, is of human tradition rather than divine origin. In another petition on the liturgy and women, the same author cited a seemingly minor point of sexual discrimination by recalling her conversation with one of the Council Fathers. When she suggested to this bishop that the words *Orate fratres* ('Pray, brothers'), spoken by the priest just before the Prayer over the offerings at Mass, be changed to *Orate fratres et sorores* ('Pray, brothers and sisters'), she found the bishop completely opposed to her request. What was significant was the reason given for his opposition. He did not reject the idea because it seemed trivial, or because he thought the proposed new formulation was too long, or because 'brothers' also implies 'sisters'. Rather he claimed that the basic reason for addressing the people as 'brothers' was that in principle a woman cannot offer sacrifice to God. He maintained that a laywoman has a much lesser share in the sacrifice of the Mass than does a layman. Frau Münch's point was that such weird and distorted theological notions are encouraged and perpetuated by practices such as exclusively masculine forms of address used by churchmen in speaking to an audience made up of both men and women.[1]

In another realm—Catholic journalism—something new for women began to happen shortly after the beginning of Vatican II. A number of critical articles appeared in the most liberal Catholic magazines, calling attention to the fact that the situation of women in the Church needed updating. The first to speak out were the women themselves; later other writings appeared by clerical authors sympathetic to their cause.[2] Usually the liberal articles were followed by strongly worded

---

[1] All of these documents are in Heinzelmann, *Wir schweigen nicht länger!*, *op. cit.*

[2] Cf. Rosemary Lauer, 'Women and the Church', *Commonweal*, vol. LXXIX, n. 13, 20 December, 1963, pp. 365–8. For letters, see vol. LXXIX, n. 20, 14 February, 1964, pp. 603–4. Cf. Mary Daly, 'A Built-in Bias', in *Commonweal*, vol. LXXXI, 15 January, 1965, pp. 508–11; and Gertrud Heinzelmann, 'The Priesthood and Women', in the same issue, pp. 504–8. An example of the open and thoughtful type of article beginning to be written on the subject by the clergy is Rev. George Tavard, A.A., 'Women in the Church: A Theological Problem?', *The Ecumenist*, vol. 4, n. 1, November-December, 1965, pp. 7–10.

'letters to the editor', pro and con. Most of the letters from women showed a keen awareness of the problem; by contrast, many letters from clerics manifested strong conservatism, failure to see the problem, and sometimes disdain. A frequent target of those on the pro-feminist side was the use made by preachers of texts of St Paul on the 'place of women', which may have been appropriate to the social situation in which he lived nineteen hundred years ago but which no longer apply.[1] The ecclesiastical custom of addressing mixed audiences as if there were no women present was also criticized. A prominent German woman pointed out that in a papal audience the Pope addressed a mixed group as 'My sons' and another mixed gathering simply as 'Messieurs'. The letter of an American woman expressed her dismay that when Pope Paul visited New York he addressed a mixed audience as 'Sons and brothers'. These objectors were not preoccupied with etiquette for its own sake, but with the thought-patterns reflected in an outdated protocol: they saw the omission as symbolic of the failure of the hierarchy in thought and action to take into account the real existence and importance of women in the Church.

On the level of serious scholarship, works dealing with the problem of women began to appear during the years the Council was in session. These generally exposed the strong antifeminist strain embedded in the Christian tradition and the need to purify theological thought of distortions. These writings also showed that the elements of a more authentic Christian doctrine had existed and had found expression in all ages, although the implications had not been fully understood and applied.

The emergence of this literature is the outcome of the rapid social changes of modern times, together with advances in science and scholarship. For once authors have the perspective necessary to begin to distinguish the authentic, personalist strain from the oppressive elements in Christian writings and practice. Among Catholic scholars whose books have opened new perspectives are: Elizabeth Schüssler, a young German

---

[1] Eleanor Schoen, 'Please! No Quotes from Paul', *National Catholic Reporter* (hereafter referred to as *NCR*), 20 January, 1965, p. 6.

theologian; Dr Govaart-Halkes, a Dutch woman; Haye van der Meer, a Dutch Jesuit; and José Idigoras, a Jesuit professor of theology at the University of Lima, Peru. Among other matters agreed upon, all of these authors conclude that the centuries-old reasons for the exclusion of women from holy orders are not of a kind clearly to exclude a claim for the future admission of women to the priesthood.

The new spirit has been manifested in yet another way. Although Catholic women's organizations have tended to be conservative, an outstanding exception is the St Joan's International Alliance. Originally founded to work for civic equality, this avant-garde organization, comprised largely of professional women, has turned its attention in recent years to achieving equal status for women in the Church. At its twentieth council meeting in 1963, the Alliance passed a number of resolutions concerning fuller participation of women in the service of the Church. It requested

'the appropriate authorities to permit women to follow courses in theology of all grades, to take the necessary qualifying examinations and to receive the diplomas and degrees now accessible only to men.'

It further asked that if diaconal duties be entrusted to laymen as an independent ministry, this ministry be open both to men and women. It requested that representatives of the laity, both men and women, be invited to attend meetings of the commissions of the Ecumenical Council as experts, and expressed the hope that the commission for the revision of canon law would give special consideration to those canons which refer to women. The Alliance moreover expressed the

'conviction that should the Church in her wisdom and in her good time decide to extend to women the dignity of the priesthood, women would be willing and eager to respond.'

In regard to the liturgy, it asked that the prayers said over the bride and bridegroom at the Nuptial Mass after the *Pater Noster* be so worded as to apply to both spouses, reminding them of their mutual obligation of fidelity.[1]

In 1964, the Alliance repeated the basic requests made the previous year and expressed satisfaction that in the Constitution on the Liturgy the prayer for the bride had been duly amended. In addition, it asked that the Council invite qualified women to attend its meetings as auditors. A new resolution petitioned the commission entrusted with the revision of canon law

'to amend those canons which concern women so that these no longer assign to women a position of inferiority which no longer corresponds with their civil and social status.'

This resolution stressed that the fundamental rights of all baptized persons, as affirmed in canon 87, should be recognized, and asked for revision of specific canons.[2]

In its 1965 meeting the Alliance, recalling the tradition of women deaconesses in the early Church, asked that No. 29 of the Constitution on the Church, which decreed the introduction of an independent diaconate, be applied to women as well as to men. It recorded gratitude to the Holy Father for his invitation to representative women to attend the Council as auditors, and the hope 'that competent women will be included in the post-conciliar commissions'. Further consideration of the ritual of marriage was asked, 'so that it may express the equal rights and duties of husband and wife as affirmed in the Encyclical *Pacem in Terris*'.[3]

The resolutions of the Alliance during the conciliar period have been substantially reaffirmed at their yearly international meetings during post-conciliar years.

Developments at the Vatican Council

The first two interventions made at the Vatican Council on behalf of women astonished many and delighted those con-

---

[1] *The Catholic Citizen*, vol. XLIX, n. 10, 15 October, 1963, p. 66. (*The Catholic Citizen* is the organ of St Joan's Alliance, 17d Dryden Chambers, 119 Oxford Street, London W.1.)
[2] *Ibid.*, vol. L, n. 10, October, 1964, pp. 72–3.
[3] *Ibid.*, vol. LI, n. 9, October, 1965, pp. 74–5.

cerned with the problem. In 1963, during the second session, Cardinal Suenens of Belgium said to the Fathers in Council that 'in our age, when woman goes almost to the moon, it is indispensable that she play a more important role in the Church'. He then proposed that women be admitted to the Council as auditors on the same terms as men. Two days later, Melkite Archbishop Hakim of Galilee, also speaking in Council, made an objection to the text of the Constitution on the Church, on the score that it was so silent regarding the place of women in the Church as to give the impression that they did not exist, and he spoke of their indispensable work in the Church. Both speeches were applauded in St Peter's.[1]

Although many doubted that Cardinal Suenens' proposal would be accepted, the feat was accomplished. In the fall of 1964 the first women auditors took their places in St Peter's for the third session of the Council. The watching world found this fact revolutionary, although sceptical observers pointed out that an auditor was only a listener and, after all, had no voice in the Council affairs. Moreover, the invitation came so late that it appeared as an afterthought, and it was observed that those chosen as auditors were in most cases more noted for qualities of tact and prudence than for demonstrated ability for progressive and creative thinking and leadership. Furthermore, it was disconcerting to hear that women were expected to attend general congregations of the Council only when questions associated with women were debated. Finally, however, perhaps as a result of a number of public complaints, women did appear at all of the sessions of the third session of the Council, and at least a few of these made fruitful use of the opportunity for influence and dialogue afforded by their presence.

Nevertheless, a disappointing incident occurred during the third session to point up the fact that the official status of women at the Council was no more than that of silent listeners. The famed woman economist, Barbara Ward, sent to the Council

[1] Cited in *The Catholic Citizen*, vol. L, n. 1, 15 January, 1964, p. 2. Cf also Eva-Maria Jung, 'Women at the Council: Spectators or Collaborators?', *The Catholic World*, vol. 200, n. 1, 199, February, 1965, p. 280.

the outline of a plan for a world-wide attack on poverty. It was received enthusiastically by some of the hierarchy, and a layman, James L. Norris, suggested that Miss Ward be invited to speak to the assembled bishops. This proposal was rejected as 'premature', and Mr Norris spoke instead. The conservative mentality which does not see beyond the scope of ancient prejudice against women had won the day. A similar incident occurred when lay auditors proposed that the president of the World Union of Catholic Women's Organizations, Miss Pilar Bellosillo, address the Council Fathers. The proposal was rejected by the Secretary General of the Council.

Even though the role of the auditors in St Peter's was a silent one, a number of eloquent and significant statements concerning women were made at the third session in connection with Schema XIII, on The Church in the Modern World. Bishop Coderre of St Jean, Quebec, told the Fathers that in a time of universal evolution, women have gradually realized their own dignity and their God-given state, which is not one of inferiority, and that the Church must accept this situation and promote it. Archbishop Malula of Leopoldville argued that the Church should call on all men to aid in the completion of the great work of civilization—the promotion of women to full human dignity and complete responsibility. Other African bishops described the plight of African women. Bishop Baurlein, of Djakovo, Yugoslavia, called for all men to be treated alike, without regard to race, sex, or social status, and said it was not enough for this equality to be recognized theoretically; it must be translated into social action. Saying that women's changed status must receive comprehensive consideration, Bishop Frotz of Cologne pointed out that modern women expect to be accepted as equal partners with men in intellectual and cultural life; the Church must therefore promote the spiritual and religious interests of woman so that she may have the opportunity of applying her special gifts to the Church. Women, he said, must be accepted as grown daughters, not as children.[1]

[1] Cited in *The Catholic Citizen*, vol. LI, n. 1, 15 January, 1965, pp. 4–5. Cf. also Eva-Maria Jung. *op. cit.*, pp. 283–4.

Throughout the discussion of The Church in the Modern World the American hierarchy was silent on the problem of women—with one notable exception. In 1965, during the final session, Archbishop Hallinan of Atlanta made very strong proposals to the Council. Although his intervention did not reach the floor, it was filed with the Council's general secretariat and given wide press coverage. The Archbishop stated that the Church must act as well as speak and he questioned whether the Church has given the leadership that Christ by word and example clearly showed he expected of her. He recommended that women be allowed to act as lectors and acolytes at Mass, and that after proper study and formation they should serve as deaconesses, preaching and administering sacraments. They should be encouraged, he said, to become teachers and consultants in theology and be included in whatever organization is established for the post-conciliar implementation of the lay apostolate. The Archbishop pointed out that the community between man and woman must not be one of subservience, but one of harmony, mutual respect, love, and responsibility.

'Therefore, we must not continue to perpetuate, in the Church of the twentieth century, the secondary place accorded to women in the past. We must not continue to be late-comers in the social, political, and economic developments that have today reached climactic proportions.'

He deplored the fact that in many places the marks of inequality still persist, in working conditions, in wages and hours of work, in marriage and property laws. He referred to the gradualism which limits the effectiveness of women and said that the Church has been slow to denounce the degradation of women in slavery and to claim for them the rights of suffrage and economic equality. 'Particularly has the Church been slow in offering to women any other vocation than that of mother or nun.'[1]

---

[1] Cited in *The Catholic Citzen*, vol. LI, n. 10, November-December, 1965, p. 88. An excellent collection of conciliar interventions concerning women exists in German: Gertrud Heinzelmann, editor, *Die getrennten Schwestern*, (Zurich: Interfeminas Verlag, 1967).

Emerging discussion of special problems: problems of catholic married women

The Vatican Council had the effect of opening the door to free discussion of all issues. Once opened, that door could not be closed. The emergence of public discussion about the increasingly problematic—sometimes desperate—situation of married Catholic women is another sign that anachronistic teaching and practice is becoming ever more difficult to defend. Much of this discussion, of course, centers around the birth control issue, which clearly touches women more profoundly than men. The vigorous and outspoken protests against the Catholic position by married women have revealed a new awareness. Particularly articulate was the protest of Dr Anne Biezanek, a physician, director of a birth control clinic outside Liverpool (at which most of her patients were Catholics), and mother of seven. Converted to Roman Catholicism many years before, Dr Biezanek has openly rebelled against the Church on the issue of the birth control pill. Not having been able to obtain clear advice on the use of the pill, she had taken it, with consequent improvement of health. Still troubled in conscience, she talked to a priest, who refused her Communion. In a press interview her spontaneous remarks revealed a basic issue of the contest with authority:

'They've never cared how much women have suffered. This is what makes me rebellious. If a priest says this is the law of God, he's prescribing martyrdom.'[1]

This drama was not new or unique, of course. But what was new was the public attention drawn to a smouldering problem.

Also in recent years we have heard the public expression of a troubled conscience on the part of priests themselves. It is obvious that not all are as traditionalist as those Dr Biezanek encountered. Some have openly opposed the traditional teaching and others express dismay. A Boston pastor is reported to have said that 'some of the fire went out' of his sermons when he

[1] *Newsweek*, 6 July, 1964, p. 42.

handled the case of a poor, hapless sort of mother who bore her fifth set of twins in as many years and whose husband deserted her.[1]

All this discussion has underlined the fact that the current crisis in the Church over birth control cannot be understood merely in terms of expediency in the face of the world's population problem. There is growing public concern over the pitiful condition of many women who are without an adequate safeguard against successive pregnancies. There is a development of awareness in the Catholic consciousness that women are persons with rights and not mere instruments for the perpetuation of the species.

Married Catholics have written articles expounding the same basic issue. Daniel Sullivan, in an enlightening historical essay, pointed to the conclusion that the misogynistic strain in the Christian tradition, linked with anti-sexuality, is largely responsible for the present crisis over birth control in the Church.[2] Rosemary Ruether, theologian and mother of three children, has presented the problematic on a personal plane, pointing out that she could not give up her studies and professional interests in order to have an unlimited number of children.

'Such a request is simply a demand that I scuttle my interests, my training, and in the last analysis, my soul. This, I feel, is not only shockingly wrong, but, for me, psychologically impossible.'

Moreover, she says, 'the inadequacies and tensions caused by rhythm were too inadequate to be endured for long'; it meant being 'the unwitting slave of biological fecundity'. In fact, rhythm turned out to be a 'sexual version of the Chinese water torture'.

The Ruethers decided against the Church's position and affirmed this as an act of conscience. Their decision was not made because the Church's position is 'hard'. Hardness is acceptable when you know

[1] *Ibid.*
[2] Daniel Sullivan, 'A History of Catholic Thinking on Contraception,' *What Modern Catholics Think about Birth Control,* edited by William Birmingham (New York: New American Library, 1964), pp. 28–69.

'that this is the way to realize the values to which you are committed. The hardness of the Church's position, on the other hand,
produces weariness and disgust, rather than joy, because it rests
on a rationale that is not convincing, because it contradicts the
emotional dynamics of the marital relationship, and finally because
it becomes an intolerable thralldom lived out of a social intimidation extrinsic to oneself.'[1]

Mrs Ruether's position, which still appeared radical to many in
1964, has been adopted in more recent years by an ever-increasing number of young Catholics.

Another aspect of conservative Catholic teaching on marriage
came under fire—the traditional opposition to working wives
and mothers. This is closely related to the birth control issue,
yet is distinct from it. A non-Catholic author, Betty Friedan, had
called attention to this opposition, claiming that the traditional
resistance of religious orthodoxy to professions and careers for
married women is masked today by the manipulative techniques
of psychotherapy. As an example, she cited the 'Suggested Outline
for Married Couples' Discussions', from the Family Life Bureau
of the Archdiocese of New York. The 'outline' was loaded with
subtle suggestions calculated to give the working wife guilt feelings; it is implied that by working she may be undermining her
husband's position and making herself sterile. Mrs Friedan was
concerned with the crippling effects of this sort of propaganda.[2]

The problems of working mothers have been further discussed by Sidney Callahan, a young Catholic author and mother
of five children. She urges a balanced solution that recognizes
the values of creative outside work as well as the values of domestic life. She asks for the abandonment of culturally imposed
stereotypes and a discovery of the true Christian ideal of personal freedom which does not exclude acceptance of family
responsibility.[3]

---

[1] Rosemary Ruether, 'A Question of Dignity, A Question of Freedom',
What Modern Catholics Think about Birth Control, pp. 233–40.

[2] Betty Friedan, *The Feminine Mystique* (London: Victor Gollancz, 1963),
pp. 351–2.

[3] Sidney Cornelia Callahan, *The Illusion of Eve* (New York: Sheed and
Ward, 1965).

Nor has the discussion of marriage and of problems of sexual morality stopped with these particular questions. Inevitably the question of the Church's position on divorce has been raised. In recent years some moralists and canonists have earnestly questioned the Church's rigid laws forbidding divorce and re-marriage and pondered how they can be liberalized. Catholic opposition to abortion, on the other hand, has remained un-animous. In the United States, where the issue of legalized abortion has been hotly debated, not only the hierarchy but also most laymen of the liberal wing have strongly opposed its legalization. They have rightly pointed out that this is a subject which must be kept distinct from that of birth control, since the life of an existing fetus is in question. However, there has been an irrational refusal to recognize any moral ambiguity, the assumption being that the moral question has been com-pletely answered in the past and need not be discussed. The general assumption has been that the only question for Catholics is one of strategy—of which tactics will win out against legalized abortion.[1]

Yet, the fact of moral ambiguity and complexity has been recognized publicly by at least one bishop, Francis Simons, Bishop of Indore, India. Bishop Simons wrote:

> 'When abortion is performed to avoid almost certain or very prob-able serious harm to the health of the mother, its licitness is at least arguable. . . . A therapeutic abortion would seem licit only at a stage when danger of death or serious injury to the health of the mother is imminent.'[2]

Problems of the emerging sisters

A special problem in the general emergence of women is the situation of religious sisters. More numerous than priests and male religious, they exercise great influence, particularly as educators, especially in the United States, with its system of

[1] Representative of this attitude was the article by Robert F. Drinan, S.J., 'Strategy on Abortion', *America*, 4 February, 1967, pp. 177–9.

[2] Francis Simons, 'The Catholic Church and the New Morality', *Cross Currents*, vol. XVI, n. 4 (Fall, 1966), pp. 429–45.

parochial schools and Catholic academies and colleges. Their public statements concerning the problem of women and the Church have not been numerous nor conspicuously progressive on the whole.[1] On the other hand, in private discussions the younger and better-educated sisters indicate an awareness of the need for radical changes in their mode of life. Some note with irony that their conspicuous and encumbering religious habits have become symbols of glaring anachronism in patterns of thinking and acting. The discrepancy between public and private utterances of sisters can be explained partly by the conservatism and timidity of some superiors, who make it morally impossible for dissenting voices to be heard publicly. Yet the phenomenon of the emerging sisters is a fact. Their participation in public demonstrations such as civil rights marches and anti-war parades indicates a change of outlook toward 'the world'. More significant is their increasing attendance at intellectual and professional gatherings, and as graduate students and visiting scholars on secular university campuses both in the United States and in foreign countries. The recent appearance of progressive, self-critical books and essays by sisters also reveals growing awareness and courage.

An important breakthrough occurred in 1965, when superiors of American nuns petitioned the Holy See to give sisters a voice in the Church bodies which rule the lives of religious women. The petition said:

'The Conference of Major Superiors of Religious Women earnestly requests that sisters be asked to serve as permanent consultative or acting members of the Sacred Congregation of Religious, of the commission for the revision of canon law and of any post-conciliar

---

[1] A few courageous voices are beginning to be raised, however. A Medical Mission sister who was appointed to the Pennsylvania Governor's Commission on the Status of Women, Sister Mary Lawrence McKenna, made a public statement that the role of women in the Church is the most neglected area of *aggiornamento*. Sister Albertus Magnus, O.P., historian and professor at Rosary College, published a letter in which she maintained that the exclusion of women from serving Mass has its roots in primitive ideas of female 'uncleanness', which the Catholic Church has never entirely abandoned. She complained that Vatican II 'did not recognize women as belonging in all things equally with men to the people of God'. *NCR*, 5 January, 1966, p. 6.

commission that may be set up for the implementing of acts of Vatican II in regard to religious.'

Explaining the petition, Sister Mary Luke, S.L., chairman of the conference's executive committee and a Vatican II auditor, was reported as saying:

'There is a serious concern on the part of major superiors that women should have something to do with the regulations that bind them. Traditionally such regulations have been made by men. We are strongly suggesting that we have representation.'

The petition was adopted by unanimous vote at a meeting in Denver, and was sent to the Pope, the Sacred Congregation for Religious, and all the bishops of the United States.

At the same conference meeting of superiors a number of speakers discussed the problems facing religious women in an age of rapid change. Sister Mary William, I.H.M., was reported to have summarized the situation in the following words:

'Either we find ways to develop and encourage this forward-looking, constantly converting type of person or, by default, we will, in my opinion, be foisting on the world psychological and spiritual pygmies who will be a scandal to religion.'

Sister Charles Borromeo, C.S.C., a teacher of theology, was quoted as saying:

'To preserve dead forms is to create museums; to grow in living and intelligent continuity with the vital past is absolutely essential. The moment of decision would seem to be upon us, as upon the whole Church.'[1]

An increasing number of progressive nuns—precisely the 'forward-looking, constantly converting type of persons' Sister Mary William described—have recently come to the decision that they can serve the Church and the world better as lay women than within the archaic structures of the religious orders. A case symbolizing this trend was that of Jacqueline Grennan, formerly Sister Jacqueline, president of Webster College in St

[1] Reported in *NCR*, 1 September, 1965, pp. 1, 11.

Louis and one of the most outstanding nuns in the United States. Miss Grennan, who left her order in 1967 but remained as president of the college, announced that she requested a dispensation from her vows because of a personal conflict between her duties as college president and her voluntary submission as a religious to the juridical control of the Church.

Most departures of nuns have been on a strictly individual basis and not widely publicized. A dramatic mass exodus occurred, however, in August, 1967 when fifty members of the Glenmary order announced they were leaving the order to work together as lay women. The sisters said they had taken the step because they felt the restrictions of religious life interfered too much with their apostolic work. A few months previous to this decision Archbishop Karl Alter of Cincinnati had restricted the sisters' hours, table reading, educational courses, and contacts with laymen. After that, sisters started leaving the order. About twenty-five sisters had left before the fifty announced their departure as a group, leaving fewer than twenty-five in the order. The departing group said their leaving should not be pinned on the Archbishop's directives as such, but that the underlying cause was the attitude in the Church about sisters which lies behind such directives.

Changes in fact

Although the Code of Canon Law has not been officially revised, changes are taking place in practice. In Latin America women have in some instances preached at Mass: in Uruguay, for example, in the fall of 1965, on one occasion an eighteen-year-old girl ascended the pulpit following the Gospel to preach at all the Sunday Masses in the Basilica of Our Lady of the Rosary in Paysandu, the country's largest city.[1] That same year the Sacred Congregation on the Sacraments gave permission to an order of missionary sisters to distribute Holy Communion. In 1966 the Holy See gave bishops the faculty to allow mother superiors of convents to distribute Holy Communion to their communities when no priest is available. Although limited

[1] *NCR*, 24 November, 1965, p. 12.

permissions of this nature had been given during the pontificate of Pius XI and later were extended under John XXIII, a new element appears here—that is, the bishops themselves are now empowered to give permission without submitting individual cases to the Holy See.[1]

Not surprisingly, changes are most evident in areas where the Church is in greatest need, and not necessarily where the status of women is most advanced in civil society. In 1964, for example, it was reported that a small community of sisters in Brazil had begun conducting a parish at Nizia Floresta, sixty kilometers south of Natal. The superior of the community technically became 'parish vicar'. So successful has the experiment been that in 1967 it was reported that the procedure is being duplicated in a number of other parishes in that country. In these parishes sisters perform all pastoral functions except for strictly sacerdotal functions (saying Mass, hearing confessions, administering the sacrament of extreme unction); they baptize, preach, teach, preside at the liturgy of the word with eucharistic benediction, distribute Holy Communion, function as witnesses for the Church at religious marriages, and conduct funerals. In an interview, the first of the nun pastors, Sister Irany Bastos, said: 'The experiment is proving that women have more success than men in matters involving human relations.'[2]

In the United States, there has been strong opposition to change. A great deal of publicity was given to one particular parish in Oklahoma where the pastor, Fr John Bloms, cited canon law in support of his policy of having girl servers. Pointing out that according to canon 813, a priest is forbidden to say Mass without a server, he claimed that there simply are not enough boys available, particularly in these days when processions are a must. Canon 813 states that if no tonsured cleric is available, a man or a boy may serve, and that if no man or boy is available, a woman may do so 'at a distance'. But what does the expression 'at a distance' mean? Fr Bloms argued that

[1] *NCR*, 26 October, 1966, p. 5.
[2] *Informations catholiques internationales*, 15 fevrier, 1967, pp. 9–10. See also the issue for 1 mars, 1964, p. 9, for earlier report.

'in our day, distance varies from submicroscopic to astronomi-
cal. No doubt the absence of any physical contact suffices for
"at a distance".' Furthermore, since the Church has removed
the communion rail from churches, it makes no sense to speak
of a 'sanctuary'. This pastor's conviction that women should be
allowed to serve Mass came from scripture itself, he said. Christ
had women ministering to him, and it was clear to him that sex is
not a source of separation from Christ.[1]

Possibly as a result of the publicity this policy received, Fr
Bloms was ordered by his bishop to stop the practice after it
had continued for almost a year. Fr Bloms complied with the
bishop's order, but his reasoning has not changed. Referring to
recent developments in South America, he asked: 'Why is it
right in one place and not in what is supposed to be the leading
country in the world?'[2]

Those who oppose the practice of women serving at Mass
seem unable to offer reasons except that it is not in accordance
with tradition nor provided for by present regulations. Opinion
in favor of the practice is growing. One priest writes:

 ' "We didn't do it in the past" is an evasion, not an argument. It's
 about time we acknowledged that women have the dignity and holiness to serve God at his altar.'[3]

In March, 1966, it was reported that girls are serving Mass in
Holland.[4]

Conservative resistance

As in the case of almost any movement that is gathering
momentum, there has been a conservative resistance. In 1965
the Vatican post-conciliar liturgical commission issued a statement to the effect that women should not serve as lectors and
commentators at Mass. Many considered the statement as a
confusing and inconsistent step backward, but timidly complied,
not realizing that the statement was not binding. Actually, it was
purely advisory and was ignored in many places.

 [1] NCR, 24 November, 1965, p. 1, 12.
 [2] NCR, 8 December, 1965, p. 3.
 [3] NCR, 15 December, 1965, p. 4.
 [4] NCR, 16 March, 1966, p. 1.

The post-conciliar liturgical commission again disappointed liberals by reconfirming the ancient restriction against women serving at Mass. This directive appeared in a document sent to the presidents of national episcopal conferences on 25 January, 1966, but its particulars were not revealed until 29 April of that year. The document left the door open for exceptions where native traditions seem to indicate, but it was for the local bishop to decide, and he was to apply to the Holy See for permission.[1] Some observers suggested at the time that this was no cause for worrying about a permanent setback, since the 'native traditions' of countries like the United States indicate the need for 'exceptions'. They also have pointed out that liturgical developments suggest that the practice of having 'servers' at Mass, whether male or female, will become a thing of the past. In any case, it is becoming evident that in some areas—Holland for example—such directives are of minimal importance.

Other varied incidents in post-conciliar years offer evidence that the spirit of Vatican II has not yet quite permeated the atmosphere of Rome. In 1966 two women journalists were barred from entry to a ceremony in the Sistine Chapel. Writing in the British Weekly, one of these correspondents, an Anglican, told that she had received an official pass to the ceremony and had been ushered to her seat. Then an Italian bishop said to her: 'This is for the Pope a special day. We must not allow a woman to sully the Sistine Chapel for His Holiness.' She was asked to leave.[2]

It is not necessary to look to Rome for incredible happenings. In June 1966 an American woman who holds a doctorate in theology traveled to Providence, Rhode Island, to attend the annual meeting of the Catholic Theological Society of America, of which she is a member. (The society admits laymen and—in very recent times—lay women who hold doctorates in theology. Priest members need not hold doctorates.) When she attempted to enter the ballroom of the hotel in which the meeting was

[1] NCR, 11 May, 1966, p. 3.
[2] Cited in The Catholic Citizen, vol. LII, n. 5, May, 1966, p. 39.

being held, in order to attend a buffet for members of the society, she was prevented from doing so by one of the officers, a priest. When she insisted upon her right to enter, the priest threatened to call the police. She replied that in this case it would unfortunately be necessary for her to call the newspapers. After a long and humiliating scene, she was finally permitted to enter. This was the debut of the female sex in the Catholic Theological Society of America.

Another form of conservative resistance to change is the suppression of inquiry and discussion, particularly in an area where a re-examination of old customs and ideas is desperately needed. Thus, early in 1967, the Milan archdiocese forced the withdrawal of an Italian seminary professor's book criticizing the failure of Italian seminaries to prepare priests for association with women. The author, Fr Tullo Goffi, in his book, *L'integrazione affettiva del sacerdote*, maintained that in the Italian seminary the affections are repressed and seminarians are taught to fear woman as temptation incarnate. He gave extensive quotations from seminarians themselves to illustrate his point. Fr Goffi thus went to the heart of a problem which is the source of many difficulties in the Church, and which will not be resolved until open discussion and criticism is possible.

A seemingly peripheral form of conservative pressure is opposition to the attempts of religious women to initiate and experiment with reform. In March, 1967, Pope Paul warned more than one hundred superiors general, representing more than a million nuns, against excessive changes of garb, although he did favor modernizing the habit. The difficulty with this is that an increasing number of nuns are experiencing the habit— any habit—as a serious obstacle to adult interpersonal relationships.

Not surprisingly, the discussion of women's predicament in the Church has awakened a conservative backlash in the form of articles, editorials and letters to the editor. A large proportion of such utterances has come from members of the clergy, who have used a variety of tactics from misogynistic ridicule to solemn claims that women's subordination is ordained by God. A priest inquired of those who might favor the possibility of women priests: 'Will they promise that alb hem-lines will never rise and fall? ... What is the future of the biretta?'[1] As another priest letter-writer pointed out, this kind of humor tends to backfire, since the clergy are about the only male professionals who still wear skirts.

A clerical version of barbershop humor has also been used in diocesan newspaper columns. In response to a statement by a Belgian theologian, Maria Schouwenaars, that the Church needs women priests, especially in women's prisons and hospitals and in mission countries, Monsignor Charles Owen Rice, in a column in *The Pittsburgh Catholic*, drew a caricature of women as capable of nothing more than 'tears, pouting, routine deviousness, catty encounters, and petty gossip'.[2] Such playful outbursts of clerical misogynism provide ammunition for the critics, who use them as illustrations of last-ditch defensiveness against the modern world and half its inhabitants. Thus, Monsignor Rice's tirade brought on strong refutations from both male and female readers in Europe as well as in America. One of these, from the University of Tübingen, Germany, pointed out that 'it is utter perversity ... that when the concern of others is about the Gospel and reform, the clergy make of it a fight for power'.[3]

Not all manifestations of conservatism, evidently, are attempts to use satire as a weapon. Completely devoid of intentional humor, for example, were the three articles on women and the priesthood which appeared in 1965 in *L'Osservatore Romano*.[4] Their antiquated theological method and biased arguments suggest the weakness of the case as clearly as does ineffective humor in the other examples. The conservative backlash has, in any

[1] *NCR*, 24 February, 1965, p. 4.

[2] Monsignor Charles Owen Rice, 'Women Priests!', *Pittsburgh Catholic*, 21 October, 1965, p. 5.

[3] Thomas L. Thompson, in *Pittsburgh Catholic*, 18 November, 1965, p. 5. Other letters appeared in the issues of 28 October, 4 November, 11 November and 9 December.

[4] Rev. Gino Concetti, 'La Donna e il Sacerdozio', *L'Osservatore Romano*, 9 November, 1965, p. 2; 11 November, 1965, p. 2; 12 November, 1965, p. 6.

case, stimulated further discussion as interest in the problem increases.

Impetus from Protestants

Impetus continues to come as a result of the generally more liberal attitude of Protestants. Quicker to recognize the need for the churches to face up honestly to the problem of the harmful effects upon women of repeated unwanted pregnancies, their leaders have been far less prone to use abstract 'natural law' arguments concerning birth control, which overstress the biological aspects of marriage. Generally they have taken a far less legalistic and more personalist view of marriage, reflected in a realistic assessment of marital problems. Unimpeded by a rigid and anachronistic code of canon law, they have been free to consider marriage primarily as a loving union rather than chiefly as a contract for reproduction, and in this perspective have been enabled to consider both spouses as persons with equal rights. That these liberal attitudes have developed recently within the Catholic Church is undoubtedly due in part to the influence of Protestant neighbors. Repeatedly it has been observed that the thinking and practice of Catholics in predominantly Protestant regions is more sensitive to the rights of women than in the so-called Catholic countries.

Another aspect of the impetus from Protestantism derives from the fact that there are women pastors in many of the countries of northern Europe—a fact often brought up in Catholic discussions. An argument often used by conservative Catholic theologians is that the ordination of women in Protestant churches creates yet another obstacle to ecumenism. The ordination of women by the Lutheran Church in Sweden evoked such reactions a few years ago.[1] The same predictable reaction occurred in 1965 when the fifty-eighth national synod of the Reformed Church in France adopted a motion to ordain women, just as men, to all the ministries, including the pastoral ministry with all its functions. Shortly after the decision

---

[1] E.g. Rev. François-Raymond Refoulé, O.P., 'Le problème des "femmes-prêtres" en Suède', *Lumière et vie*, t. VIII, n. 43, juillet-août, 1959, pp. 65-99.

was announced, Charles Boyer, S.J., member of the Secretariat for Christian Unity, complained publicly that such decisions place an insurmountable obstacle to Christian unity.[1] The same argument was used in England in support of the negative stance of the Anglican Archbishops' Report on Women and Holy Orders, in 1966.

Critics of this sort of 'ecumenical argument' point out that since the knife cuts both ways, such polemic is futile. A persistent adherence to outmoded traditions can also be a grave obstacle to union with those whose views are shaped to the needs of the times. Proponents of the 'ecumenical argument' must consider in what direction the future lies. One signpost for the future has been the position of Episcopal Bishop James A. Pike, formerly Bishop of San Francisco, who made the following unequivocal statement:

'I am for women being ordained. I feel the question is exactly parallel to the question of race relations. There is no integral reason why any person—regardless of race or sex—should not have the same opportunities as any other.'[2]

Continuing momentum

Although some of the data we have presented may be interpreted in various ways, the indisputable fact is that the question of women's situation vis-à-vis the Church has been raised and that momentum continues.[3] During the Council and within a short period of time thereafter a number of theologians including Fathers Bernard Häring, Jean Daniélou, Georges Tavard, and Gregory Baum all publicly stated that they thought

[1] Rev. Charles Boyer, S.J., 'L'ordination des femmes', *La documentation catholique*, t. LXII, n. 1450, 20 juin, 1965, col. 1101–5.

[2] *NCR*, 1 September, 1965, p. 2.

[3] Cf.: Catherine Beaton, 'Does the Church Discriminate against Women on the Basis of their Sex?', *The Critic*, June–July, 1966, pp. 21–7; Arlene Swidler, 'The Male Church', *Commonweal*, 24 June, 1966, pp. 387–9; Rosemary Lauer, 'Women Clergy for Rome?', *The Christian Century*, 14 September, 1966, pp. 1107–10; Monsignor John D. Conway, 'Question Box', *NCR*, 16 November, 1966, p. 8; Dan Sullivan, 'Sex and the Person', *Commonweal*, 22 July, 1966, pp. 460–4; 'The Woman Intellectual and the Church', A Symposium, *Commonweal*, 27 January, 1967, pp. 446–58; Josefa Münch, 'Pourquoi je veux devenir femme prêtre', *Réalités*, juillet, 1966, pp. 79–81.

progress is possible on the question of the ordination of women. A leading Jesuit sociologist, Joseph Fichter, speaking at the National Conference of Diocesan Vocation Directors in Milwaukee in 1966, affirmed his opinion that the Church should consider ordaining women as well as married men to the priesthood. In that same year a group of thirty-five scholars (canonists, theologians, sociologists and historians) who met in Pittsburgh sent to Rome numerous proposals for the reform of canon law. Among other things, in calling for 'full participation of women in the life of the Church', certain of the group conceded that 'full participation' could be interpreted to include ordination.

No doubt many hope that if they just close their eyes the whole thing will quietly blow over—that the 'new breed' and the *avant-garde* types will eventually fade into merited oblivion, and then we can 'get back to normal'. Such wishful thinkers might ponder the following item which appeared in the Catholic press—an item small in size but large in significance:

'To the Editors:
Dear Brothers in Christ,
Why do you think that we should not have girl servers? We should be a family. We would rather have girls and boys serving. Just because boys are stronger than girls it doesn't mean that boys have to serve everyday. Are there some of you who don't like girl servers? Please tell us why you don't like them? We can't think of any good reason. I am a girl and I would really aprishiate it if girls could serve at the altar. If everyone would only try it. After all we are a Christian family, and Christ wants us to do things together.
Love,
Rita Martin
Ada, Ola.
I am in the third grade. From St Joseph School.'[1]

On the basis of such evidence, it seems reasonable to suspect that something even more disturbing than the 'new breed' lurks menacingly on the horizon. The breed of tomorrow will have many questions.

[1] *NCR*, 15 December, 1965, p. 4.

CHAPTER FOUR

The Pedestal Peddlars

'The conditions and the aims of life are both represented in religion poetically, but this poetry tends to
arrogate to itself literal truth and moral authority,
neither of which it possesses.'

George Santayana

Despite the steady progress toward recognition of women's personal rights and autonomy, stereotypes concerning their supposed 'nature' have continued to reappear in modern and
contemporary thought. This tendency toward stereotypes is not
limited to theologians. It is to be found in the works of philosophers (e.g. Teilhard de Chardin, Jaspers, Edith Stein,
Whitehead, Berdyaev, Buytendijk), psychoanalysts (e.g. Freud,
Jung, Deutsch), poets (e.g. Claudel, Dylan Thomas), as well as
on the popular level in the women's magazines and in adver-
tizing. Somewhat counterbalancing these, there are thinkers of
the environmentalist school, who stress the impact of cultural
institutions in forcing people into stereotyped sex roles. These
include theologians (e.g. D. S. Bailey), philosophers (Sartre,
S. de Beauvoir, E. Metzke, A. Jeannière), psychoanalysts
(Horney, Laing), sociologists (Riesman, Rossi), anthropologists
(Mead).

The myth of the 'eternal feminine'

Although among progressive Catholic theologians and writers
there is an increasing trend away from the stereotypes, there
has been a continual stream of Catholic works of a semi-theo-
logical nature, which are based upon the 'eternal feminine'
motif. Fundamentally, their authors are not at all disposed to

abandon the ancient prejudices. Thus the French Dominican theologian, A.-M. Henry, writing within the past decade, apparently saw nothing incongruous in the following assertion:

'In that balanced century (the thirteenth) St Thomas had a notion of the respective situations of the spouses in the home which, even despite certain exaggerations, appears sound to us today.'[1]

For the most part, these authors would keep woman on a pedestal at all costs, paralyzing her will to freedom and personhood. A classic of this brand of Catholic thinking is Gertrud von le Fort's book, *The Eternal Woman*, first published in Germany in 1934. Over one hundred thousand copies of the German original were sold, and the book was translated into French, Italian, Spanish, Portuguese, and English. Its influence can be traced in a number of derivative works which perpetuate its basic fallacy, namely the confusion of 'symbolic significance' with concrete, historical reality.

Gertrud von le Fort's book develops many of the key themes of the 'eternal feminine' school. It claims to interpret

'the significance of woman, not in the light of her psychological or biological, her historical or social position, but under her symbolic aspect.'[2]

Such a project was doomed to be abortive, since it did not recognize the truth that man's symbolism is derived precisely from psychological, biological, historical, and social facts. Moreover, these facts are changing. Since Von le Fort and others of this school are fundamentally anti-evolutionistic as concerns women, they attempt to draw from contingent and changing situations certain 'immutable' symbols and then to arrest the evolution of the situation by forcing it into the mold of these symbols drawn from past experience. This process has a great attraction for a certain type of mentality (that of William James's 'tender-minded' variety), which prefers easy metaphors to a critical

---

[1] A. M. Henry, O.P., 'Pour une théologie de la féminité', *Lumière et vie*, t. XIII, n. 43, juillet-août, 1959, p. 123.
[2] Gertrud von le Fort, *The Eternal Woman*, translated by Placid Jordan O.S.B. (Milwaukee: Bruce, 1962), p. xiii.

examination of the facts of concrete experience. It is also a useful rhetorical method for those who have some psychological motivation, either conscious or unconscious, for attempting to preserve the *status quo*. Inevitably the writer is unable to stay on the high level of pure symbolism, and continually descends to the level of historical fact, making dogmatic assertions about what should or should not be the 'role' of existing individuals, in order to keep them in line with the immutable symbols.

The characteristics of the Eternal Woman are opposed to those of a developing, authentic *person*, who will be unique, self-critical, self-creating, active and searching. By contrast to these authentic personal qualities, the Eternal Woman is said to have a vocation to surrender and hiddenness; hence the symbol of the veil. Self-less, she achieves not individual realization but merely generic fulfillment in motherhood, physical or spiritual (the wife is always a 'mother to her husband' as well as to her children). She is said to be timeless and conservative by nature. She is shrouded in 'mystery', because she is not recognized as a genuine human person. Thus, the poet Claudel in his preface to *Partage de Midi* wrote of woman that she is 'someone on whose brow is inscribed the word "mystery"'. It is, of course, the 'symbol' of woman that these authors are talking about, but the symbol turns out to be normative for the individual. It is significant that the same alienating procedure is not attempted with the same degree of thoroughness for the male. There are only hints in the writings of the Eternal Woman devotees of what the Eternal Man might be. The androcentric society which engenders this type of speculation tends to see men, but not women, in personalist rather than in static, symbolic categories.

Characteristically, the 'eternal feminine' school is radically opposed to female emancipation. For Von le Fort, the feminist movement had a 'tragic' motivation. It was a result of the 'dissonance which had come about in feminine nature'.[1] She imagines that prior to this time the home had offered the possibility of absolute fulfillment for the married woman and

[1] Von le Fort, *op. cit.*, p. 48.

even for the unmarried woman. Unable to focus on the advantages of the movement, she writes of its 'tragic drawbacks'. For example, it is hard to get women 'to do the work of domestic servants which is so rewarding and so naturally in keeping with woman's calling'.[1]

Von le Fort also distrusts technical progress which emancipates women from some of the burdens of maternity:

> 'The advantage that the future mother derives from the clinic, for her own health and that of her child, is purchased at the expense of tearing away the mystery of birth not only from the shared experience of the family . . . but also from the awesomeness of the primal powers that are its carriers.'

This brings about 'a disappearance of respect for the sovereignty of nature'.[2] Consistently with all of this, the ultimate achievement of emancipation within the Church, accession to the hierarchy, is viewed as forever impossible:

> 'The priesthood could not be confided to woman, for thereby the very meaning of woman in the Church would have been eliminated.'[3]

Thus on all fronts the Eternal Woman is the enemy of the individual woman looking for self-realization and creative expansion of her own unique personhood. As Von le Fort admitted: 'The mother as such does not bear the individualizing marks of the person.'[4]

A clue to the fears and motivations behind the opposition to emancipation can be seen in the repeated use of the term 'masculinization'. It is indeed characteristic of the opposition that it interprets woman's efforts to become more completely human as efforts to become 'masculine'. Nicholas Berdyaev, for example, thought that the modern movement for the emancipation of women 'seeks to lead them along masculine ways'. This interpretation has been applauded by Catholic

[1] *Ibid.*, p. 53.
[2] *Ibid.*, p. 66.
[3] *Ibid.*, pp. 94–5.
[4] *Ibid.*, p. 64.

authors. Such confused thinking arises from the fact that in the past and still today many functions and activities which are quite naturally human and which have nothing specifically sexual about them have been appropriated by the males. Yet there is more involved than a mere naive confusion based on custom. This can be seen from Berdyaev's remark that the drive for emancipation is 'an anti-hierarchic, a leveling movement'. The opponents of emancipation have always wanted to keep the *hierarchical* form of man-woman relationship, which implies all the not all easily relinquished privileges of male headship.

A similar theme is found in the writings of Teilhard de Chardin. Though he was a vigorous evolutionist with many optimistic and liberating ideas about sexual relationship, Teilhard failed to extend the implications of his dynamic vision to the feminine half of the human race. Thus, while he favored 'a certain emancipation', he was fearful lest this go so far as to 'masculinize' her, or 'take away the character of illuminating and idealizing power which she exercises by the simple action of presence and as at rest'. He even praised—as 'the most perspicacious of all'

'the old French conception (doubtless a little narrow and jealous) which made of the woman a luminous and inspiring influence, and placed her outside the tumult and prose of action.'[1]

The last words are especially significant, for they express a desire, dear to all of the 'eternal feminine' school, that woman should be kept out from where the action is, not for her sake, but for man's sake. Deprived of the means to achieve her own personhood, she presumably will inspire the man to achieve his. Even if this would 'work'—and there is no reason to think that an underdeveloped person should be more 'inspiring'—it is impossible to justify the thesis that one half of the race should automatically be sacrificed for the sake of the other half.

For the symbolic, non-empirical thinker, disturbing facts cause no snags in the well-ordered dream world of symbols, for the

---

[1] Teilhard de Chardin, *Genèse d'une Pensée* (Paris: Grasset, 1961), pp. 154–5.

basic ambiguity of the symbols renders them elastic, and by a selective presentation and interpretation of facts he can place these intruders at the service of a thesis to be preserved at all costs. Thus, even the woman who is a person capable of achievement preserves the veil motif, according to Von le Fort, because 'woman's contribution at best can occupy but a secondary place'.[1] Inconsistently enough, she admits the disturbing fact that some few women do reach the heights but, without missing a beat, she quickly veils these cases:

> 'The veil motif is still discernible, however, when woman actually does attain to some ultimate height of achievement, for then a charismatic vocation becomes more evident in her work than in the work of a man.'[2]

Even such phenomena as the Church's 'apparent lack of estimation of the mother' are smoothly taken care of. This attitude of the Church

> 'accentuates her actual dignity because it is an attitude signifying the utter humility of nature in its complete surrender . . . yet by this very attitude rising above itself to the level of the words of the Magnificat: "He hath exalted the humble".'[3]

It seems that there is no veil thick enough to hide the multitude of inconsistencies of the Eternal Woman thesis.

The 'eternal feminine' symbolism is almost invariably flattering to the male. The built-in bias is sometimes so irrational and loaded with unintended irony as to be truly comic. Thus the poet Claudel wrote in *The Tidings Brought to Mary*:

> 'Man is the priest; but woman's privilege is to sacrifice herself.'

Louis Bouyer proclaims:

> 'Femininity is a sign of the essential incompleteness of the creature.'[4]

---

[1] Von le Fort, *op. cit.*, p. 27.
[2] *Ibid.*
[3] *Ibid.*, p. 88.
[4] Louis Bouyer, *The Seat of Wisdom* (New York: Pantheon, 1962), p. 87.

Teilhard de Chardin tended to see woman as analogous to matter; man, to spirit; and matter is, of course, for the sake of spirit, which emerges from it.[1] Subtly flattering to the male is the invariable tendency of the Eternal Woman school to describe woman strictly within the categories of virgin, bride, and mother, thus considering her strictly in terms of sexual relationship, whether in a negative or a positive sense. It would not occur to such writers to apply this reductive system to the male, compressing his whole being into the categories of 'virgin, husband, and father'.

Recent attempts to rejuvenate the Eternal Woman

Especially instructive are more recent attempts of the 'eternal feminine' writers to sustain their thesis in the face of continuing social evolution. Often, these attempts involve incredible inconsistencies. Thus, Father F. X. Arnold bends over backward to identify and criticize the antifeminist errors of the past, and then proceeds to perpetuate them. Having condemned the notoriously negative remarks of Nietzsche on the subject, in the very next chapter he cites that unhappy bachelor as an authority, heartily agreeing with one of the most alienating theses of all:

'Man's happiness, as Nietzsche said, is "my will". Woman's happiness is "his will".'[2]

Once this biased hypothesis is granted, of course, the way to social evolution is blocked; justification for the continued, or renewed, oppression of women is there in full measure. And this, in a kind of modified, adapted way, is what Father Arnold wants. In fact, he praises the 'prophetic vision' of Pius XI's Encyclical Letter, *Casti Connubii*, which condemned the 'threefold emancipation' of women. Father Arnold even goes so far as to call the father 'the head, the king, the appointed representative of authority in the family', and the *episcopus*

---

[1] Cf. André A. Devaux, 'Le féminin selon Teilhard de Chardin', *Recherches et débats, op. cit.,* cahier n. 45, décembre, 1963, pp. 125–6.
[2] F.X. Arnold, *Woman and Man: Their Nature and Mission* (Freiburg: Herder, 1963), p. 47.

of his house.[1] Such patriarchal, regressive terminology is ironic, confirming the evidence given in support of the first sentence of his book:

'Far too often the world and the Church, as well as secular and ecclesiastical history, have been looked at totally and exclusively from a masculine viewpoint.'[2]

Typical of the method of those who would perpetuate woman's imprisonment on her time-honored pedestal is a pseudo-psychology, which is manifest in their uncritical interpretation of certain behavior patterns as coming from some immutable 'nature', without considering the possibility that this behavior is in large measure the effect of early and subtle conditioning. Thus, evidence of the 'spiritual and mental distinction between the sexes' is seen by Father Arnold in the fact that boys play with steam engines, 'giving early evidence of the signs of coming power', whereas girls play with doll houses.[3] The fact that boys are given steam engines and forcefully discouraged if they show any signs of interest in dolls is simply not taken into account. So also, Fathers Danniel and Oliver, in their revealingly entitled book, *Woman is the Glory of Man*, make undemonstrated universalizations. Thus woman, 'whose entire psychology is founded upon the primordial tendency to love',[4] is said to have 'a natural spontaneity toward submission',[5] and to be 'more easily subject to illusions'.[6] Those who fail to fit into this pattern are dismissed as not being 'true women'.

Not only a pseudo-psychology, but also a pseudo-biology becomes the instrument of the contemporary pedestal peddlers. Danniel and Oliver resort to some amazing hypotheses from biology. Thus: 'Her brain is generally lighter and simpler than man's, which may explain her lesser capacity for

---

[1] *Ibid.*, p. 149–50.
[2] *Ibid.*, p. 9.
[3] *Ibid.*, p. 49.
[4] E. Danniel and B. Oliver, *Woman is the Glory of Man*, translated by Angeline Bouchard (Westminster, Maryland: The Newman Press, 1966), p. 21.
[5] *Ibid.*, p. 24.
[6] *Ibid.*, p. 81.

deduction.'[1] Apparently aware that her alleged 'lesser capacity for deduction' is less than self-evident and can easily be disputed on the basis of widely recorded academic achievement, these authors have a ready explanation:

> 'The natural plasticity of girls enables them to adapt quite easily to masculine methods. Girls often prove to be more diligent workers, and so make better grades than boys.'[2]

No hearing at all is given to the obvious objection that superior achievement on the part of some girls just might be due to a superior native intelligence and to a natural aptitude for methods which are quite normally human and by no means specifically 'masculine'.

Intimately connected with the pseudo-science of the contemporary pedestal pushers is the elasticity of the notions employed, which can be stretched to cover any embarrassing facts of experience. Thus, Danniel and Oliver note that men, too, as well as women, are intuitive, emotional, have a sense of unity, are influenced by likes and dislikes, etc. However, men are said to have these qualities in a 'different' way. Thus:

> 'Man looks to intuition merely as a stimulus and a guide, and constantly submits its ideas to the grueling examination of his logic.'[3]

However, if women attempt to control intuition in this reasonable way, they are accused of becoming 'too intensively intellectualized by masculine methods' so that they 'gradually lose many of their intuitive qualities'.[4]

Obviously, within the artificial world of this ideology, there is no room for development. The formula is very simple: once the *a priori* norms of femininity have been set up, all of the exceptions are classified as 'de-feminized'. Criticism is directed exclusively toward individuals who fail to conform; never is it directed to the assumptions of the ideology itself. This can be seen in the way in which the question of 'women in authority'

[1] *Ibid.*, p. 12.
[2] *Ibid.*, p. 10.
[3] *Ibid.*, p. 8.
[4] *Ibid.*, p. 12.

is handled. There are 'two pitfalls' for the woman exercising authority 'of the masculine type'. These are 'the danger of becoming masculine' and 'the danger of transforming into faults normal feminine reactions'.[1] What this means is that if the woman fails to exercise authority well, she is being 'feminine'; if she succeeds, this is a sure sign that she is too 'masculine'. Moral: she cannot win.

Unwittingly, Gertrud von le Fort herself suggested the most efficacious means of defeating the Eternal Woman game:

'But when the woman seeks herself, her metaphysical mystery is extinguished; for in raising up her own image she destroys the image that is eternal.'[2]

It is precisely this—the emergence of a significant number of creative women who will *raise up their own image*—that can significantly weaken the hold of the paralyzing stereotypes upon human consciousness. There are signs of hope, as the 'eternal feminine' writers themselves note with alarm. Danniel and Oliver have remarked that the number of 'de-feminized' women is constantly growing. And Gertrud von le Fort wrote, in *The Eternal Woman*:

'Modern woman is to some extent no longer the one with whom this book is concerned.'[3]

Theological distortions

Another aspect of the 'eternal feminine' phenomenon must be considered in this context, and this is the use of Catholic doctrine to perpetuate the symbol syndrome. Before we do so, we need to agree that there are many other contributing sources which have nothing directly to do with the Church, although they undoubtedly influence Catholic authors. These non-church sources include the myths of advertisers who reduce the image of woman to that of sex object; the theories of educators

[1] *Ibid.*, p. 27.
[2] von le Fort, *op. cit.*, p. 7.
[3] *Ibid.*, p. 54.

who promote a rigid, role-determining program of studies for girls; theories of doctrinaire Freudian psychologists who classify women's efforts at being human as 'penis-envy'; and the operative philosophy of the editors of women's magazines that glorify only the 'happy housewife heroine'. These have been studied in other books. What we are concerned with here is a species of delusion peculiar to Catholic thinking which is especially potent because it surrounds itself with an aura of alleged divine approval. This delusion is rather complex. It can best be described in connection with two phrases familiar to Catholic ears which, though they may be innocuous in themselves, tend to accumulate assumptions and associations which are highly questionable. These two phrases are 'the divine plan' (with its variations, such as 'God's plan', 'God's ordinance', 'divinely ordained', 'Christ's plan', 'inspired by God'), and 'Mary as the model of all women'.

'The divine plan', to start with, is often used by religious authors and speakers to buttress claims for which there is no conclusive argument. Generally, the phrase or one of its variations is accompanied by some claims about 'nature' and her 'laws'. Since the various sciences keep turning up with more and more disconcerting facts and theories which defy the old simplifications about mother nature and her 'laws', the need is seen to appeal to a higher court. What could be higher or more unassailable than 'the divine plan'? Thus, Father Arnold alludes to 'the divinely ordained hierarchy between man and woman in marriage, in the family and in public life'.[1] Monsignor Alberione, Italian author of a work on women which was translated into English and published in the United States, illustrates the technique so obviously that the unconscious parody would make even the Eternal Woman see the point and laugh behind her veil:

'Lest we forget, let it be repeated here once more: Woman's true sphere is within the family circle. He who would substitute any-

---

[1] Arnold, *op. cit.*, p. 148.

thing else, frustrates her true nature, disrupts the providential plan of God and creates serious problems for society at large, which becomes filled with neurotic, unhappy, useless and very often, and worst of all, disruptive women!'[1]

There are several points to be noticed about the use of the 'God's plan' terminology. First, as is generally recognized by those who study the uses of language, words and phrases are often used (consciously or unconsciously) for purposes other than that of communicating ideas. They may be used to arouse a desired emotional response, unaccompanied by any critical understanding, as all good orators know. The eighteenth century philosopher George Berkeley accurately described this phenomenon:

'At first, indeed, the words might have occasioned ideas that were fitting to produce those emotions; but, if I mistake not, it will be found that when language is once grown familiar, the hearing of the sounds or sight of the characters is oft immediately attended with those passions, which at first were wont to be produced by the intervention of ideas, that are now quite omitted. . . . For example, when a schoolman tells me, "Aristotle hath said it", all I conceive he means by it is to dispose me to embrace his opinion with the deference and submission which custom has annexed to that name.'[2]

If 'Aristotle' can elicit such a reaction, how much more so can 'God'.

When an audience which has been conditioned by Catholic training hears or sees the words 'divine plan', 'divinely ordained', etc., there tends to be a response of awe and reverence, and an inclination to assent to whatever is being proposed as God's plan. This effect is greatly increased if the people are made to feel that the speaker or writer has a position of authority in the Church and a claim to some esoteric body of know-

---

[1] Very Rev. James Alberione, S.S.P., S.T.D., *Woman: Her Influence and Zeal as an Aid to the Priesthood*, translated by the Daughters of St Paul (Boston: St Paul Editions, 1964), p. 40.
[2] George Berkeley, *A Treatise Concerning the Principles of Human Knowledge*, n. 20.

ledge which they themselves lack. Therefore the popularity of such devices as the 'God's plan' rhetoric among clerical authors and speakers is not surprising. Nor is it surprising that the phrase occurs with great frequency when the doctrine proposed is open to attack as contrary to reason, or to custom, or to social justice. 'God', after all, could propose nothing unreasonable, unfitting, or unjust. The Eternal Woman proponents are now especially in need of such a device, since they are working against an aspect of social evolution which is constantly gaining momentum.

In the second place, the 'God's plan' theme is very frequently used to close discussion on positions which are not only open to challenge from the various 'profane' sciences, but from theology as well. These authors take advantage of their readers' ignorance of the fact that theology, too, is evolving, and of the fact that there is a variety of opinion among scholars and theologians on the interpretation of nearly every significant document and on the approach to nearly every important problem. The fact is that theological opinion concerning the man-woman relationship is evolving, and shows every sign of continuing to do so, largely because of pressure from social processes and because of new insights from non-theological disciplines. Theological opinion about the place of women in the Church is also changing. There are all shades of opinion on the many issues surrounding these two central themes. The writers who are prone to invoke the 'divine plan' hide this variety behind the monolithic mask of a supposedly changeless ideology.

We may say, in the third place, that the use of such terminology not only suggests the user's rhetorical purpose but also reflects a naive simplicism. It requires a lack of appreciation of the complexity of reality, and a lack of insight concerning the limitations, projection mechanisms and other 'tricks' of one's own mind, to be able to set down with a clear conscience the specifics of the 'divine plan'. To whom has God confided his blueprints? Upon reflection, therefore, it appears that such verbal devices, which are meant to arouse reverence, should instead be recognized as warning signals.

The second seemingly innocent but loaded phrase deserving review—a phrase which is often both the effect and the cause of delusions—is 'Mary as the model of all women'. The dimensions of the problem with which we are confronted here are suggested by the following remark:

'Devotion to Mary is, without fail, the best experience capable of opening to the priest "the metaphysical world of woman".'[1]

It does not require a specialized knowledge of psychology to be aware of some of the difficulties involved in supporting this hypothesis. First, there are the projection mechanisms by which one may be deluded in his well-meaning 'devotion to Mary'. Not to be forgotten is the fact that the promotion of Marian devotion has largely been the work of a celibate clergy, whose manner of life has cut them off not only from marriage and sexual experience, but also from most of the normal day to day personal relationships which alone can provide a realistic understanding of persons of the opposite sex. The confessional is hardly a situation for normal dialogue, and it is probable that the types of women who turn consistently to the clergy for advice are often over-dependent and obsessive. Even in apparently normal social contacts between a woman and a priest, there are psychological barriers on both sides. The isolated seminary education of the priest has ill-prepared him for such social encounters, so that what takes place is often play-acting rather than honest dialogue. Not infrequently, therefore, one finds among the Catholic clergy a warped and pessimistic view of women which is based upon narrow, selective, or even vicarious experience.

Some of the excesses of Marianism may well be accounted for by this situation of the celibate clergy. There is evidence enough to give rise to suspicions that compensation mechanisms have a great deal to do with some forms of devotion to Mary. A seminarian in Rome remarked that his 'spiritual director' told him that when he was troubled by 'bad thoughts' he should immediately try to think about Mary. Such advice ap-

[1] Devaux, 'Le féminin selon Teilhard de Chardin', op. cit., p. 134.

pears to be rather common, if not always as crude and obvious as this. In any case, the 'beloved in heaven' idea leaves something to be desired. What it can spawn is that dream world which is precisely 'the metaphysical world of woman', the ideal, static woman, who is so much less troublesome than the real article. Since she belongs to 'another world', she cannot compete with man. Safely relegated to her pedestal, she serves his purpose, his psychological need, without having any purpose of her own. For the celibate who prefers not to be tied down to a wife, or whose canonical situation forbids marriage, the 'Mary' of his imagination could appear to be the ideal spouse.

While none of this precludes a genuine devotion to Mary on the part of men or women, married or celibate, it does suggest the real possibility of self-delusion. Is it mere coincidence that the countries most noted for their 'devotion to Mary' are those in which the clergy have the greatest power and in which the legal and social situation of women is demonstrably the most retarded? This schizophrenic situation appears to be a peculiarity of Catholic culture, especially in countries where the culture bears most clearly the marks of clerical influence, without the challenge and modifications arising from opposed influences, as is the case in pluralistic societies.

The idea, then, that 'devotion to Mary is, without fail, the best experience capable of opening to the priest "the metaphysical world" of woman' is highly questionable. How does the priest know that his devotion is not, at least in part, a confused product of his own psychology? The realism that comes from dialogue, from the realm of concrete human experience, is a more trustworthy source of understanding of the opposite sex. Moreover, when this understanding is developed, it will be discovered that there is no 'metaphysical world' peculiar to women, except in the foggy realm of the mind's own symbols. But women in fact are not symbols; they are people, and each person is a unique subject. To consider a person—a subject—as a symbol is to treat him or her as an object, which is fundamentally an egoistic and hostile act.

As remarked earlier some questionable assumptions have attached to the idea of 'Mary as the model of all women'. In the first place the phrase assumes that a great deal is known about that historical personage. In fact, very little is known. Deficiencies in historical knowledge have been filled in by creative imagination, often in the circumstances just described. Furthermore, it has also been falsely assumed that historical circumstances are irrelevant, and so it has been argued that since Mary did not act as a leader, modern women should not attempt that role. The greatest confusion, however, comes from the assumption that the relationship between Christ and Mary should serve as a model for the man-woman relationship.

All three of these assumptions are operative in much writing on woman's place in the Church, notably in that of the Jesuit theologian J. Galot, who attempts to outline in detail the 'divine plan' for women on the basis of a universalization of certain ideas about Mary contained in Vatican II's Dogmatic Constitution on the Church (*Lumen Gentium*). Admitting that the Council did not have the purpose of envisaging the mission which God assigns in general to women in the Church, but rather confines itself to some statements about Mary, Father Galot seizes upon these statements and adds to them considerably:

'In Mary are revealed the intentions of the divine plan concerning the whole of femininity.'[1]

This assumption invokes the whole fallacious process of spinning a 'theology of woman' out of Marian doctrine, in which process fantasy fills the void left by unknown historical fact and universalizes with naive abandon.

The most catastrophic aspect of this method is its simplistic analogizing from the Christ-Mary relationship to the man-woman relationship in general. The inevitable fruit of this method, despite the elaborate precautions of its proponents, is the relegating of the woman to a hopelessly inferior situation. Thus, Father Galot argues that as Christ *operated* and Mary, being totally dependent, merely *cooperated*, so it is, analogously, with the respective roles of men and women in the Church.

[1] J. Galot, S.J., *L'église et la femme* (Gembloux: J. Duculot, 1965), p. 6.

The clue to the meaning of women's 'cooperation' is 'receptivity'. Thus it follows, we are told, that man has the mission to preach and woman has the mission to listen. However, we are assured this does not reduce the feminine role to something small, for 'in willing to listen and assimilate, woman is rendering service to the man who speaks'.[1] There is no evidence that the author intends the obvious irony. With incredible naiveté the argument concludes with the affirmation that this silence is what permits woman to play a veritable role, that of receiving the word of God and thus of making it penetrate more deeply into humanity.[2] If logic were at all operative here, it would follow that, given this total identification of the individual with a fixed sex 'role', it should be impossible for the male to receive the word of God, and then, of course, it would follow that he could not transmit it. However, in this happy dream world of reified symbols, no embarrassing logic or facts are admitted.

Inevitably, given this framework, woman is seen as a 'relative being'. Submission and self-effacement are her lot. Since it is impossible to stay on the wave length of the Christ-Mary analogy without becoming at least subliminally aware of interference from reality, the analogy is generally supported with affirmations about woman's 'nature' which make it all appear to turn out just right. She is said to be 'disposed by nature' to subordinate her nature to another, to be 'docile', to be 'less apt at reasoning'. Thus, Father Galot supports his flimsy analogical argument for the exclusion of women from preaching with a pronouncement about 'her' (never 'their') capacities. 'God's choice', he writes, 'is based upon masculine aptitudes.' Having spent two hundred pages exaggerating woman's 'receptivity', he now comes to the real issue:

> 'She is less capable of receiving the doctrinal deposit objectively, of mastering its essential lines by a vigorous synthesis, of submitting it to a rational work of elaboration and of explicitation, and of transmitting it objectively after having re-thought it.'[3]

[1] *Ibid.*, p. 57.
[2] *Ibid.*
[3] *Ibid.*, p. 200.

The generalizing 'she' suggests that all women are inferior in this respect, or should be, according to their 'nature'. Regressing to the stage of theological development represented by the most antifeminist of the Fathers, Father Galot sees woman as a weak daughter of Eve:

'She has not lost the dispositions of impressionability and mobility which Eve had manifested in the initial drama of humanity. She remains fragile, more subject to an unreflected impulse, and more accessible to seduction.'[1]

It is characteristic of this species of symbol-oriented writing that it nearly always refers to 'woman', rather than to 'women'. The static, symbolic point of view does not take into account plurality, which implies variety. It is hierarchical, but not pluralistic. It sees polarity, but not individuality; specific complementarity, but not the likeness and autonomous self-realization which are the basis of all genuine friendship.

Although symbols play an irreplaceable part in man's thought processes, there is always the danger that they will distract him from the arduous work of wrestling with the problems presented by the complexity of reality itself and of his own mind. Symbols, which record human experience in shorthand, stress similarities—some of the frequently repeated elements of experience. What they leave out are the differences. It is especially the uniqueness and dynamism of the person which cannot be captured in the symbol.

The symbol, however, has seductive power. It is grasped without effort, and it generally conveys some recognizable truth. Distortion occurs when this truth is accepted as the whole truth. The 'old man' serves well enough as a symbol for wisdom and the 'step-mother' for wickedness, but old men are not always wise, nor are stepmothers always wicked. To use the symbol, which is largely derived from collective past experience, as a norm for the future development of individuals is to confer upon it an adequacy and an authority which it does not possess, and to take up arms against the dynamic potential of persons.

[1] *Ibid.*, p. 79.

Symbols 'like living beings, grow and die', as theologian Paul Tillich pointed out. 'They grow when the situation is ripe for them, and they die when the situation changes.' It is no secret that the 'eternal feminine' is fading. Berdyaev and Rilke have written hopefully, but without evidence, of its future resurrection. Some persist in advertising a remodeled pedestal, but their success is comparable to that of antique dealers who manage to do a thriving business with a narrow range of customers, but hardly can be said to be altering the course of history.

CHAPTER FIVE

The Demon of Sexual Prejudice:
An Exercise in Exorcism

'Exorcism is that process by which the stubborn deposits of town and tribal pasts are scraped from the social consciousness of man and he is freed to face his world matter-of-factly.'

Harvey Cox

A striking characteristic of the 'eternal feminine' phenomenon is that it is both cause and (to a degree) effect of insensitivity to injustice. So seductive is the ideology that the concrete problems of individuals seeking liberty escape the attention of its adherents, whose eyes are fixed upon the static symbol, rather than upon the varied and dynamic beings who exist in this world. Thus, the dehumanizing aspects of exclusive male headship are discreetly passed over. So too, the effects of inferior education and opportunity are ignored, while energy is expended in describing the imagined 'evils' of equality.

The breeding of insensitivity to the situation of another through stereotypes is a widespread phenomenon, which is not confined to the problem of women. The images of the 'greedy Jew' and the 'lazy Negro' have the same effect. In each case, the victim is seen as completely 'other', not as a person with whom one can identify or enter into a relationship of friendship and respect. The stereotype provides a built-in excuse for not taking the necessary steps to discover its unreliability.

Failure to resist exploitation

There is much more to the problem than this. One complication is that many women themselves seem to justify the insensitivity to the 'feminine problem'. Some of them have been ardent promoters of the 'eternal feminine' (Gertrud von le Fort, Ida Görres, Phyllis McGinley). More important perhaps, the majority of women have never protested their relegation, in theory and in social fact, to sub-human categories. African women, on the whole, did not rebel against such horrors as ritual mutilation or such indignities as the bride-price. Moslem women for the most part did not protest against the institution of the harem. The majority of European and American women did not go out and campaign for the vote, for equal education and professional opportunity, or for legal reforms. And the vast majority of Catholic women have not protested their passive and voiceless position in the Church. All of this would seem to support the 'eternal feminine' conception of women as naturally passive and docile beings.

This failure to oppose exploitation might be explained in part by lack of opportunity to protest and by the fear characteristic of those who are in a subordinate position. It might also be explained partly by ignorance of the facts—the euphemisms about women's privileged position disguise antifeminist theories and attitudes which are operative in society. There is also a strong probability that pre-occupation with self-interest obscures the problem for many who vaguely feel that the given system has worked out well enough for themselves, and are too comfortable to bother to abstract from their own condition and see the more general aspects of the situation. Female antifeminists are often members of a privileged class who are blind to the problems of their less privileged sisters. Thus Gertrud von le Fort could write about how 'rewarding' is the work of a domestic servant, never having had to bear the 'rewards' of such an existence. Then too, there is the lulling effect of habit and custom. The reminder that 'everyone' behaves this way, or that things have 'always' been this way has stopped many a logical train of thought from pursuing its course.

The foregoing explanations have value but they are not completely satisfactory.

Why do so many, who should be able to see through the

euphemisms, not see? Why is there not a greater effort to abstract from one's own particular situation. Why has custom had such a stranglehold in this area?

Evidently a psychological mechanism is operative at a deeper level than that touched by any of the reasons we have given so far. This mechanism is not peculiar to women, but is common to those who belong to an oppressed class. Richard Wright gave a simple but apt description of how this mechanism operates in the case of Negroes in *Black Boy*:

> 'I began to marvel at how smoothly the black boys acted out the roles that the white race had mapped out for them. Most of them were not conscious of living a special, separate, stunted way of life. Yet I knew that in some period of their growing up—a period that they had no doubt forgotten—there had been developed in them a delicate, sensitive controlling mechanism that shut off their minds and emotions from all that the white race had said was taboo. Although they lived in America where in theory there existed equality of opportunity, they knew unerringly what to aspire to and what not to aspire to. Had a black boy announced that he aspired to be a writer, he would have been unhesitatingly called crazy by his pals. Or had a black boy spoken of yearning to get a seat on the New York Stock Exchange, his friends—in the boy's own interests—would have reported his odd ambition to the white boss.'

A similar process takes place in other groups who are forced to accept a stunted manner of living. This is also true of women, who in the past and to some extent even today (in varying shades of subtlety according to various cultural patterns) have been conditioned to accept a mutilated existence as normal.

Help in understanding how this mechanism is developed comes from the psychoanalytic theory of repression and projection. Since certain feelings are not permitted by society to have expression, these are often projected to other persons or to whole groups. Thus, the Jews in Germany and Negroes in the United States and South Africa serve as receptacles for the repressed problems of the majority in those societies. This, of course, requires a corresponding mechanism, which Freud called 'introjection', by which the 'inferior' accepts the role imposed upon him. Sartre has illustrated this in describing what happened to Jean Genet, who as a child was accused by the 'honest' villagers of being a thief. Thus the 'honest' people were able to use Genet; they could hate in him that part of themselves which they had denied and projected into him. As Genet became the 'thief' which the villagers wanted him to be, so a Negro child becomes the 'lazy nigger' which the white citizens want him to be. So, too, do girls accept a limiting and stunting role for themselves in a society which expects this of them. This whole process of 'role psychology' or 'self-fulfilling prophecy' involves a vicious circle. Members of the oppressed or minority group have no other images with which to identify than those forced upon them by the dominant class. Slowly these persons learn to live out what is expected of them. Since they do, in fact, become inferior in just the way society desires, the prejudice is reinforced. If someone questions the prejudice, numerous examples can be pointed to as 'evidence' that the stereotype is well grounded in 'nature'. The 'niggers' who are thieves, the Jews who are sly and greedy, the 'true women' who are naively spontaneous, self-abasing, and narcissistic are there in abundance, frustrating attempts to break out of the magic circle. Which is to say that the images are self-perpetuating.

Demonic distortions

In his stimulating book, *The Secular City,* theologian Harvey Cox has described with logic and power the need for the Church to fulfill its role as cultural exorcist. This means that the Church has the duty of exorcising the 'demons' which are born of the projection-introjection mechanisms.

> 'Jesus calls men to adulthood,' he says, 'a condition in which they are freed from their bondages to the infantile images of the species and of the self.'

If the Church is to perpetuate this work, this means that

'men must be called away from their fascination with other worlds
... and summoned to confront the concrete issues of this one.'[1]

There must be a community of persons who 'are not burdened
by the constriction of an archaic heritage'.

What are some of the demonic distortions which plague contemporary society? Cox writes of the humiliating role in which
our culture has tried to cast the Negro. He writes of the un-
exorcised demons associated with sex, and maintains that twentieth century American culture has set up an idol which is a kind
of anti-Madonna, that is, The Girl who appears in modern
advertising, beauty contests—who is, in fact, ubiquitous. Cox
does not give any space to the Eternal Woman; the assumption
is perhaps that she is dead, at last.

In the mentality of conservative Roman Catholicism, however, the Eternal Woman—the Madonna of the imagination—
is not dead. The Girl is recognized as a deadly enemy, for it
is characteristic of those who live on the level of ideology,
safely away from the facts of experience, that the 'good guys'
and the 'bad guys' are neatly divided. For conservative Catholic
theologians and journalists, the 'good girl', who is the Eternal
Woman, is the only answer to the challenge of the 'bad girl', who
is The Girl of the world of James Bond, of *Playboy,* of advertising. If Cox fails to see the Eternal Woman as a demon to be
exorcised, this is undoubtedly because, being Protestant, he is at
a distance from the sub-culture of the Catholic ghetto.

The Church does, in fact, have the duty of exorcising the
Eternal Woman as well as The Girl, for both myths are destructive. Being two sides of the same mirage, they are, not surprisingly, quite similar. Both the Eternal Woman and The Girl
are, in the ultimate analysis, passive, abject, relative and irrelevant beings. If the one appears to be the antithesis of the other,
the opposition does not hold up under careful scrutiny. True, the
one is represented in spiritualistic terms, while the other em-
bodies the values of so-called secular materialism. The Eternal
Woman delights in being relegated to her pedestal, while The

---

[1] Harvey Cox, *The Secular City* (New York: Macmillan, 1965), p. 154.

Girl enjoys being used as a footstool. However, if the one appears as supra-human and the other as sub-human, the distinction is nevertheless trivial. Both are abysmally, hopelessly, non-human.

In the Catholic world, the Eternal Woman is not yet dead, and there is a web of ironies involved in the Church's failure to exorcise her. There is, first of all, the fact that the Church, by reason of inertia, has not merely failed in a purely negative fashion to exorcise her but has even actively promoted her, often with fanatical zeal. Moreover, failing to realize that The Girl is the Eternal Woman face-lifted and rejuvenated, the ecclesiastical ideologists have tried to send forth the Eternal Woman to do battle against her. If this has any effect at all, it can only be to help promote The Girl, who is an ideological reaction to the Eternal Woman and, being a reaction, will thrive as long as the threat of the Eternal Woman is there to support her.

The final solution for both of these demons, who are but the opposed faces of the same illusion, does not lie in the realm of ideology, where there is only a self-perpetuating vicious circle. It can come only from an honest confrontation with all information that can be wrested from the world of experience. This implies an openness to relevant data from any of the sciences, and a willingness to give up, if necessary, cherished notions of 'femininity' which are shown to be the products of social conditioning, particularly if these are revealed to be harmful.

Effects upon intelligence

Psychological studies conducted within the past few decades have in fact yielded results which strongly suggest that the effects of the 'eternal feminine' image are more subtly damaging than readily can be imagined. Some psychologists claim that it is possible to predict, from knowing the personality characteristics of young children, which ones will have rising, and which falling, IQs. Psychologist Eleanor Maccoby has pointed out the general lines of differentiation:

'Here is what a child is like at age six if he or she is among those whose IQs will increase during the next four years: he or she is competitive, self-assertive, independent, and dominant in inter-action with other children. And the children who will show declining IQs during the next four years are children who are passive, shy, and dependent.'[1]

It is evident that the characteristics associated with a falling IQ are those which are encouraged in girls by the 'eternal femi-nine' mystique.

Convincing evidence has been marshalled in support of the thesis that the sort of analytic thinking required for high level intellectual creativity is developed in children who are encour-aged at a very young age to take initiative. Creativity and produc-tivity require independence of mind and ability to detach oneself from others. The Eternal Woman image militates against initi-ative and independence. The Eternal Woman is 'by nature' pas-sive, dependent, totally relational. If given this image as an ideal, and subtly encouraged in many ways to conform to it, the girl child is very seriously handicapped.

Undeniably some girls do succeed in acquiring and develop-ing the necessary qualities of independence, dominance, and initiative. Studies indicate that many such girls have known a close relationship with their fathers. Sometimes, too, the mother is unusually liberated from the chains of the feminine mystique. The fact is, however, that these girls are developing in a way which is counter to society's conventions, to its subtle demands. For this, they may have to pay a terrible price. That price is called anxiety, and it may account for the sparse creativity even of many gifted and trained women who managed to defy society's effort to cast them into a passive, unthinking role. Eleanor Maccoby has summarized the ironic situation:

'We are beginning to know a good deal about the effects of anxiety on thinking: it is especially damaging to creative thinking, for it narrows the range of solution efforts, interferes with breaking set, and prevents scanning of the whole range of elements open to perception. When anxiety facilitates performance, as it sometimes

---

[1] Eleanor E. Maccoby, 'Woman's Intellect', *The Potential of Woman*, edited by Seymour M. Farber and Roger H. L. Wilson (New York: McGraw Hill Book Company), 1963, p. 33.

does, it facilitates already well-learned tasks; it does not contribute to breaking new ground. From the standpoint of those who want women to become intellectuals this is something of a horror story.'[1]

The psychologists who point out the powerful effect of conditioning in hampering mental development and creativity do not overlook biological differences; indeed they are very much aware of biological discoveries and theories concerning sexual differentiation. It is very possible that genetic factors dispose boys to be more aggressive than girls. At the same time, there is evidence pointing to the conclusion that conditioning has grossly exaggerated and caricatured the aggressive-passive polarity and has created differences where biology has nothing to say. Role differences which are cultural inventions have varied startlingly in different cultures, as anthropologists such as Margaret Mead have shown. We have come far enough to see that rigid, imposed dichotomies ignore the uniqueness of the individual, curtailing human liberty and depressing human potential. It is time, therefore, to challenge anachronistic patterns, which may have been necessary at an earlier stage of human development, but whose survival constitutes an obstacle to human progress.

Effects upon man-woman relationship

There is reason to think that the 'eternal feminine' also has a devastating effect upon the man-woman relationship, and clearly this is not unrelated to its limiting of women's creative potential. Sociologist Alice Rossi put it very simply:

'Social and personal life is impoverished for some part of many men's lives because so many of their wives live in a perpetual state of intellectual and social impoverishment.'[2]

Moreover, the woman who is victimized by this myth is damaged

[1] *Ibid.*, p. 37. Additional material can be found in *The Development of Sex Differences*, edited by Eleanor E. Maccoby (Stanford, California: Stanford University Press, 1966).

[2] Alice S. Rossi, 'Equality between the Sexes: An Immodest Proposal', *Daedalus*, Spring, 1964, *The Woman in America*, p. 614.

in her potential to love as well as to think. Passive and narcissistic, paralyzed and alienated from her deepest self, she cannot enter into an authentic union because she is not an authentic person. She desires to be desired; everything turns back upon herself. Not surprisingly, Claudel, who was able to think of women only in the form of the Eternal Woman, wrote that 'Woman is a promise that is never kept'. This mutilated creature cannot be a true partner; she throws man back upon his solitude. And as one author pointed out, 'solitude is relatively less anguishing without, than with, the company of the "eternal feminine" '.[1] The harmfulness of the myth, then, is contagious; it affects men, too.

Especially disastrous for marriage is an element of the Eternal Woman myth which has been dear to popes and theologians as well as to non-Christians: the virtual identification of women's being with the relational roles of wife and mother (with the stress upon mother). Psychoanalyst André Lussier states that therapy often reveals a woman who has an impression of non-existence, resulting from the annihilation of her personality identity by her duties as wife and mother. Therapy also reveals that there are men—and they are legion—for whom the person in the wife is non-existent. These men know the wife as a possession and the mother of their children.

> 'This way of thinking,' Lussier explains, 'stems from foggy religious standards, as well as a biased interpretation of the texts of St Paul on the supposed authority of the husband over the wife. The complacent male wallows in it. . . . Unconsciously the woman then feels encouraged to regress to the pre-genital role of possessed object. If she resists and does not give in to this regression, marital conflicts inevitably follow.'[2]

While responsibility for such nightmarish situations cannot be laid exclusively at the door of the Church, it is certain that much clerical writing on marriage promotes this sort of

---

[1] Dan Sullivan, 'Beast in the Belly vs. Union with the Beloved', NCR 29 June, 1966, p. 6.
[2] André Lussier, 'Psychoanalysis and Moral Issues in Marital Problems', Cross Currents XV, Winter, 1965, p. 59.

destructive relationship. A treasure house of bad advice is *The Catholic Marriage Manual* by Rev. George A. Kelly, who served as director of the Family Life Bureau of the Archdiocese of New York. Monsignor Kelly asserts:

> 'Nothing gives a man greater satisfaction and sense of fulfillment than a realized sense of importance. Men want recognition. They thrive on it. . . . Nothing like this is natural to the woman. If she is aggressive or domineering it is because she has been made so, and that is not good. Two egotists do not easily make a harmonious pair.'[1]

Not surprisingly, Monsignor Kelly thinks that the father's example 'will probably be the most important influence in the development of his son's personality'.[2] Obviously, the abased wife in this 'ideal marriage', could hardly have much positive influence upon a developing *personality*. Sometimes, self-appointed marriage authorities of this breed will write of the wife as the man's 'reward' after a hard day's work. It is characteristic of these marriage counselors that they oppose work outside the home on the part of the wife, since this fosters 'undesirable traits', such as independence.

Since it is chiefly as mother rather than as partner that the Eternal Woman is envisioned, the maternal role tends to be exaggerated into grotesque proportions which have pathological implications for sexual relationship. Devotees of the mystique often proclaim that the wife should be a mother not only to her children but also to her husband. This encourages infantile, obsessive men to 'marry a mother', in order to perpetuate the advantages of infantile dependence. Lussier points out that a psychological evolution sometimes takes place in such men, so that they eventually discover the true nature of their marriage. When this happens, the man begins to see his wife as dominating, much as an adolescent boy reacts against his mother. Often he will then try to prove his independence of her by seeking

[1] Reverend George A. Kelly, *The Catholic Marriage Manual* (New York: Random House, 1958), p. 6.
[2] *Ibid.*, p. 20.

affairs with other women.[1] It is clear that the total identification of the woman with the mother image is a source of sickness
in both sexes.

This identification can also be harmful to the children. It
would seem that the better educated and more energetic the
woman is, the greater is the chance that she will suffocate her
children, if she has no other outlet. Betty Friedan has pointed
out that

> 'the mother whose son becomes homosexual is usually not the
> "emancipated" woman who competes with men in the world, but
> the very paradigm of the feminine mystique—a woman who lives
> through her son, whose femininity is used in virtual seduction of
> her son, who attaches her son to her with such dependence that
> he can never mature to love a woman, nor can he, often, cope as an
> adult with life on his own.'[2]

The task of exorcism

In view of the psychological and sociological data now at our
disposal, it is irrelevant to support the 'eternal feminine' on the
basis that many people, including many women, are satisfied
with it in theory and in practice. When human consciousness had
evolved to the point where it became clear that slavery is harmful, abolition became morally imperative, even if some slaves
were satisfied with their shrunken existence. Although the
'chains' of sexual prejudice are invisible and psychological, their
coercive strength is nonetheless real. Not least among the demonic aspects of the 'eternal feminine' is the blindness which
it brings about.

The task of exorcising this demon is one of the great challenges of our era. It can be said with justice that the Church has
failed to rise to this challenge. Indeed, there is abundant evidence that as a power structure it has tended to ally itself with
the powers of darkness. Inevitably, the people of God have been
wounded by this alliance. The Church has been wounded in its

---

[1] Lussier, *op. cit.*, p. 64.
[2] Betty Friedan, *The Feminine Mystique* (London: Victor Gollancz, 1963),
p. 275.

structures, for it has deprived itself of the gifts and insights of more than half of its members. It has been grievously hurt in its members of both sexes, for in a society which welcomes and fosters prejudice, not only is the human potential of the subject group restricted, but the superordinate group also becomes warped in the process.

The need for exorcism is clear, but the method cannot be substitution of a new simplistic ideology for an old one. What this would come to in the end would be merely a face-lifting for the Eternal Woman. Efforts should be made, certainly, to improve the quality of Catholic writing and publishing, which still harbors strong inclinations toward serving up archaic myth to support traditional teachings and antiquated canon law. However, since the roots of sexual prejudice are deep—in fact, since this represents the neurosis of a whole culture, it cannot be expected that logical arguments will convince the official exponents of the 'eternal feminine' myth. The problem is compounded by the fact that sometimes those who are most influential in Catholic organizations and communications media are there precisely because they are given over to simplistic ideological thought patterns. It will be necessary, then, to look for a way of exorcism which strikes at the roots of the problem.

The answer, in a general sense, was suggested by Simone de Beauvoir and unintentionally by Gertrud von le Fort. This answer is, that women who have a consciousness of the problem, and who have the required creative vigor and independence, have the responsibility of changing the image of woman by raising up their own image, giving an example to others, and especially to the young. The thought of the immeasurable influence which Indira Gandhi may have upon the self-images of girls in India suggests the potency for image changing which a great woman can have. Such influence can be exercised in varying ways and degrees by others. The point is not to set up another stereotype, such as that of the stateswoman, to replace the old, but to manifest the unreliability of all stereotypes by showing the immense variety in the potential of women. Many girls would be encouraged to realize this potential if they could see that normal, attractive persons are in fact doing the things they want to do.

Despite the fact that the answer lies in the 'raising up' of new images, it is doubtful that women will rise to the task in sufficient numbers until favorable conditions are not only allowed but also encouraged. As far as the Church is concerned, this will require a work which has both a negative and a positive aspect. The work of removing impediments to evolution of personality and of fostering an atmosphere in which such evolution can best take place is equivalent to the task of exorcism, which is an essential part of its ministry. Furthermore, this changing of atmosphere must take place on the two levels of theory and of practice. The following chapters examine some dimensions of the work ahead.

CHAPTER SIX

Theological Roots of the Problem: Radical Surgery Required

'The attack by Christian apologetic upon the adult-hood of the world I consider to be in the first place pointless, in the second ignoble, and in the third un-Christian.'

Dietrich Bonhoeffer

If the change of atmosphere which is so badly needed is really to come about, the best talents and concerted efforts of many persons working in different areas will be required. In this chapter we shall indicate some theological inadequacies which are at the source of Catholic androcentrism. To become aware of the scope and context of the work of ridding theology of its ancient bias is of first importance, not only for theologians but for all who are interested in the women-Church problem.

Once having taken note of the more obvious misogynistic notions which have become embedded in Christian tradition, one begins to see that the roots of these are profound and that they are interrelated. Theology is comparable to an organism: a disease affecting one part quickly spreads to another part. Moreover, it is not enough to cure a symptom. In fact, instant cures of surface manifestations might simply disguise the fact that the disease is still present at a deeper level, ready to manifest itself in other forms.

From one point of view, antifeminism in Christian thought can be looked upon as a symptom. We shall consider it here from this aspect. This is by no means to deny that misogynism can be and is a psychological origin of the very doctrinal disorders which, in turn, serve to perpetuate it. The cause-effect relationship is not one-way. It is more accurate to describe it as a vicious circle. We are now approaching that circle from the point of view of the internal structure of theology itself. That is, we shall examine those inadequacies in the conceptualizations of basic doctrines which sustain and perpetuate androcentric theological teachings.

Ideas about God

In theology, at the root of such distortions as antifeminism is the problem of conceptualizations, images, and attitudes concerning God. Many intelligent people are not aware of the depth and far-reaching consequences of this problem. It appears to such persons that an image of God as 'an old man with a beard' who lives 'up in heaven' is too childish to be taken seriously by any adult. They feel certain their own belief is on a level far above these notions, and that the same is true of every educated adult. In actuality their confidence in themselves and in others like them is groundless. They fail to realize what a powerful grip such images have upon the imagination even after they have been consciously rejected as primitive and inadequate. Indeed, shades of 'the old man with a beard'—his various metaphysical equivalents—continue to appear even in the most learned speculations of theologians. They appear even more obviously and frequently in the watered-down, popularized versions of these speculations, for example, in text books, religion classes, and sermons.

What does the abiding presence of such images have to do with the problem with which this book is concerned? On one level the answer to this question may be glimpsed when one considers that the image in question is, obviously, of a person of the male sex. Of course, no theologian or biblical scholar believes that God literally belongs to the male sex. However, there are bits of evidence that the absurd idea that God is male lingers on in the minds of theologians, preachers and simple believers, on a level which is not entirely explicit or conscious. One has only to think of the predictable and spontaneous reaction of shock and embarrassment if a speaker were to stand before a group and refer to God as 'she'. Indeed, many would find it unfitting, not quite 'normal' to refer to God as 'she', and chances are that if forced to choose between 'she' and 'it' to refer to the divinity, many would prefer the latter pronoun, which, although unsatisfactory, would appear to them less blasphemous than the feminine.

Even the best theological writing can occasionally reflect the confusion over God and sex, even when a conscious effort is being made to avoid confusion. The following passage, from a well-known scholar, is an interesting specimen:

'We have already noticed that in the Mesopotamian myths sex was as primeval as nature itself. The Hebrews could not accept this view, for there was no sex in the God they worshipped. God is, of course, masculine, but not in the sense of sexual distinction, and the Hebrew found it necessary to state expressly, in the form of a story, that sex was introduced into the world by the creative Deity, who is above sex as he is above all the things which he made.'[1]

What is fascinating here is that in a passage which patently explains that the God of the Old Testament is above sex, in which the author goes to great pains to make this clear, we find the bland assertion that 'God is, of course, masculine'. The meaning is, of course, not clear. In fact, this is the sort of nonsense statement which philosophers of the linguistic analysis school delight in dissecting. What can 'masculine' mean if predicated of a Being in which there is no sex? Is this a statement about God or is it rather a statement of the author's and/or the Hebrews' opinion of the male sex? In any case, the subtle conditioning effected by the widespread opinion that God is masculine, whatever that may mean, is unlikely to engender much self-esteem in women, or much esteem for women.

There are other distortions in traditional notions of the divinity which are quite distinct from vague identifications of God with the male sex, although they may very well be connected with these identifications. Many of these distortions have

[1] John L. McKenzie, S.J., *The Two-Edged Sword. An Interpretation of the Old Testament*, op. cit., pp. 93-4.

recently come under criticism by some theologians, who attribute them to an exaggerated influence of Greek philosophy upon Christian thought, and who now advocate a 'de-hellenization' of Christian doctrine.[1] It is important to be aware of these perverted notions and of their bearing upon the problems with which we are concerned in this book.

Among the misleading and harmful notions about God which the modern 'de-hellenizing' theologians have in mind are certain concepts which occur in connection with 'divine omnipotence', 'divine immutability', and 'divine providence'. The classical formulations of the doctrine that God is omnipotent bear with them associations and images which modern man tends to find alienating. This is especially the case because these formulations involve the idea that God is immutable. The picture which comes through is of an all-powerful, all-just God who evidently wills or, at least, permits oppressive conditions to exist. Moreover, this God is said to be changeless. In the face of such a God, man is despairing and helpless. He wonders why he should commit himself to attempting to improve his lot or trying to bring about social justice, if such a God exists.

In fact, then, such notions can and do have the effect of paralyzing the human will to change evil conditions and can inspire callousness and insensitivity. This effect upon attitudes is reinforced by certain ideas of divine providence as a fixed plan being copied out in history. With such a frame of reference, there is a temptation to glorify the *status quo*, to assume that the social conditions peculiar to any given time and place are right simply because they exist. Evidently, if one wishes to arouse theological awareness concerning problems of social justice, such as those which concern women, he should take into account the built-in resistance arising from such thought-patterns.

Scholastic theologians can argue that this is a caricature of the traditional doctrines of divine immutability, omnipotence, and providence. They can point out that classical theology has always stressed charity, that it has always insisted upon man's free-will,

[1] See Leslie Dewart, *The Future of Belief* (New York: Herder and Herder, 1966).

which is not destroyed by divine omnipotence. They can point to the thousand refinements in scholastic thought which are ignored in such a representation as we have given. The difficulty is, however, that these efforts to 'save' man's freedom have never been particularly convincing, despite their subtle and elaborate logic. What comes through to modern man is a picture of God and of man's situation which is paralyzing and alienating.

The static world-view

The central characteristic of the world-view which results is changelessness. The frame of mind which it engenders is hardly open to theological development and social change. It is therefore not sympathetic to the problem that women and other disadvantaged groups face in relation to the Church and to other cultural institutions. Consistent with this static view is a limited conception of biological nature and of the 'natural law'—interpreted as God's will. A mentality conditioned by such ideas instinctively opposes radical efforts to control and transcend the limits imposed by biological nature. The typical conservative theologians who have opposed change in the Catholic Church's position on birth control have this frame of reference. And, of course, it is consistent with this line of thinking that the myth of 'immutable feminine nature and masculine nature', which is in reality a pattern of images derived in large measure from social conditioning, be set up as normative.

The resistance which the static world-view presents to ideas of social change is fortified by another idea which must be considered inimical to healthy development. This is the idea that divine revelation was given to man in the past, once and for all, and that it was 'closed' at the end of the apostolic age. There can easily follow from this the idea that certain statements in the Bible represent descriptions of an unalterable divine plan, and that these statements must be accepted now and forcibly applied even though the social context in which we find ourselves is vastly different from the situation in biblical times. We have seen in a previous chapter how disastrous this attitude has been in relation to the texts of Paul and to the opening chapters of Genesis concerning women.

Contemporary theologians are beginning to take account of the inadequacies of the old notion of revelation as closed. Of course, there has always been some awareness of these inadequacies since, in fact, there has been doctrinal development in every age. Traditional theologians have tried to reconcile this undeniable fact of development with the doctrine that revelation is 'closed' by arguing that content which was implicitly contained in revelation becomes, in the course of time, more explicit. Complex theories have been developed elaborating upon this, but these have been less than completely satisfactory. They tend to overemphasize the need for justification of every change in terms of the past. Some contemporary Catholic theologians, notably Gabriel Moran, are beginning to insist that revelation is an event, and that it exists today as a present event.[1] This implies a radical openness to the facts of contemporary experience. We are in need of such a concept of revelation, which will help to create the atmosphere needed for honest re-examination of contemporary issues, such as the Church's attitude concerning women.

Other theological developments required

The healing of Christian antifeminism will require still other theological developments. It will be necessary that the institutionalist view of the Church—a root of many evils—be transcended. A theology which overstresses the institutional character of the Church tends to be preoccupied with defending positions held by authorities in the past and to close its eyes to present realities. It is wary of all attempts at development of doctrine, since change appears to weaken respect for authority. While the Church can certainly be considered as an institution, this should be balanced by an understanding of another side of its reality. What is needed is a more prophetic vision of the Church as a movement in the world, concerned primarily with better-

---

[1] Gabriel Moran, F.S.C. 'The God of Revelation', *Commonweal*, vol. LXXXV n. 18, 10 February, 1967, pp. 499–503.

ment of the human condition, and seeking to cooperate with all who are striving for this goal. As this attitude develops, with its emphasis upon the work to be done rather than upon vested interests and personal and institutional prestige, women will come more into their own among the people of God. Both the Old and the New Testaments recognize that women as well as men have the gift of prophecy. As Christian theology comes to see institutional structures more in the terms of the prophetic mission of the Church, it will become evident that the exclusion of women from ministerial functions is unreasonable.

In order to create the theological atmosphere which we are seeking, it will also be necessary to develop an understanding of the Incarnation which goes beyond the regressive, sin-obsessed view of human life which colored so much of the theology of the past. Thought about this doctrine must become consonant with evolutionary awareness of modern man, welcoming and encouraging human progress on all levels as continuing the work of the Incarnation. It must encourage active personal commitment to the work of bringing about social justice and to creative work of all kinds.

One of the chief obstacles to envisaging the Incarnation within an evolutionary context has been a literalist interpretation of the story of the Fall of Adam and Eve. Teilhard de Chardin, in 'Christologie et Evolution', an article which appeared in 1933, wrote of this:

> 'Not only must history, in order to accept Adam and Eve, be strangled in a quite artificial way, on the level of the appearance of man, but—in a more immediately vital area, that of belief—the expansion of our religion is constantly stifled by the present formulation of the doctrine of original sin. It clips the wings of our expectations and inexorably leads us back into the shadows of reparation and expiation.'

Paul Tillich in his *Systematic Theology* called literal belief in the story of the Fall 'a distinct disservice to Christianity'.

It is not by accident that two such prophetic thinkers as Teilhard de Chardin and Paul Tillich focused attention upon theological distortions connected with the story of the Fall. The effects of these distortions are far-reaching. As long as theology is obsessed with a conception of human nature as fallen from a state of original integrity, and considers that state to have actually existed in the past, it must be pessimistic about the present and the future. It tends to see human life chiefly in terms of reparation and expiation. As long as this is the atmosphere of theology, Christianity cannot fully recognize itself to be what theologian Karl Rahner called it: 'the religion of the absolute future'.

This static, sin-haunted view of human life reflects and perpetuates a negative attitude toward sexuality, matter, and 'the world'. In such an atmosphere antifeminism has thrived. To some theologians, 'woman' came to personify all those aspects of reality which they believed should be feared, fled from, denied and despised. We have already examined some of the tirades of the Fathers against the 'daughters of Eve'. It is necessary to face the fact that there are warped attitudes deeply embedded in Christian thought which have continued to sustain the 'daughters of Eve' theme, despite the fact that inconsistencies and absurdities should have been self-evident to reason.

The disease of sin-obsession and antisexuality has spread from the roots to the branches of theology. As a result, the growth of sacramental theology has been in some ways stunted and one-sided. This can be seen in the cases of the two sacraments most directly related to the problem of women in the Church, matrimony and holy orders.

Theological treatises on marriage have, until very recently, tended to view the man-woman relationship in sub-personal categories. They have heavily emphasized the canonical distinction between 'primary and secondary ends' of marriage, stressing that the union is primarily for the production and education of offspring. All of this has been quite consistent with the tacit assumption that women are not fully human. It was difficult to think of marriage as primarily a personal union, when one partner in the union was thought to be not quite a person. What is required now is a clear rejection of the biologism which gave the dominant motif to the older theology of marriage. In place of it there should be an ever increasing stress upon personalist values and goals. The theology of marriage is in a state of transition, but the work is by no means completed. As long as Catholic doctrine keeps women in a state of bondage to biological fertility and paralyzes them by a degrading doctrine of exclusive male headship, there is little hope of their achieving adulthood without separating themselves from the Church in some way—if not completely and openly, then partially and clandestinely.

The theology of the sacrament of Holy Orders has also suffered from lack of balance. There has been a disproportionate emphasis upon the exalted status of the priest, rather than upon his mission to serve. One is tempted to conclude, upon reading some theological treatises, that there is a kind of phallic symbolism involved in the exaggerated emphasis upon the dignity of the priest. This has been especially in evidence when the question of the ordination of women has been raised. Thomas Aquinas, for example, wrote that women cannot receive Holy Orders because 'eminence of degree cannot be signified in the female sex, since woman has the state of subjection'.[1] (It is interesting that he listed the feminine sex first among a group of six impediments to reception of Orders—the others being lack of the use of reason, the state of slavery, homicide, illegitimate birth, and lack of physical members.)

Some of Thomas's disciples have gone even further. An American Dominican theologian wrote that a woman cannot be ordained because 'to the gathering of the Church her feminine nature cannot represent "male", which is precisely the symbolic sacramental distinction Christ possesses in relation to his Church'.[2] This example illustrates very well the fact that the theological argumentation used against the ordination of women is sometimes rooted in a Christology which tends to see greater significance in the maleness of Jesus than in the central fact of his humanity. Obviously, this is somewhat out of perspective. We

[1] Thomas Aquinas, *Summa theologiae*, Suppl. 39, 1.
[2] Edmund Manchak, O.P., 'More from St Paul on a Female Priesthood', *NCR*, 26 May, 1965, p. 4.

shall consider at greater length the question of women and the priesthood in the next chapter.

We are now in a position to see that the healing of theology's built-in misogynism is related to the advancement of doctrine on many levels. Development of doctrine on one point does not normally occur independently. Advocates of progress on the women-Church issue should keep this in mind, if they hope to have deep and lasting influence. Since the roots of the disease are profound and complicated, again let us recognize that there are no instant cures. A constant effort should be made at seeing relationships, at sustaining a wide vision.

Needed: special attention to the problem

The fact that there is need for breadth of vision does not, however, imply that special attention and effort should not be directed to the problem of women and the Church. We have seen that inadequacies in the understanding and formulation of basic doctrines, such as those concerned with the divine attributes, the Incarnation, the nature of the Church, will be reflected in thought on sexual relation and the situation of women. However, it would be a mistake to think that the cause-effect relationship moves only in one direction. In fact, as we have already indicated, there is reason to think that there is a reciprocal causality. From the point of view of psychological origin, warped notions of sexual relation and of woman may be the roots of weak and inadequate conceptions concerning God, Christ, revelation, the Church and the sacraments. For example, images of God as jealous and vengeful, which historian Arnold Toynbee has judged to have had a devastating effect upon Christian civilization,[1] may well be projections and justifications of the role of the tyrant father in patriarchal society. That is, they may be the effects of imbalance in sexual relation. It is important, then, for the health and authentic evolution of Christian theology, that the question of the man-woman relationship and the problems arising from androcentrism be made a special focus of attention.

[1] Arnold Toynbee, *Christianity among the Religions of the World* (New York: Charles Scribner's Sons, Scribner Library Books), 1957, p. 19.

A more enlightened understanding in this area will have far-reaching effects.

Another point which needs to be stressed in connection with theological reform on the question of women is this: if a radical re-thinking of the subject is to take place, it is necessary to opt for a clear-cut rejection of that approach which is suggested by the expression, 'theology of woman'. This approach contains a built-in assumption that 'woman' is in fact a distinct species which can be understood apart from the other sex. It is founded on the unproved supposition that there is an innate psycho-sexual complementarity. Invariably, attempts to develop a 'theology of woman' fall on their various faces because they naively assume that the sex images of a patriarchal culture infallibly correspond to 'nature' and to God's will.

The bias which is inherent in this approach becomes evident when one attempts to state the corresponding formula: 'theology of man (male)'. Whereas the idea of a 'theology of woman' is frequently proposed, few would seriously suggest that there should be a 'theology of man'.

Men have been regarded as having full human status and therefore are not seen as posing a special problem, whereas women, who have not yet achieved this status, seem mysterious. Because of its assumptions, a 'theology of woman' helps to perpetuate and justify this situation. It is misbegotten in that it places sexual differentiation above personhood. Moreover, it misconstrues the problematic of sexuality itself for, as we have said, it assumes that one sex can be understood as if it were a complete essence existing in isolation. In fact, the sexual differentiation has to be understood within the category of relation. Men and women as they are, are the products of complex social relations which are constantly in flux. That is to say, they have a continuing history.

What is needed is creative effort to develop a theological anthropology which will study the dynamics of human personality and social relationship from a radically evolutionary point of view. Within this context there needs to be developed a theology of the man-woman relationship which rejects as alienating to both sexes the idea of a sexual hierarchy founded upon 'nature' and defined once and for all. This much needed theology will recognize that the relationship between the sexes evolves, that its forms must change according to the conditions of diverse historical epochs and according to individual differences. It will reject any conception of 'the common good' which would diminish the potential of one sex for the sake of the other. It will place value in personal liberty and growth, which must be seen not as opposed to, but as essential to, love and commitment. Rejecting the old obsession with sex roles, it will be concerned with the problems of persons in relation to others. It will be honest enough to admit the ambiguity of concrete reality, which the theologian's abstractions cannot fully clarify or encompass.

Obstacles to theological development

It is essential to be aware, however, that there are obstacles to the eradication of theological misogynism and to the development of a dynamic and liberating theological anthropology—obstacles arising from the society in which the theologian lives and works. The fact is that he does not live in a Platonic 'world of ideas' but in human society. It would be naive to suppose that the ancient bias could persist in doctrine if this were not given support and apparent justification by the actual condition of women both within the Church itself and in the secular milieu.

Within the Church itself, the exclusion of women from the hierarchy and, until very recent years, from access to theological education has perpetuated an atmosphere in which theologians—all male—felt no pressure to give serious attention to the problems of the other sex in their struggle to achieve first-class citizenship. These could be dismissed as unimportant. Kept in ignorance of theology and canon law and of the political realities of the Church, women have until recently lacked even an awareness of their own situation. When questions did arise, they were intimidated by their lack of knowledge from challenging the situation of subservience imposed upon them. This is to some extent still true. Even in those cases in which women have become knowledgeable and articulate, they have found that there were few channels of communication open to them. It has been easy for the theologians to ignore weak protests.

Moreover, it would be unrealistic to suppose that the status of women in secular society does not affect the thinking of theologians. If complete and genuine equality of opportunity for women did exist in Europe and the United States, the absurdity of anachronistic theological ideas concerning them would be so blatantly obvious that such notions would rapidly be discarded. The existing situation in America, Britain, and most of the northern European countries is, in varying styles and degrees, one of semi-equality. The possibility of professional and political equality exists in theory, but a combination of negative influences—not least among them psychological pressures—hinders full realization of the ideal. In the Latin countries, the situation is even more unbalanced.

Inevitably, then, the progress of theology is hindered by prevailing conditions in ecclesiastical and civil society. To the problems and challenges posed by these conditions we shall next turn our attention.

CHAPTER SEVEN

Toward Partnership: Some Modest Proposals

'God created man in his image. In the image of God
he created him. Male and female he created them.'

Genesis 1:27

'There is neither Jew nor Greek, there is neither
slave nor free, there is neither male nor female; for
you are all one in Christ Jesus.'

Galatians 3:28

Some believe that those concerned with the problem of eradicating sexual discrimination should concentrate their energies
upon the secular milieu rather than upon the Church. It is said
that if truly equal educational, professional and political opportunities are attained for women in secular society, and if psychological and social pressures which hinder them from using these
opportunities can be combatted successfully, the Church will
grudgingly but inevitably follow suit. There is something to be
said for this approach, but it is incomplete. First of all, it is seen
as incomplete by those who recognize value in the Church itself
and who therefore feel the urgency of the need for its reform.
Furthermore, it is incomplete because it considers the Church
simply as a superstructure without influence upon society. This
view fails to take into account the great power which the Church
has as pressure group and image maker. It would be as foolish
to ignore its power at this point in history as it would be to ignore
that of any great cultural institution. It is important to take into
account the fact that, while it is true that ecclesiastical attitudes
are conditioned by the secular milieu, it is also true that the
Church has influence upon the whole environment.

Our problem now is to understand the basic nature of our task of exorcising, on the level of practical activity and within the context of evolving structures, the 'demon' of sexual prejudice in the Church. We have already seen the need for exorcism on the level of theory, particularly through the expulsion of the demonic myth of the eternal feminine from theology. Now we must ask what will be the operative principle which will direct our efforts on the level of social action.

The answer to this question must be sought by first considering the nature of the disease which we are attempting to cure, for an adequate cure must be appropriate to the illness. We have seen in an earlier chapter that the disease can be understood in terms of self-fulfilling prophecy, a process by which the dominant class projects its unwanted characteristics, its lower self, upon the members of the oppressed class, who in turn introject the despised qualities. Thus, the creation story speaks the truth in declaring that Eve came from Adam. Moreover, the workings of the process—the whole vicious circle of role psychology—are understood neither by the oppressor nor by his victim, both of whom are inclined to accept the myths, such as the myth of fixed natures, which serve as its justification.

If the resultant fixed roles were harmful only to the class of persons who have been made inferior (the slave, the Negro, the woman) there would be compelling enough reason to seek a cure. However, there is more to it than this. Thus the white supremacist is rent at the core of his being. Thus also the male, through the mutilation of woman, has been caught up in a process of self-destruction. In relation to woman as mother, wife, companion, he is doomed to frustration if he cannot find in the other an authentic, self-activating person—with precisely the qualities which are stunted by the imposition of the eternal feminine. Fated to partnership with 'true woman', he may find this dissociated, narcissistic being less satisfactory than the companion of his dreams. What is more, the 'eternal masculine' itself is alienating, crippling the personalities of men and restricting their experience of life at every level. The male in our society is not supposed to express much feeling, sensitivity, aesthetic appreciation, imagination, consideration for others, intuition. He is expected to affirm only part of his real self. Indeed, it may be that a good deal of the compulsive competitiveness of males is rooted in this half existence.

It is the nature of the disease, therefore, to inhibit the expansion of the individual's potential, through conditioned conformity to roles, and through a total identification of the individual with them. It contrasts starkly with free acceptance of roles by integrated personalities, for its effect is to hinder the integration of personality. The healing which we seek must not be understood as a return to a state of health presumed to have existed in the past. This would be nothing but an abortive quest for the state of dreaming innocence, for primitive unconsciousness, or for the paradise lost by the Fall. Rather, we must strive for that forward leap into the future of human history which is now demanded of us. Then perhaps it will be understood that our sickness was only the growing pains of a species on its way to maturity.

The nature of the effort demanded of us is revealed by the nature of our predicament, of our alienation. Disintegrated and dissociated by processes which may have been necessary for the development of civilization, we must seek integration by confronting each other in a way which is qualitatively different from that of the past. Men and women are in history, in time, existing only in dynamic relationship to each other. We have in the past been chained to the wheel of psychological processes whose nature was not understood, living out roles which seemingly were predestined, written in the heavens. There is evidence that a few privileged souls in every age transcended the blindness of the culture and achieved communication which was profound and genuinely personal, but the literature of all ages attests to the general failure. In our time, however, we appear to be at the threshold of liberation from this ancient servitude. The developing sciences, particularly psychology and anthropology, have given us insight at last into the mechanisms which had enslaved us. The advance of technology has provided us with a situation in which, for the first time in history, we have the required leisure, mobility, control of our environment to experiment on the basis of this insight.

Our efforts, then, must be toward a level of confrontation, dialogue, and cooperation between the sexes undreamed of in the past, when the struggle for biological survival of the species and numerical multiplication had to take precedence over any thought of qualitative development of relation between the sexes. The directing principle of our thoughts and plans concerning the future relations of men and women in the Church and society must be commitment to providing the possibility of ever more profound, complete, dynamic and humanizing relationships, in which we may hope to transcend our alienation through understanding of each other and of ourselves.

It should become axiomatic that if the vicious circle of imposed roles and of self-fulfilling prophecy is to be overcome among the people of God, if the level of dialogue and cooperation between men and women which we are seeking is to be attained, then all automatic exclusion from any Church office or function on the basis of sex is to be eradicated.

A concerted effort should be made, then, to work toward this eradicating of discrimination on all levels. On the parish and diocesan levels, wherever boards and councils of laymen are established, women should be represented, significantly and proportionately, not merely by a few token appointments. They should be found in positions of importance in the national Catholic organizations. In particular, efforts should be directed to seeking out and using the talents of gifted and highly trained women specialists in influential and decision-making roles within the Church. Relevant areas of specialization in which competent women are now to be found include advanced theological research and teaching, sociology, political science, psychology, educational administration, business administration, journalism, law, social work. Such specialists should be recruited for postconciliar commissions and other organizations which may be set up to continue the work begun by the Vatican Council.

In liturgical affairs, as participation of the laity becomes more active, equally active participation of both sexes must be insisted upon. If laymen serve as lectors and acolytes, if they preach and distribute Holy Communion, then women should do the same. Moreover, it is evident, if one faces the problem with consistency, courage and sincerity, that the process of eradicating discrimination must not stop here. The question of women clergy must be faced.

The question of women priests

In the question of whether women may be ordained priests, the whole problem of the situation of women in the Church is reflected, symbolized, and crystallized. Indeed, it is evident to anyone who has repeatedly engaged in discussions of the subject that this can serve as a touchstone for attitudes concerning women and the man-woman relationship. Many who would see the appropriateness of some kind of active role for women in the Church recoil in horror when the priesthood is mentioned. Often, conversations which had been rational up to this point suddenly become wildly emotional and hidden prejudices blossom forth, dramatically revealing the insincerity of earlier admissions that women should be recognized as equal to men in the Church.

The power of the issue of women priests to unmask hidden attitudes is demonstrated in statements of a German author who wrote:

'Picture the relations between priestesses and men, if you have any experience of life, any acquaintance with human nature, above all, any imagination. What a kaleidoscope of situations we should have—embarrassing, grotesque, delicate, amusing, and quite intolerable. Supposing there were no theological argument, I cannot see a single reason for discarding the logic and religious experience of thousands of years in order to gratify the longing a handful of women have for recognition and power.'[1]

It is interesting that it does not occur to the writer of this passage, apparently, to 'picture the relations between priests and women'. Yet here one could find a storehouse of situations

[1] Ida Friederika Görres, 'Women as Priests?', *Herder Correspondence Feature Service*, 3 December, 1965.

which are grotesque, delicate, etc.—situations which need not be conjured up by the imagination, since they exist in fact. This peculiar one-sidedness of vision reflects the deep-seated prejudice which totally identifies women, but not men, with their sexual function. Also noteworthy is the assumption that everyone who argues that both sexes should be represented in the hierarchy is a woman, and moreover a woman with a 'longing for recognition and power'. In fact, at least as many men as women have argued the affirmative on the question of women in the hierarchy. Moreover, only a very small percentage of the women who have publicly taken an affirmative position on the question have expressed a personal desire to become priests. What they have in common is some ability to transcend stereotypes and to abstract from the immediate situation. What is at stake in this issue is more radical and more universal than the specific ambitions of a few persons.

What is at stake is the character and quality of the man-woman relation in the Church of the future. There will be no genuine equality of men and women in the Church as long as qualified persons are excluded from any ministry by reason of their sex alone. Those who point to the rising position of the laity in the Church and then argue that women are attaining equality because of this are ignoring the fact that the situation of men and women is not the same here. Men have the option of becoming priests or remaining laymen. Women have no choice. As long as the Church maintains a significant distinction between hierarchy and laity, the exclusion of women from the hierarchy is a radical affirmation of their inferior position among the people of God. By this exclusion the Church is in a very real and effective way teaching that women are not fully human and conditioning people to accept this as an irremediable fact. It is saying that the sexual differentiation is—for one sex—a handicap so crippling that no personal qualities of intelligence, virtue or leadership can overcome it.

That there is no valid theological objection to the ordination of women has become increasingly evident in recent years. Discussion by scholars in the various Protestant Churches which have decided to ordain women has helped to manifest the absurdity of objections on theological grounds. Of particular interest is the dispute which occurred concerning the ordination of women in Sweden in the 1950's. Biblical scholar Krister Stendahl has pointed out that scholars on both sides of the dispute were in agreement concerning the historical meaning of the texts of St Paul concerning women. The real problem and disagreement concerned application to modern times. Those who took the conservative position assumed that Paul's view could be taken as a generally valid Christian view, normative for all times. This is precisely the weakness of the conservative position. Professor Stendahl maintains that in all the texts where the New Testament speaks about the role of women in the Church, when a reason is given, it is always by reference to the subordinate position of women in creation. In fact,

'the question of women's place in the cult and ministry and in the Christian home and in society is dealt with on the selfsame principle: the subordination in creation'.[1]

This implies that the question about the ordination of women cannot be separated from the total problem of the emancipation of women in our society. Thus, Professor Stendahl argues, it is almost impossible to assent to the political emancipation of women while arguing on biblical grounds against the ordination of women.

There is further reason to reject the position of those who accept the political emancipation of women but, on supposedly scriptural grounds, reject their ordination. The New Testament (Galatians 3:28) suggests that if there is to be a change in the man-woman relationship, it will be in Christ. It is a peculiar reversal of this to claim that emancipation is all right in 'the world' but not in the Church. It would be more consistent, although quite mad, to crusade in the name of the Bible against all emancipation and try to regain the social situation of the first

[1] Krister Stendahl, *The Bible and the Role of Women: A Case Study in Hermeneutics*, translated by Emilie T. Sander (Philadelphia: Fortress Press, Facet Books, Biblical Series 15, 1966), p. 39.

century. Professor Stendahl summarizes the case succinctly:

'If emancipation is right, then there is no valid "biblical" reason not to ordain women. Ordination cannot be treated as a "special" problem since there is no indication that the New Testament sees it as such.'[1]

A frequent type of objection takes the form of an argument from fact. Some have based their opposition upon the fact that Jesus called only men to be his apostles. The weakness of this sort of reasoning is evident. It is impossible to move with logical certitude from this to the conclusion that only men should be priests—such a conclusion requires quite an unjustifiable leap. How do we know that this was the point of his choice? He also chose only Jews, which hardly can be interpreted to mean that only Jews can be priests. The objection fails to take into account the cultural climate of the time. It reflects a kind of Docetism, which refuses to recognize the implications of the full humanity of Jesus. That is, it simply does not take into account the fact that, being truly human, Jesus lived and thought within the cultural context of his age.

Similar to this objection is the argument based upon the fact that Jesus was male. It is argued that the priest represents Christ and therefore must be male. This type of fuzzy, symbol-oriented thinking leaves itself open to objections at both ends. It betrays a distorted understanding of the meaning of Christ (a point which we have already touched upon in the last chapter), giving prior importance to his maleness, rather than to his humanity. Moreover, it is forced to be inconsistent in order to avoid the assertion that women cannot represent Christ at all—and few would want to go this far.

Some forward-looking Catholic writers (notably Monsignor J. D. Conway) have suggested that Pope John was opening just a crack the door to the priesthood for women, perhaps without realizing it, when he wrote in *Pacem in Terris*:

'Human beings have the right to choose freely the state of life which they prefer, and therefore the right to establish a family, with

[1] *Ibid.*, p. 41.

equal rights and duties for man and woman, and also the right to follow a vocation to the priesthood or the religious life.'

After quoting this passage, Monsignor Conway commented:

'Pope John might object to my taking his words literally but they deserve meditation. He noted with approval the fading of a stratified society, in which some persons are put in an inferior condition, and others assume superior position, "on account of economic and social conditions, of sex, of assigned rank".'[1]

It is possible that Pope John's words have prophetic implications which will be recognized only after the passage of time.

A procedure similar to that employed by Monsignor Conway could be used in connection with a passage already cited in an earlier chapter from Vatican II's *Pastoral Constitution on the Church in the Modern World*:

'With respect to the fundamental rights of the person, every type of discrimination, whether social or cultural, whether based on sex, race, color, social condition, language, or religion, is to be overcome and eradicated as contrary to God's intent. For in truth it must still be regretted that fundamental personal rights are not yet being universally honored. Such is the case of a woman who is denied the right and freedom to choose a husband, to embrace a state of life, or to acquire an education or cultural benefits equal to those recognized for men.'[2]

It is clear that women cannot 'embrace a state of life' on the same terms as men, as long as they are excluded from the hierarchy.

The vast theological developments which have taken place in recent years have implications for the specific question of women's ordination which have not been lost upon progressive theologians. Recognizing the weakness of theological objections, they have openly shifted the whole question to the arenas of sociology and psychology. Thus, in 1966, Father Hans Küng stated:

[1] *NCR*, 16 November, 1966, p. 8.
[2] *Pastoral Constitution on the Church in the Modern World*, n. 29.

'There are two factors to consider regarding the ordination of women to the Sacred Ministry of the Church. The first is that there are no dogmatic or biblical reasons against it. The second is that there are psychological and sociological factors to be considered. The solution to the problem depends on the sociological conditions of the time and place. It is entirely a matter of cultural circumstances.'[1]

It can hardly be denied that cultural circumstances, as far as women are concerned, have changed enormously during this century. We live in an age in which women have gained access to nearly all the professions, including the Protestant ministry, and have demonstrated their competence in them, often to an unusual degree. There are few thinking people who would deny this, or who would deny that in the face of this social evolution the situation within the Church is anachronistic. However, there is by no means unanimity concerning the nature of the problem and its solution.

Among those who recognize that something is amiss and who do sincerely wish to see the female situation improved, a variety of attitudes exists. We shall consider two extremely opposed approaches, both of which betray inadequate understanding of the dimensions of the problem at hand. The first approach favors some modest reform of women's situation among the laity but looks upon the question of women priests as premature, peripheral, and unrelated to the more immediate problems of women and of the Church. It ignores the fact that exclusion of women from the clergy not only reflects but also serves to perpetuate a certain restrictive style of man-woman relationship. The second attitude supposes that the ordination of women will be a panacea for the ills of the Church in general and women in particular. It naively ignores the complexity of the problems which are the concern of sexual anthropology. We shall examine each of these approaches in turn.

Despite the evidence of social evolution, there are many—

---

[1] Hans Küng, quoted in *Progress Report to the House of Bishops* (Episcopalian), from The Committee to Study the Proper Place of Women in the Church's Ministry (an unpublished report), October, 1966, p. 111.

including many women—who feel that people are not ready
for so radical a change as the introduction of women priests.
They choose to keep a prudent silence on this issue, or at least
leave the matter in abeyance. They wish to avoid what they consider to be extremism and to work realistically for small changes.
Briefly, they think that the question of women's ordination has
surfaced prematurely. Although this position may appear to
reflect a sense of 'balance' and good judgment, it has inherent
difficulties.

First of all, the question simply cannot be ignored as premature, since many Protestant churches now ordain women.
Thus it inevitably enters into the ecumenical frame of reference.
This is not to say that the 'argument from ecumenism'—i.e. what
one church does, another must do—is valid. It does mean that
the question has been raised and must be faced.

Second, the argument that it is 'too soon' to consider seriously
women's ordination puts an exaggerated emphasis upon the
factor of psychological resistance to social change. There is always some resistance to any social change. This will be the case
no matter how delayed the reform movement may be in coming. Indeed, if there were no unwillingness to change, there
would be no discriminatory situation. In fact, it is to a large
extent true that prejudice is overcome only by the fact of change
itself. A prejudice against women university professors, for
example, is not overcome by refusal to hire them. Rather, it is
defeated by demonstration, that is, by the presence and influence of excellent women professors.

Nevertheless the factor of psychological resistance should not
unrealistically be ignored. If in a given time and place the opposition to change is overwhelming, and if it is reinforced by
other cultural institutions, then delay or gradualism will be
necessary. Today, however, it is clear that in the United States
and a great part of Europe, the basic conflict is not between
cultural circumstances and the admission of women to the ranks
of the clergy. On the contrary, there is a basic incongruity between present social conditions and the absolute exclusion of
women from the official ministry of the Church. Indeed, at this

point in history the Church is in the somewhat comical position of applauding women's legal, professional and political emancipation in secular society while keeping them in the basement of its own edifice.

Those who use the 'people are not yet ready' argument are in fact often projecting feelings of resistance within themselves. The irrationality of these feelings is revealed in the tendency to speak as if large numbers of women priests threaten to appear on the scene immediately. Even the mention of the idea appears to suggest to some that hordes of women priests (all resembling traditional Mother Superiors) will descend like invading soldier ants upon the heretofore all-male stronghold, thus producing a cultural shock of titanic proportions. Clearly this will not happen, except perhaps in the nightmares of insecure curates. Since girls have not been encouraged in this direction, it is unlikely that more than a very small number of them would consider the priesthood, were it opened to them as a possibility. By the very nature of the situation the change would be effected gradually. The issue at stake is not one of numbers but of principle: no human being should be disqualified from any Church office on the basis of sex. The same criteria should be applied to candidates of both sexes.

Much of the insistence that the discussion of women's ordination is premature is rooted in the belief that it is a peripheral and unimportant issue, having little relevance for the immediate problems of men and women. Thus, many will dismiss this topic as unimportant but will favor raising the status of women among the laity. This reveals a notion of the man-woman relation which is narrow and short-sighted. Such persons are willing to accept discrimination on the basis of sex up to—or rather down to—a point, and fail to affirm that this is wrong in principle and justifiable only when circumstances make it impossible to avoid. This position is weak and inconsistent. It would be more consistent to hold that whatever deficiency or mysterious difference makes women universally unfit for membership in the hierarchy would also disqualify them from equality with men among the laity. If sexual discrimination is desirable or at least justifiable where the hierarchy is in question, there is no compelling reason for not perpetuating it where the functions of the laity are in question.

When this principle of consistency is understood, it throws some light upon the unfortunate fact that in post Vatican II years, rather than gaining ground at an equal pace with laymen, women have been kept in an inferior status. This has become so painfully obvious that in 1967 the executive director of the National Council of Catholic Women in the United States—traditionally a very cautious organization—publicly issued a strong protest. Her comments had been prepared for discussion by the National Council of Catholic Bishops, which was held in Chicago in April of that year. Significantly the topic was never discussed, but the report was issued to newsmen who were covering the bishops' meeting. In it the NCCW director stated that women now seem destined to become third class Christians, despite the emphasis upon the laity as the 'people of God', which was voiced at Vatican II. She said:

'As the participation of laymen in liturgical and ecclesiastical affairs continues to increase, it becomes painfully obvious that women are being left behind in a class by themselves. The position of the Catholic woman in the spiritual worshipping community is exactly the same as it was before the Council.'

The statement further bemoaned the fact that women still have no active role in the liturgy, that they are very much in the minority on parish boards and councils, that they are not in positions of importance in national Catholic organizations. Finally, it declared that the present situation is 'an unhealthy climate' for the Catholic woman, who 'waits for her talents and abilities . . . and, indeed, her personhood, to be recognized and acknowledged by the Church'.[1]

The difficulty is that the Catholic woman will wait in vain for such acknowledgment, unless organizations such as the NCCW come to see and publicly affirm the full implications of the

---

[1] Quoted in *The Catholic Transcript*, Hartford, Conn., 21 April, 1967 (Religious News Service).

personhood which they want to be recognized by the Church. Because Catholic women and their organizations have been too timid in affirming their worth and their rights, because they have asked for too little, they have in fact failed to make progress. Until they have the clear-sightedness and courage to reject discrimination totally, it is to be expected that women will be the losers on all levels. The perverse consistency in the present trend toward third-class citizenship in the Church can be challenged only by those who think and act with consistency.

Just as it is short-sighted to dismiss the question of women in the hierarchy as premature and irrelevant, so also it is a mistake to think of their acceptance as a panacea. There are lessons to be learned in this matter from the experience of Protestant churches which have ordained women. From the testimony of these women ministers it is clear that being ordained does not guarantee the removal of all discriminatory practices. In fact, they do suffer from such practices in a variety of ways. This experience indicates that the problems involved in relations between the sexes in the Church, as in any society, are profound and complex. There is no instant cure for them. Progress on any level toward recognition and development of the full potential of women should be the occasion of rejoicing but not of unrealistic optimism. In the long run, particular advances will not be very effective unless they are accompanied and supported by developments in many parts of the social organism.

When studying the problem of women's situation vis-à-vis the Church, it is essential to realize that the solution is inseparably bound up with the whole issue of evolving structures. It would be rash to pretend that one can predict with certainty what form the Church community of the future will take. However, there is a serious danger of short-sightedness, of being fixated upon presently existing forms which are already fading into the past or which are doomed eventually to disappear. A consciousness of social evolution counteracts the temptation to simplistic activism, to the search for panaceas for a problem which is all-pervasive and extremely complex. This is not to say that an awareness of evolution should spawn a sort of quietism which chooses to 'wait and see' what will happen. On the contrary, it is essential to see that man is the being who shares in the shaping of his own destiny. Thus it is necessary to work within the existing situation, to rectify injustice within existing structures insofar as this is possible, and at the same time to anticipate and direct toward future developments.

It is most important, then, to go beyond thinking in terms of the institutional Church as it has existed until the present time. We are living in a time of social upheaval. Indeed, it appears that we are entering upon a new stage in human evolution, and it may be that many social structures which are still with us and many accepted patterns of behavior are really dead remnants of an earlier stage. Characteristic of our age is the breakdown of class distinctions which have persisted for thousands of years—indeed, since the human race moved from its infancy, the state of primitive society, into its adolescence. These class distinctions have been expressed in hierarchical patterns of society. Master and slave, feudal lord and serf, husband and wife—all lived out their existence in fixed roles, more or less modified according to circumstances and individual disposition. The fundamental dialectic was between oppressor and oppressed. This hierarchical vision of the world was reflected in the structures of the Church and justified by her theology. Today these structures remain, but modern man is experiencing them more and more as suffocating anachronisms.

At the same time, modern man experiences an anxiety about the disappearance of these structures. There is an awareness, in some cases, explicit, in others half-buried in the unconscious, that we stand at a turn in the road and that there is no going back. This is the reason for the strange power of the women priests issue to arouse violent and irrational responses. In fact, the very expression 'women priests' juxtaposes in the most striking way two symbols which in a former age, the age from which we are emerging, had been understood as occupying opposed positions in the hierarchical scheme of things. The very suggestion that the same individual could be the bearer of these two images is a declaration that an age has ended and another has begun.

It is quite possible, many would say inevitable, that the distinction between hierarchy and laity as we now know it will disappear. Since our age is characterized by the emergence of oppressed minorities, it is unlikely that the Church can hold out against this rising tide. The existence of a separate and superior priestly caste, of a hierarchy, appears to modern man as a quaint leftover from an earlier stage of human development. Modern theologians, recognizing this, stress the point that the clergy exist in order to serve the faithful, not in order to accumulate power, honors and prestige. A prominent theologian has pointed out that whereas for several centuries the Catholic idea of the priest was almost exclusively that of an 'offerer of sacrifice', doctrinal development has moved away from this. Vatican II's Constitution on the Church reflects growth from a cultic notion of the priest to a ministerial one.[1]

This is an important transition. The priest, formerly detached, a 'sacred person', an object of veneration and almost superstitious awe, is beginning to be seen as a presence in the midst of the world rather than an overseer, as brother rather than as father. Thus there is a shift toward democratization. The priest now sees himself and is seen in terms of mission to the world, which requires dialogue and cooperation with his fellow men. Since dialogue and cooperation are two-way processes, the priest's temptations to accept false prestige and to appraise himself unrealistically will be greatly diminished.

The emphasis upon service and cooperation has the effect of putting sharply into focus the problem which is nagging many priests, who discover that they are, in fact, in a less advantageous situation for serving the Christian community than many professionally competent laymen. Indeed, a large percentage of the clergy, in this age of specialization, are in the uncomfortable situation of being non-professional dabblers competing with experts in a variety of fields. Their work touches many areas requiring special competence: theology, teaching, preaching, social

[1] Gregory Baum, in *The Ecumenist*, November-December, 1965, p. 6.

service, counseling psychology, business administration, recreational leadership. Any of these areas of work can be handled by qualified members of the laity, men and women, and any of them can be handled better by lay specialists than by clerical non-specialists. It is not surprising, then, that some are beginning to look upon clerical caste as we now know it as irrelevant and doomed to extinction, and to envision the Church of the future as a community based upon charismatic ministries, and transformed into a higher and more adequately human social order.

It is essential that those who are concerned with relations between the sexes in the Church give serious attention to this modern development in the direction of democratization and specialization. When the emphasis is shifted away from symbolic roles which are identified with fixed states of life and toward functional roles freely assumed on the basis of personal qualifications and skills, away from caste systems and towards specialization based on ability, there will be hope for realization of that higher level of dialogue and cooperation between men and women which we seek.

The nun

We have not yet discussed one of the most fascinating and paradoxical figures involved in the drama of transition from the era which is ending to the new age which has begun. This is the figure of the religious sister, the nun. There is a sense in which the nun appears to embody the eternal feminine, the stereotype of woman. She wears a veil and lives under a vow of obedience. Traditionally, she has led a life of silence, except when speech is necessary, demurely carrying out the humble tasks apportioned to womanhood.

Yet, individual nuns have transcended the eternal feminine to a greater degree than most of their married sisters. We have seen that there were extremely powerful abbesses in the Middle Ages, who ruled vast territories with skill and authority. There was the brilliant and active figure of Teresa of Avila, and there were the daring women such as Mary Ward, whose struggle we have described, who established the first active communities of religious women away from the cloister. In our own time, a large proportion of Catholic professional women are religious sisters. Among their numbers are outstanding scholars, scientists, artists, administrators. Some of these have recently come into the limelight, and one speaks of 'the emerging nun'. Indeed, more and more frequently these very modern women are to be seen at professional gatherings, or on the campuses of great secular universities, attired in medieval garb, vividly exemplifying the paradox of the Catholic nun.

Throughout centuries in which women were under the tutelage of father, guardian or husband, the nuns enjoyed a kind of liberation from subjection to the male. True, they had vows of obedience and were subject to masculine jurisdiction on the higher and more remote levels, yet there was also always a kind of autonomy which even Thomas Aquinas acknowledged. These consecrated virgins were recognized as symbolizing the value and dignity of the human person, which transcends sex roles and functions, and at least in some individual cases they actually realized this transcendence in their thoughts and activities. The nun has always been the image of the old and of the new woman, bearing in an extraordinary way the burden of the eternal feminine mystique, yet at the same time anticipating symbolically and sometimes in concrete reality the emancipation which has only recently begun to take hold in the world.

It it not by accident that none of the outspoken advocates of women clergy are nuns, even though some of them privately favor this movement. Leaving aside the psychology of vested interests, which may help to explain this lack of enthusiasm, there is the fact that the sisterhoods have introjected to a great extent the attitudes of the eternal feminine. Still wearing veils, still partly cloistered, nuns are, symbolically speaking, the antithesis of women in the active ministry. Many still seek fulfillment in ways which are as anachronistic as the garb which symbolizes their ancient bondage. At the same time, the tremors of change are being felt in even the most conservative of convents. Even in these isolated places the message that an age is coming to an end is being heard.

At this point in history the nun, more than ever before, is a walking paradox. All the discussion and confusion over modifying or eliminating the habit signifies far more than a superficial concern with style or convenience. At the heart of it is a question of acceptance or rejection of the feminine stereotypes. The intransigent reluctance of male ecclesiastical superiors, who still govern the lives of religious women to permit elimination of the habit is rooted in resistance to liberation of nuns from these depersonalizing images.

Strong resistance to the phenomenon of the emerging nun comes not only from conservative prelates in Rome but also from some who are considered to be spokesmen for the liberal side. A particularly instructive example of this can be seen in the statements of a priest counseling psychologist who has expressed his unhappiness over the image of the new nun, as 'the dynamic college president, the flashy fund-raiser, the grant-laden scientist'.[1] These he sees as 'masculinized women'. What are the sisters to do, then? Their counselor is a little hazy on this, but the words are familiar. They are to be 'handmaids of the spirit', 'real women'; they are to accept 'Mary's role'. Rather than be great college presidents (an 'aggressive and faulted model of sisters'), they should 'surrender themselves to their womanhood'. Side by side with this terminology, reminiscent of Gertrud von le Fort and Pius XII, one finds a term greatly favored by psychologists—'healthy'. Their critic is concerned that the sisters become healthy and adult, yet the very images which he perpetuates present a formidable obstacle to healthy maturity. He writes nostalgically of the women 'who stood always in the shadow of great men, helping them, reassuring them, opening them to the possibilities of their services to mankind', yet gives no indication of recognizing that fact that such a relationship would be richer if reciprocal, or that to be healthy a person might need to emerge from the shadows. What is in fact being proposed is that the sisters serve as sublimated, 'spiritual' and psychologically useful objects. Yet it may be optimistic

[1] Eugene Kennedy, M.M. 'The Women who are More than Poor', *The Critic*, December, 1966-January, 1967, pp. 31-9.

to hope that not many sisters can be persuaded by such 'psychology'.

The nuns, we have said, have always presented a dual and paradoxical image. It could not have been otherwise. However, we have arrived at that point in time when it is possible, at last, for religious women to emerge from the cloister and veil of the eternal feminine mystique and to realize in their lives the rich possibilities which their unique vocation offers—possibilities which were suggested and anticipated in the lives of great religious women of the past. The tension of opposites in which they have lived can be transcended if there is enough courage and optimism.

The emergence of the nun is bound up with the emergence of the married woman. Throughout an age in which only a small percentage of offspring might be expected to survive to adulthood, married women literally were considered to exist for the reproductive function. The marriage act, significantly referred to by theologians as 'the *use* of the woman', could not really be understood as the expression of mutual love between persons, since one of the parties was looked upon more as instrument than as person. The husband had to be the head, since an instrument can hardly be a partner.

Standing in extreme contrast to the situation of the married woman, the situation of the nun was also to some extent dehumanizing. A compensatory figure, liberated from the burden of reproduction, the nun was in a sense society's affirmation—almost a token affirmation—of the latent humanity of women. However, she paid the price of isolation from the male. Of course, some nuns did manage to overcome the obstacles and form deep and enriching friendships with men. It is not by coincidence that the greatest personalities among them did so.

Now, however, in a society which is no longer desperately bent upon excessive reproduction for survival of the species, which in fact begins to see a decrease in reproduction as required for suvival, the same forces which are freeing married women to realize their personhood are creating a new situation for, and image of the nun. There begin to emerge vast possibilities for more fully humanizing relations between men and women, married and celibate.

The basic obstacle to the attainment of these more completely human relationships, and to the achievement of integrated, self-activating personhood, is isolation. 'Isolation' here is to be understood not simply in the obvious sense of physical separation, although it may include this, but also and more importantly in its more subtle significations. Thus, one may be isolated within an organization if he or she is not allowed to participate to a meaningful degree in its decision-making and in its activities. A husband and wife may be isolated from each other if they do not have a range of common interests. Therefore, continuous effort is needed to expand opportunities for broadened experience, and for cooperation and dialogue between men and women.

In the case of religious women this will entail the elimination of archaic rules and of outmoded garb, which erect barriers to communication. It will entail the abandonment of the style of life which prevails in 'total institutions', in which the inmates sleep, eat, study, play and pray in the same building or compound. It will involve attendance at coeducational secular universities, adoption of contemporary dress, experiments in living and teaching in the secular milieu, and working together with men and with other women in a wide variety of forms of cooperative endeavor. It will also mean that those who are qualified should, together with other qualified women, move into influential and decision-making roles in the Church as well as in other cultural institutions.

In the process of making decisions concerning new activities for sisters, and in carrying out these decisions, it should be clearly affirmed that the risk of an individual's losing her commitment to 'the religious life' is incomparably less grave than the risk of foreshortening her potential as a human being. If this principle is understood, and if its implications are courageously followed through, we may witness the time when 'the new nun' is truly in the avant-garde, living out the possibilities of personhood which her veiled and cloistered predecessors for the most part merely symbolized, and realizing in this world what had been thought attainable only in the next. When this occurs, the apparent opposition between 'religious women' and 'women in the sacred ministry' will be overcome. Indeed, in a humanized, democratized Church of the future, in which systems of caste have been transcended, it may be discovered that men and women, married and celibate, are called in abundance to minister to the people of God.

Reform in the Church and in the world

It is painfully obvious, however, that the reformed, democratized Church of the future is not yet here, although the seeds of it are present in the living faith, hope and courage of the Christian community. Moreover, there is no divine guarantee that it will come into actuality automatically. Human beings have the power to choose, which implies capacity for failure. The people of God have responsibility for the future of the man-woman relationship on all levels.

The primary responsibility of the Church in this regard is the reform of its own doctrine and practices. It is here above all that one has the right to expect to see the old order overcome. The New Testament, still partly immersed in the old order, nevertheless points beyond it: just as there is neither Jew nor Greek, neither slave nor free, so there is neither male nor female in Christ. That is to say, the old oppressive form of relationships is to be transcended. It is the Church's mission to work toward this transcendence in history. However, the Church hardly seems to be in any position to be 'God's avant-garde', working as a leaven in society, if in fact it incongruously refuses to progress within its own structures.

It is precisely this incongruous situation which we now witness: although Vatican II's Pastoral Constitution on the Church in the Modern World speaks out against discrimination on the basis of sex, the situation of women in the post-conciliar Church has not changed greatly. There has been failure to see that the fundamental problem of the right relation between men and women is basically one, whether we are talking about education, professional opportunity, political life, home life or ecclesiastical affairs. The first and most essential way, then, in which the Church ideally should carry out its mission to bring about a development toward right relation between men and women is by demonstration through reform of itself, in its theology and in its life. If it did this, it would present to 'the world' a model and an ideal.

However, there is a sense in which it may be too late to expect the Church as institution to act as model. 'The world' is already far ahead, and there are many who think, as does Karl Rahner, that the Church is already in *diaspora*, or at least well on its way. Thus, while total reform 'at home' would seem logically to precede the reform of the secular milieu, in practice it is not advisable for individual Christians or groups to wait for this transformation before directing their efforts toward bringing about desirable reforms in society. This is not to say that they should neglect the Church, but that it can be considered as one cultural institution among others in need of reform. Moreover, they can be reasonably certain that in bringing about reform in the wider milieu, their efforts will ultimately have an effect upon the institutional Church.

The people of God as the Church in diaspora have a mission, then, to bring about in society what the Church as institution has failed to do within its own doctrine and structures. This will involve many different tasks and procedures, some requiring highly specialized training, others not. We shall consider some of these.

Since the most theoretical work is sometimes the most practical in its results, it is important to emphasize the work of research in various branches of learning which contribute to our understanding of the sexual relation. It is important that specialists in such disciplines as biology, psychology, sociology, anthropology and philosophy bring the fruits of their labors to bear upon our understanding of the problem, especially upon the problem of the effect of environment in producing psychological differences between the sexes. Without such stimuli from other sciences, theology will not advance.

Furthermore, those who are in the field of education have opportunities not only to communicate understanding of the problem in the classroom, but also to remedy situations which support the feminine mystique and the masculine mystique, and to create new situations which foster dialogue and cooperation. The elimination of arbitrary distinctions in the education of boys and girls will cut deeply into the heart of the problem. In particular, single-sex educational institutions are difficult to justify in principle, and should wherever possible evolve into, or be replaced by, coeducational institutions. Even though girls' high schools and colleges sometimes have better professors and more gifted students, the prevailing feminine attitudes and images on their campuses can inhibit creative and critical thinking. It is sometimes argued in favor of separate schools that girls can develop leadership qualities there which would be encouraged less in a mixed school. The difficulty with this is that learning to lead in an unnaturally segregated environment might not prove too useful in the normal world, comprised of two sexes.

The advantages of coeducation are evident. It provides opportunities for normal day to day encounters, on a level other than that of dating. The two sexes learn to work together. They learn to compete as individuals who are interested in the same projects—which is something quite other from the hostile competitiveness which acccompanies the exaggeration of sex differences. In a coeducational environment, boys who have been conditioned to think of girls as sex objects can make the exciting and enriching discovery that friendship, interesting discussions and shared insights are possible with the other sex. They can discover that there are girls with minds every bit as good as their own. Girls, many of whom are inclined to accept notions of male intellectual superiority, can learn confidence in discovering their equal ability and in developing it, whereas they are inclined to doubt this when kept in isolation.

Isolation in one-sex institutions promotes unrealistic notions about the other sex, as well as about one's own. In the vacuum of the imagination which is not supplied with general experience of personal encounter and dialogue, the sexual stereotypes thrive. Obsession with sex then plays a compensatory role. The temptation for boys to see girls only as prey and as objects, and for girls to look upon themselves in the same way, is not counterbalanced.

This is not to say that all the presently existing single-sex schools and colleges must be abandoned, but it suggests the direction in which they should plan future development. Their transformation into coeducational institutions might be the ideal, but there are other possible solutions. In the cases of men's and women's colleges which are in proximity to each other or to coeducational universities, every effort should be made to encourage participation in the same classes, seminars and activities. In some cases, it may be desirable to move an entire institution to the campus of another.

The most extreme cases of sexually isolated institutions are, of course, novitiates and seminaries. We have already suggested that it would be helpful if religious women could be given the opportunity of studying in non-sectarian coeducational institutions, on both the undergraduate and graduate levels. The same holds true for seminarians, priests and male religious. Priests who have spent long years in seminaries, often preceded by all-male high schools and colleges, have not had much opportunity for recognizing in women the fact that they are fellow human beings. Not infrequently, therefore, they are inclined to accept the woman-as-object attitude, transposing this view to an unrealistically 'spiritual' level. The urgency of changing the situation of seminarians can hardly be over-emphasized. Moreover, a radical change is required. Thus, those who advocate bringing a few women professors into seminaries are not offering an adequate solution. It will be more in accord with real needs, and more in line with the secularization process, if efforts are directed to moving away from the seminary as it is now known. In some cases, seminaries are close enough to coeducational universities so that their students could attend classes and participate in student affairs. In other cases, seminaries could be transported to the campuses of large secular universities, where they could share resources with students of other denominations and of both sexes. There should also be more experiments in regard to living quarters, such as living in dormitories with other students, in apartments and in families.

The value of the whole movement toward coeducation will of course be undermined unless there is an effort to achieve truly equal education for both sexes. So, for example, a university which admits girls to its school of nursing and of education but denies them access to its more highly selective college of arts and sciences is not truly coeducational. By such a policy it is discriminating precisely against the most ambitious and gifted girls, the potential scholars, university professors, scientists, doctors, lawyers. By such a policy, moreover, the image of the female student on campus is restricted to that of the girl who chooses the traditionally feminine and less intellectually demanding occupations, and thus the old stereotypes are perpetuated. In fact, the forms of discrimination which vitiate coeducation are many: quotas, denial of loans and fellowships, discouragement of girls from the more demanding and rewarding fields by counselors and educators, to mention a few.

In contrast to all this, a truly equitable and truly coeducational system would take seriously the principle that it is just as important for every girl to be educated to her full potential as it is for every boy. It is essential that educators not only cease to discourage girls, but that they make a special effort to encourage them, in order to counterbalance their disadvantaged situation. Since it is generally true that education is only taken seriously when there is expectation that it can be used in society, it follows that educators who are truly committed to the realization of the full potential of girls must earnestly seek to make their charges aware of professional opportunities and must strive to increase such opportunities. Moreover, such committed educators will see the necessity of providing educational possibilities for women whose course of study or career was interrupted while they were raising their families, and who now wish to return to the professional world.

The mere opening of the doors of universities and professional schools to women is not of itself adequate to bring about radical change. Today in the United States only one in three of the

B.A.'s and M.A.'s granted are earned by women, and one in ten Ph.D's. Some observers have noted with alarm that despite a few widely publicized token appointments of women to high positions in government in the United States, and despite all the talk about America having become a 'matriarchy', there is an increasing tendency in recent years for women to be concentrated at the bottom of the job ladder in the more menial and routine jobs. Only 7% of doctors in the United States are women, less than 4% of lawyers, and less than 1% of federal judges.

All this suggests that the realization of the potential of women and the attainment of a higher level of cooperation between the sexes in society will require still other forms of effort, since there are many factors in society which militate against high ambitions on the part of young women. Obviously a society which expects women to retire from the professional or business world for fifteen or twenty years in order to raise a family, sets up a most effective deterrent to high aspirations. Yet there is no reason why social innovations could not be worked out, such as networks of child care centers, or flexible and part time work schedules.

There is need that efforts be made in other areas as well. Thus, it is essential that birth control information and medical assistance be made readily available to all women, regardless of economic status. It is particularly important that this help be extended to women who are living in poverty and whose condition, together with that of their families, is rendered subhuman by repeated, undesired pregnancies. However indifferent the official Church may appear to be to their plight, it is clear by now on which side true humanism stands, and on which side the Church in diaspora must direct its efforts.

Another area requiring attention is that of the mass media, which are universally conveying an image of women as mindless sex objects and therefore conditioning the masses of people to accept the image as reality. Influence must be brought to bear upon advertisers, publishers and editors to change their policies in this regard. Finally, it is essential that special efforts be devoted to the problems of realizing equal opportunity in employment[1] and equal responsibility in politics.[2]

It is painfully evident that there is a long road ahead. Christianity, and the Catholic Church in particular, has not yet faced its responsibility to exorcise the devil of sexual prejudice. In fact, it has lagged behind the rest of the world on this issue. Other groups have been in the avant-garde and, ironically enough, their efforts have more often than not met with ecclesiastical opposition. The Church must admit its past failures. However much social conditions of the past excuse those failures, the times no longer offer an excuse. If the institutional Church has not accepted its responsibility to do battle against the powers of darkness, nevertheless individuals and groups of Christians bear that responsibility. If they fail now, there will be no answer to the mounting suspicion in the minds of many that Christianity— particularly as it is embodied in the Catholic Church—is the inevitable enemy of human progress.

[1] In the United States, discrimination in employment on the basis of sex is now prohibited by federal law, in Title VII of the Civil Rights Act of 1964. However, the Equal Employment Opportunity Commission has not demonstrated that its commitment to enforcement of the law in the case of women is as serious as in the case of other groups suffering from discrimination.

[2] In the United States, the practice of having separate 'ladies' auxiliaries' within the political parties has not been conducive to giving to women a proportionate share in political decision making. What is needed is representation according to numbers in the regularly constituted party committee on all levels, and in the informal power structure. Militant organizations such as the recently constituted National Organization for Women are necessary, and they will play an indispensable role in bringing about reform in this area as well as in all of the other areas we have mentioned.

CONCLUSION

The Second Sex and the Seeds of Transcendence

'I do best by obeying and serving my sovereign Lord
—that is, God.'

Joan of Arc

We have seen that Simone de Beauvoir's position on the role of Christianity in the oppression of women is in large measure justified. We do not—nor does she—believe that the Church alone can be 'blamed' for the oppressive situations which have arisen in the process of the evolution of humanity. The Church condoned slavery but it did not originate that institution; it has approved of the subjection of women, but it did not initiate it. In the larger perspective, these institutions which have been so destructive for large segments of humanity may be seen as necessary survival techniques for the race as a whole during one phase of the evolutionary process.

We are now witnessing and participating in a period of growth beyond that phase. The slaves have been freed, the Negroes are no longer willing to play the subservient role assigned to them, the women are beginning to become conscious of their latent potentialities. The archaic heritage is being shaken off. Humanity appears to be in a transitional stage and is therefore haunted by unnamed anxieties, for it is not possible to predict with certainty what the next stage will be or where we are going, ultimately. In this situation, we are experiencing a dramatic cleavage between those who, looking to the horizon, affirm that the world is moving, and those who stubbornly insist that nothing changes. This fundamental division between liberal and conservative cuts across all others. Thus, for example, a liberal Christian feels more at home talking to an open and honest agnostic than to his conservative fellow believers, who cling to their vision of a static Church.

In this situation, it is not astonishing that many of those whose psychic structures are robust enough to welcome change have lost all patience with organizations and ideologies which appear to hold back the evolutionary process. To these, total rejection of the old appears to be a normal and necessary part of maturation. This could in some cases be a neurotic reaction, just as clinging to the past can be a sign of immaturity. However, there is no reason to think that it is always so. Thus, an *ad hominem* attack upon Simone de Beauvoir's rejection of Christianity is not an answer; it is an escape.

We have said that we are in fundamental agreement with de Beauvoir concerning the facts of history. Is there no disagreement, then? We have already suggested the answer to this. Disagreement may bear more upon the attitude concerning the facts and interpretation than upon the facts themselves. It also may bear more upon what a critic has omitted than upon what is actually said.

The fundamental difference between Simone de Beauvoir's vision of the Church and women and that which motivated this book is the difference between despair and hope. For this reason our approach is fundamentally far more radical than that of the French existentialist. De Beauvoir was willing to accept the conservative vision of the Church as the reality, and therefore has had to reject it as unworthy of mature humanity. However, there is an alternative to rejection, an alternative which need not involve self-mutilation. This is commitment to radical transformation of the negative, life-destroying elements of the Church as it exists today. The possibility of such commitment rests upon clear understanding that the seeds of the eschatological community, of the liberating, humanizing Church of the future, are already present, however submerged and neutralized they may be. Such commitment requires hope and courage.

De Beauvoir herself has acknowledged that religion has been able to work a transformation, enabling women to perform works comparable to men, although the only examples she cites are

Catherine of Siena and Teresa of Avila. We have seen that she becomes quite lyrical concerning the case of Teresa who, it is claimed, lived out the situation of humanity, taking her stand beyond the earthly hierarchies, and setting her pride beyond the sexual differentiation. We could well argue that there have been others in all ages who have transcended 'the earthly hierarchies', and, although they have been comparatively few, they have served as beacons, signalling to others the fact of undreamed of possibilities in themselves. We can truly say that the Church has, indeed, worked to bring about this transformation, that it has inspired men and women to reach beyond the limitations imposed by their environments, even beyond the limitations imposed by itself as institution.

It is essential, however, that we do not dupe ourselves, supporting our optimism with a facile apologetic. It is easy to say that Christianity has 'always taught' the dignity of the human person, and indeed it is true that the prophetic voice has always called out from the depths, however muffled that voice may have been by alienating notions spawned in an alienated society. However, it is not necessary to belabor this point defensively. Our optimism is not dependent upon the past; rather, it arises from a call, a summons into the future. Harvey Cox expressed the Christian condition accurately when he said that Jesus Christ comes to his people not primarily through ecclesiastical traditions, but through social change, that he 'goes before' first as a pillar of fire. There is no need, then, to be obsessed with justification of the past. In fact, while it is necessary to watch the rear-view mirror, this does not tell us where we are going, but only where we have been.

Simone de Beauvoir rejects Christianity as burdensome baggage inherited from the past. The life-affirming alternative to this is response to that liberating Power which calls us to transcend the archaic heritage and move toward a future whose seeds are already within us. Our response to the French existentialist is one of friendly respect and gratitude, for without her light we may not have recognized so acutely our own darkness and therefore may not have discovered the dimensions of our own light. Rather than a philosophy of despair, we choose a theology of hope, not because the former is 'false', but because we think it represents an incomplete and partial vision.

It is part and parcel of Christian hope and courage that these qualities do not allow us ultimately to rest in the illusion that we are in possession of fixed blueprints for our future. God is present, yet always hidden, and the summons from that Presence gives a dimension of transcendence to our activity, by which we are propelled forward.

In the exercise of self-transcending creative activity, inspired and driven forward by faith and hope, sustained by courage, men and women can learn to 'set their pride beyond the sexual differentiation'. Working together on all levels they may come at last to see each other's faces, and in so doing, come to know themselves. It is only by this creative personal encounter, sparked by that power of transcendence which the theologians have called grace, that the old wounds can be healed. Men and women, using their best talents, forgetful of self and intent upon the work, will with God's help mount together toward a higher order of consciousness and being, in which the alienating projections will have been defeated and wholeness, psychic integrity, achieved.

Index